THE GOLDEN
ENCYCLOPEDIA OF FRESHWATER
TROPICAL
AQUARIUM
FISHES

Cichlasoma biocellatum (C. octofasciatum)

Symphysodon aequifasciata aequifasciata

THE GOLDEN
ENCYCLOPEDIA OF FRESHWATER
TROPICAL
AQUARIUM
FISHES

Dick Mills
Dr. Gwynne Vevers

Consultant
Douglas G. Campbell

Golden Press • New York
Western Publishing Company, Inc.
Racine, Wisconsin

Published by
Western Publishing Company, Inc.,
Racine, Wisconsin.

Golden® and Golden Press® are
trademarks of Western Publishing
Company, Inc.

Library of Congress Catalog
Card Number: 82-82792

ISBN 0-307-46633-7

All correspondence concerning
the content of this volume should
be addressed to Salamander Books Ltd.

This book may not be sold outside
the USA and Canada.

Credits

For Western Publishing Company, Inc.
Jonathan P. Latimer, Editorial Director,
    Adult Books
Susan A. Roth, Senior Editor
Karen Stray Nolting, Copy Editor

For Salamander Books Ltd.
Editor: Geoff Rogers
Designer: Roger Hyde

Color separations: Bantam Litho Ltd.,
    England. Rodney Howe Ltd., England.

Filmset: Modern Text Typesetting,
    England.

Printed in Belgium by

THE AUTHORS

PART ONE

*Dick Mills has been keeping fish for over 20 years. During this
time he has written four books as well as many articles
for aquatic hobby magazines. A member of his local aquarist
society, for the past 12 years he has also been a council member
of the Federation of British Aquatic Societies, for which he
regularly lectures and produces a quarterly news bulletin. By
profession, Mr. Mills composes electronic music and special
sound sequences for television and radio programs —
a complete contrast to fishkeeping, the quietest of hobbies.*

PART TWO

*Gwynne Vevers, M.B.E., M.A., D.Phil., F.L.S., F.I. Biol.,
is well qualified to write about aquarium fishes. Dr. Vevers'
distinguished academic career in the zoological sciences
culminated in his appointment as Curator of the Aquarium at
the London Zoo, a post he held until 1981. In addition to
undertaking biological expeditions to places as far away as
Iceland and the Solomon Islands, Dr. Vevers has found the time
to write, translate, and edit many books on aquarium fishes.*

THE CONSULTANT

*Douglas G. Campbell, currently an aquarist at the Houston
Zoological Gardens, has both practical and academic knowledge of
fishkeeping. He has spent six years in the retail fish trade, and
written over 50 articles on fish subjects. He was formerly a
Contributing Editor of Freshwater and Marine Aquarium magazine.*

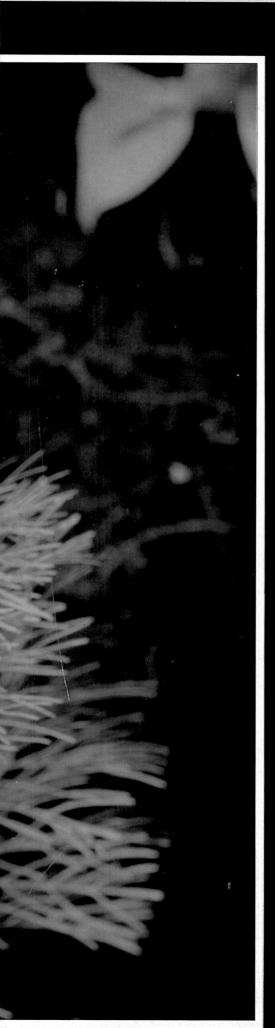

CONTENTS

PART ONE PRACTICAL SECTION

A complete practical guide to setting up and maintaining a tropical freshwater aquarium, from selecting a tank to exhibiting fishes at a competitive show.

PART TWO SPECIES GUIDE

A detailed survey of 200 tropical freshwater fishes. These are presented in family groupings that are arranged in order of evolutionary development, from the more primitive to the more specialized. Within each family the fishes are presented in alphabetical order of scientific name. The principal families featured are listed below.

Publisher's note

Fishkeeping is a hobby full of technical terms and scientific names. This book tries to avoid becoming too complicated, but understanding a technical language is a necessary part of this hobby, as it is with many others. When technical terms are introduced they are explained in the text. However, if questions should arise, the glossary contains clear descriptions of all the terms used in this book. The scientific names of fishes, plants, disease organisms, etc. may seem awesome at first, but anyone seriously interested in fishkeeping as a hobby will soon realize that understanding these standardized terms makes life easier. Measurements in the book are quoted in the units in everyday use in the United States, i.e. feet, inches, pounds, ounces, US-gallons, degrees Fahrenheit, etc. The metric equivalents, which are used in scientific circles, are given in parentheses where necessary. British Imperial equivalents are also given where appropriate. To show the sex of fishes, the standard scientific symbols have been used — ♂ male, ♀ female. In the end, however, as the authors are quick to point out, the rewards of fishkeeping will not come from a preoccupation with the technical details and scientific names, but from the pleasure of nuturing and displaying some of the world's most beautiful living things.

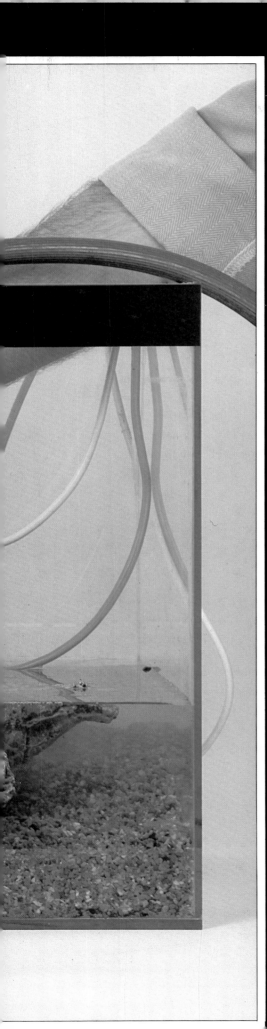

PART ONE

PRACTICAL SECTION

Fishkeeping, although not a new hobby, now bears little resemblance to its form of 100 years ago. Technical advances, especially fast air transportation, have resulted in a modern, satisfying hobby that appeals to people everywhere.

Concentrating on the history of fishkeeping would not necessarily introduce the newcomer to the hobby. Naturally, he wants to 'get on with it' as soon as possible. Therefore, the first section of this book will concentrate on preparing a modern-day aquarium for its living occupants, whether they are fishes or plants. However, respectful recognition is given to those pioneering aquarists whose efforts have made the hobby as popular as it is today.

Compared with other hobbies and pastimes, fishkeeping requires relatively little time from the hobbyist. Even when increasing costs are considered, the rewards, when compared with the capital outlay, seem to be proportionately higher than with other hobbies.

Fishkeeping is a quite, self-contained interest and has little nuisance value either to the neighbors or to the hobbyist's vacation plans. If the aquarium is prepared correctly and the guidance on aquarium management is followed, this should be a very fulfilling pastime. The only real problem will be finding room for those extra tanks!

Left: Filling the aquarium should be done carefully to avoid disturbing the gravel and other furnishings.

SELECTING A TANK

An aquarium makes good use of a corner.

Selecting a tank is very similar to choosing a house. It should be big enough for the number of occupants (including room for any possible increases); it must be in the right location and of sound construction; you must be able to live with it; and it must be within your price range. The style and design are personal choices. The main aim should be something that fishes can live in comfortably, and that will remain functioning with a minimum of maintenance. Carry out a survey of existing aquariums in your neighborhood. Make friends with their owners and ask all the questions you want. Find out from them which types have stood the test of time. Your local aquatic store will have all the information about modern tanks and which ones are the best buys. Be guided by people with practical experience, not seduced by a gimmick-laden creation. You owe it to your fishes.

Think reasonably big. There are several good reasons for this: Conditions in a large aquarium remain more stable (and therefore more controllable) than in a small one; more fishes can be kept; and the overall appearance of the aquarium when fully furnished will be more pleasing. Any tank longer than 24in (60cm) with a width of 12in (30cm) and a water depth of 12 to 15in (30 to 38cm) is suitable.

The overall water capacity of the tank is not the most important contributing factor to the tank's fish-carrying capacity. Fishes do have more room to swim and set up their territories in a larger tank, but much more important than size is the shape or proportions of the tank. A tall, slim tank may well hold the same amount of water as a shallow, wide tank, but the latter will house more fishes. The reason for this is that the oxygen content of the water depends upon how easily it can be supplied: The only place that this can occur is at the water surface, so the larger the water surface offered to the atmosphere, the better. The shallow, wide tank outscores the narrow tank in this respect.

Similarly, the opportunity for carbon dioxide (exhaled by the fishes) to be expelled from the water also occurs primarily at the water surface, and again a large water surface area is preferable.

In terms of numbers of fishes that may be stocked in any particular size tank, the following guide may be usefully considered:

Freshwater tropical species
   $12in^2$ per inch body length.
   $(75cm^2$ per cm body length.)
Freshwater coldwater species
   $30in^2$ per inch body length.
   $(187.5cm^2$ per cm body length.)
Marine tropical species
   $48in^2$ per inch body length.
   $(300cm^2$ per cm body length.)

Note: In all fish measurements used in these calculations the tail (caudal fin) is excluded.

An example: A tank 24x12x12in (60x 30x30cm) has a water surface area of

Right, from the top: Three types of tanks. Angle-iron framed with inset glass panels; all-glass, adhesive bonded construction; one-piece molded acrylic tank.

Angle-iron tank

All-glass bonded tank

One-piece acrylic tank

Freshwater tropical

Freshwater coldwater

Marine tropical

Above: Two tanks of identical water volume. One has twice the water surface area of the other and will hold more fish.
Left: The surface area of a 24x12x12in tank is divided here to show recommended maximum stocking levels. Each symbol represents 1in (2.5cm) of fish length.

$288in^2$ $(1800cm^2)$ and will comfortably hold:
   24in (60cm) of freshwater tropical fishes
   10in (25cm) of freshwater coldwater fishes
   15cm (6in) of marine tropical fishes.

Consideration must be given to the final sizes that the fishes will reach in the aquarium; fishes bought from dealers are usually juveniles and can be expected to double in size at least.

Types of tank

There are three main types of tank to choose from: Angle-iron frames with glass panels inset with putty; all-glass tanks made from five panes of glass bonded together with silicon-rubber adhesive; and one-piece, plastic tanks.

Until recently, the plastic types were best forgotten for long-term fishkeeping use, being used mainly for nursery, breeding tank, hospital, or quarantine quarters. The main drawback was that they were generally of small dimensions, and the plastic soon became scratched and discolored. Modern acrylic tanks are gaining popularity, particularly in the U.S., where such tanks may be found in all sizes, and reports indicate that discoloration is no longer a problem.

Apart from aesthetic considerations, there is little difference between the framed tank and the all-glass type, although for a marine (saltwater) aquarium you must use the all-glass tank, because

the salt water would soon corrode an angle-iron tank.

Tanks are commercially available in standard sizes (quoted either by dimensions or by water capacity), but the hobbyist can make his own tank to suit his exact requirements. Any glass used should be optically clear, free from distortion and of sufficient thickness to withstand the considerable water pressure exerted on it.

Secondhand tanks are occasionally available and, if of sound construction, are a good buy.

Siting the tank

Given a free choice of possible locations for the tank, there are several places that are definitely not suitable. A window location, especially one that faces the sun, is probably the worst place of all, because in hot weather the amount of light reaching the tank would be excessive and would not only result in the rapid growth of unwanted and unsightly algae, but also cause the water temperature to rise too high. In cold weather, a tropical aquarium thus situated will be fighting to conserve heat.

An aquarium should not be placed directly opposite a constantly opening door, since an accidentally slammed door will frighten the fishes and may even crack a glass panel. Again, a heated

Above: This splendidly furnished aquarium not only provides a focal point in the apartment but also acts as a very decorative room divider. Filtration equipment is hidden beneath the aquarium and is easily accessible.

aquarium may be subject to cold drafts.

Another important factor to keep in mind is that a fully furnished aquarium is heavy. A conveniently placed bureau or sideboard may seem an ideal site, but at best any drawers or doors in it will become unopenable under the weight of the aquarium, and at worst the legs may collapse. A strong stand or plinth is recommended, and the site should be located over the floor joists in such a way that the load is spread. Specially made aquarium stands are available commercially; these are designed to accommodate 'standard' sized tanks, and are usually made of wrought-iron. Provision should be made to protect decorative floor coverings from damage by the metal legs.

The ideal location for an aquarium is in a dark alcove. Here, the lighting conditions can be carefully controlled, there are unlikely to be cold drafts or physical disturbances, and as a bonus the illuminated aquarium will liven up that dark corner!

An aquarium can be placed in an unused fireplace, used as a free-standing room-divider or built in alongside book

shelves. Wherever the tank is finally sited, it must be accessible for regular maintenance and for feeding.

Additionally, whatever type of aquarium is planned, coldwater or tropical, there should be an electrical socket nearby to power the tank lights, air pump, filtration equipment, and heating (if required).

Installing the tank

Having chosen the tank's permanent position, make sure that, in addition to being firm, it is also level. An uneven supporting surface will produce stresses in the glass base of the tank, which could crack when the aquarium is filled. Place a thick slab of polystyrene (cut to the tank's base dimensions) beneath the tank to cushion it and even out any irregularities in the supporting surface. It will also conserve heat in a tropical aquarium.

A frequent fear, if not of the aquarist then certainly of other members of the family, is that of a leaking tank—a reasonable concern when considering the mess that 15 gallons of water might make!

It is wise to check any tank (even a new one) for leaks before final installation. Glazed, angle-iron framed tanks may leak as the glass panels 'bed down' under the initial water pressure and excess putty is forced out. These early leaks may well cure themselves but, to be on the safe side, the tank should be emptied and dried out, and all internal seams sealed. All-glass tanks are not likely to leak, but if a leak is found, it is easily repaired by applying the silicon-rubber sealant straight from the tube or from a cartridge used in a sealing gun. The sealant gives off strong fumes smelling of vinegar, and repair work should be done in a well-ventilated area. This is particularly important since one tends to bend over the work closely.

It is important to use only sealants specifically approved for aquarium use; the sealants used in bathrooms and for window-fixing contain mildew retardants that are toxic to fish.

If you want the aquarium to have a decorative background, it must be fixed in place before the tank is put in its final position. Or you may paint the outside of the rear and side panels a dark color.

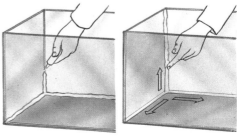

Above: Aquarium sealant should be applied in a continuous bead to all interior seams, and then smoothed over with a finger. It is vital to allow the sealant to cure for 24 hours before using.

11

HEATING, LIGHTING, FILTRATION, AERATION

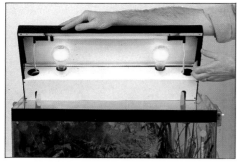
Fluorescent and tungsten lamps in one hood.

Before furnishing a tank, the newcomer should have a clear understanding of how the environment for fishes in captivity is maintained. For many decades it was believed that an aquarium should be self-cleaning and—apart from the addition of food by the hobbyist— self-perpetuating. Modern understanding has revised that thinking and it is now agreed that technology may be allowed to lend a hand. There are four areas in which the hobbyist has the controlling influence: Heating, lighting, filtration, and aeration. Today's aquarium equipment is completely reliable and almost foolproof. Very little technical knowledge, beyond the ability to wire up an electrical plug, is needed to install and operate the equipment safely. But never place your hands in the aquarium without first disconnecting the electrical power supply.

The majority of fishes kept are tropical species. Since many fishkeepers live outside the tropical areas from which their fishes come, it is necessary for them to heat the aquarium water to the temperature of the fishes' natural waters, approximately 75°F (24°C).

Aquarists with several tanks in one room may find it to their financial advantage to heat the room rather than each individual tank, but for the purposes of this book it is assumed that only one tank is planned at the outset and therefore only individual tank heating will be examined.

Aquarium heaters are heat-resistant, submersible glass tubes containing a wire heating element wound on a ceramic former. Electricity is supplied via a cable, which enters the tube through a watertight cap. It would be impossible to choose a heater of any particular size that would exactly counterbalance heat losses for any tank, bearing in mind the diversity of likely ambient temperatures around the world, and so the aquarium heater needs to be thermostatically controlled.

The thermostat may be contained in a waterproof tube similar to that of the heater, or it may be clamped externally to the glass wall of the aquarium. In recent years a combined heater and thermostat has been developed sharing the same outer casing. This is a standard item of aquarium equipment in the U.S. although separate heaters and thermostats are still widely used by European fishkeepers. The very latest line in thermostats is one controlled by the ubiquitous microchip.

Thermostats effectively stabilize the water temperature by switching off the supply to the heater when the required temperature is reached and switching it on again when the water has cooled by a degree or two. These temperature fluctuations occur quite slowly, particularly in a tank of the recommended size.

If you have a number of tanks, provided that equal-sized tanks are to be heated by equal-sized heaters, one master thermostat can control several heaters as long as its electrical current-carrying capacity is not exceeded.

The size of heater (measured in watts) should be selected with care. An overlarge heater will cause a rapid rise in water temperature (which could be fatal to the fishes), should the thermostat fail while in an 'on' position. On the other hand, a small heater may have to work overtime to keep up, with the result that the thermostat's contacts will become burned and pitted, with eventual failure.

Allow 10 watts per gallon (3.8 liters) as a rough estimate when choosing a heater. For large tanks, 36in (90cm) and over, two heaters may share the total required wattage and be controlled by one thermostat.

Do not worry about severe temperature loss in the event of electrical power failure. This will not occur for hours following the cut in electrical supply. You can take immediate steps by wrapping the tank in a blanket or with thick layers of newspaper. Bottles of hot water (heated by alternative means) can be placed in the aquarium if the power remains off for too long and the temperature appears to be falling to a critical level. Some aquarists insulate the outside of the sides and rear

Right: Combined heater/thermostats are usually mounted on the rear wall of the aquarium, either at an angle or near vertical in a corner. Check whether the unit is suitable for total immersion before use. Temperature adjustment is made by means of the protruding knob.
Below: Extra heaters may be connected to a separate thermostat and heater system as required for use in large tanks. The thermostat must be able to carry the total heater current. Heat is distributed throughout the aquarium by means of water currents created by convection.

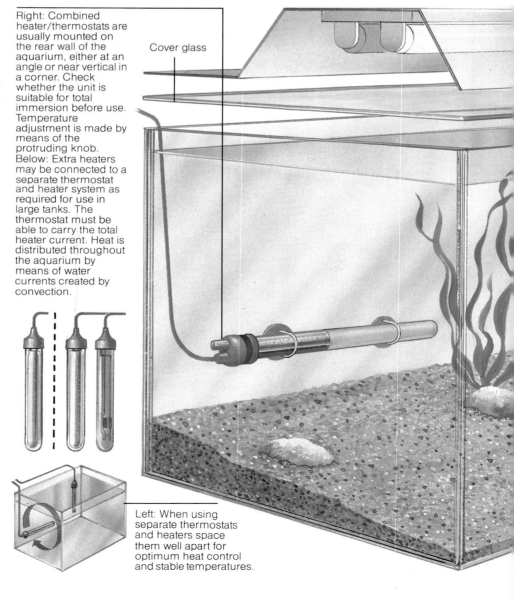

Cover glass

Left: When using separate thermostats and heaters space them well apart for optimum heat control and stable temperatures.

of a tank with polystyrene sheeting to conserve heat.

The temperature is easily measured with an aquarium thermometer. This may be one of several types: Floating or stick-on internal models, or a liquid-crystal display external type. Although water temperatures will vary by a degree or so over a period of hours, this is nothing to worry about; this fluctuation is far less than the fishes experience in nature, where the day-night-day differences can be quite considerable.

Lighting

Light is not provided just to enable the hobbyist to see his collection of fishes. It acts as a stimulus to the fishes, and is needed by aquatic plants for photosynthesis. This latter function is most important, for while the plants photosynthesize they absorb carbon dioxide from the water, thus lowering the level of this unwanted gas.

The amount of light is fairly critical, and the final balance between the brightness and the illumination time is best found by trial and error. Naturally the hobbyist will want the aquarium lit to suit his viewing habits (usually in the evenings), and the plants will also require a certain minimum amount of light to flourish properly. Fortunately, these two requirements are quite compatible and the aquarium is normally lit for 10 to 15 hours each day.

It will suffice to say at this point that two types of lighting can be used, either independently or in conjunction.

Tungsten lighting: Conventional light bulbs or filament strip lights.

Advantages: Inexpensive to install and replace.

Disadvantages: Short lamp life, high running costs, and may overheat the aquarium.

Fluorescent lighting: Tube lighting.

Advantages: Long lamp life, inexpensive to run, cool running, even light distribution, various colors available to enhance fish colors and to promote plant growth.

Disadvantages: More expensive and slightly more complicated to install. Lamp length may not correspond exactly to choice of hood size.

Both systems can be combined to suit aquarium plant requirements and both may be operated by means of a time-switch for accurate and regular light control (convenient during vacations.)

It is normal practice to use a cover glass between the tank top and the hood to prevent excessive water evaporation, fish escape attempts, and damage to the light fittings by condensation. If tungsten lighting is employed, it is essential that the hood/reflector is well ventilated; this will prolong lamp life and also disperse excessive, unwanted heat.

Plants do best in light with certain wavelengths predominating—blue-green and orange-red. Fluorescent lamps that provide this spectrum are available but aquarists usually supplement these lamps with the more normal 'warm-white' tubes to give better colored light for viewing.

Although bright light may well suit the viewing fishkeeper, too much light results in excessive growth of algae (remember the warning against window locations). The amount of light may be reduced by installing lower wattage lamps, reducing the illumination time, or providing a cover of floating plants. Alternatively, an increase in the number of aquatic plants may well do the trick by out-competing the algae for the available light.

Light should be used as efficiently as possible. The reflector can be painted white inside or lined with reflecting metal foil. Direct the light downwards and slightly backwards into the tank to avoid casting shadows on the undersides and viewer-facing sides of the fishes. Keep cover glasses meticulously clean so as not to reduce the brightness of the light.

Another factor affecting efficiency is the clarity of the water—water containing particles of dirt in suspension will cut down the amount of light reaching the plants. It is to the aquarium's advantage if the water can be maintained in a clear condition at all times.

Filtration

The efficiency of any filter is often gauged by its ability to maintain crystal clear water, but modern filters can also be used to alter the water's pH or hardness to some degree in addition to just removing suspended matter. Filters, depending on design and mode of operation, can provide three methods of filtration—mechanical, chemical, and biological. Filters may be fitted either inside or outside the tank and be operated by either compressed air or electrically powered water pumps. Most filters that provide mechanical and chemical processes are box- or cylindrical-shaped containers holding the necessary filter media through which the water is passed.

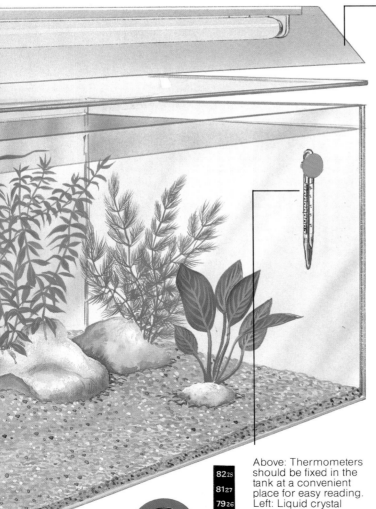

Left: A combination of types of lighting can be fitted in the hood. Where tungsten lamps are used, a well-ventilated hood is essential to disperse their heat. Here a tube designed to promote plant growth is paired with an ordinary fluorescent tube.

Back   Front

Above: The position of the light in the hood affects the aquarist's view of the fish. With a center position (top) any fish near the front glass will cast a shadow towards the viewer. A front-located lamp (below) will cast all shadows behind the fishes being viewed, thus showing all the fishes' colors and beautiful iridescences.

Above: Thermometers should be fixed in the tank at a convenient place for easy reading. Left: Liquid crystal types are fixed externally and may be affected by room temperatures. Dial-type thermometers are fixed internally.

82 28
81 27
79 26
77 25
75 24
73 23
72 22

Biological filters are slotted plates or perforated tubular constructions. They utilize no filter medium and work through bacterial action beneath the gravel.

Mechanical and chemical filters

Compressed air is used either to draw water through internal types or to return filtered water from an external type back into the aquarium.

Internal filters are best used in sparsely furnished tanks, such as those used for raising young fishes, because the necessary regular maintenance would otherwise disturb a heavily planted tank. Internal filters can be of a very simple or very complicated design.

The widely used outside filter has few maintenance problems, although when it is initially installed some cutting of the tank hood may be necessary. Outside filters cannot overflow—as soon as the water in them rises to the same level as that in the main aquarium the inlet siphon action stops. When sufficient clean water has been returned to the tank the level in the filter falls and the siphon starts again.

Electrically powered filters

Usually referred to as 'power filters', these filters have a far greater water flow and may be of an 'open' or 'closed' type. The 'open' type is merely an upgraded version (by virtue of the motorized pump) of the outside box filter. The 'closed' type—the cannister type favored by European aquarists—can be fully submersible, semi-submersible, or situated outside the tank, even some distance from it. To prevent accidental emptying of the tank when using an external power filter, make sure that all water hose connections are firmly made and that the return tube and spray bar are securely fixed.

Filter media

In filters used as trapping devices, matter suspended in the aquarium water is removed by filter 'wool', usually a man-made fiber. Glass-wool must *not* be used because tiny particles of it can find their way back into the tank and irritate and damage the fishes' delicate gills. Filter wool can be re-used (after washing) to some degree. This poses the question how often should the filter medium be changed. There is no definite answer to this because it depends on how dirty the water was in the first place and how fast the filter does its job. But regular filter maintenance should be the rule rather than the exception.

Other types of filter media are available—sand, pebbles, diatomaceous earth, foam rubber. Polyurethane foam (as used in upholstery) may not be safe—check a small sample for toxicity on a dispensable

fish first. Whatever material is used, it should not be packed into the filter too tightly or this will impede water flow through the filter.

Although the water in an aquarium may appear to be quite clear of suspended matter, it will contain dissolved waste products excreted by the fishes and organic materials from decaying matter such as dead leaves. Some of these unwanted substances can be removed by the use of activated carbon in the filter. One drawback of this material is that it will also absorb any medication added to the water when treating the aquarium for sickness. Filters that contain activated carbon should be turned off during the period of treatment. Alternatively the carbon can be removed and the filter left running to provide water circulation and aeration since many medications reduce the oxygen content of the water.

Peat and ion-exchange resins may also be used within the filter body to alter the water chemistry but these sophisticated uses are beyond the scope of this book.

Some aquarists argue that they have never seen a stream or pond fitted with a

filtration system and they scorn such devices. Unfortunately the static aquarium does not benefit from the cleansing actions of wind, rain, and water movements enjoyed by natural bodies of water, so the modern aquarist has to employ artificial aids (including partial water changes) to keep the aquarium in top condition.

Biological filtration

Working with no moving parts and no filter media and needing no maintenance except a periodic stir of the gravel to help remove detritus, the biological filter is probably the most misunderstood piece of aquarium equipment and is often blamed for poor plant growth. If a sufficient depth of gravel (of correct particle size) is used above the filter plate, there should be no problems.

The newcomer to the hobby ought to be warned that the biological filtration *versus* plant growth debate is a controversial subject among aquarists everywhere, although a few minutes' examination of the function of this type of filter will reveal just what a naturally

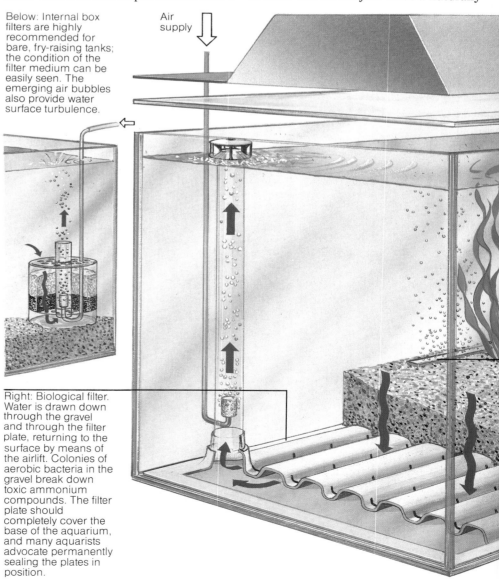

Below: Internal box filters are highly recommended for bare, fry-raising tanks; the condition of the filter medium can be easily seen. The emerging air bubbles also provide water surface turbulence.

Air supply

Right: Biological filter. Water is drawn down through the gravel and through the filter plate, returning to the surface by means of the airlift. Colonies of aerobic bacteria in the gravel break down toxic ammonium compounds. The filter plate should completely cover the base of the aquarium, and many aquarists advocate permanently sealing the plates in position.

efficient job it can usefully perform.

Water is drawn through the aquarium gravel in either a downward or an upward direction depending on the filter's design. This oxygenated water flow encourages aerobic bacterial growth, which continues to thrive only as long as the water flow continues. For this reason, the air supply to a biological (or undergravel) filter system should never be disconnected.

The bacterial colony in the aquarium gravel breaks down toxic substances such as ammonium compounds into less harmful forms by a three stage process. Ammonia is produced by the fish either directly from the gills during respiration, or indirectly because their fecal material is further metabolized by bacteria that produce ammonia as a waste product. *Nitrosomonas* bacteria metabolize ammonia and in doing so produce a waste product called nitrite. Next, *Nitrobacter* bacteria turn the nitrite into a waste product, nitrate. Ammonia and nitrite, both toxic to fish, have now been changed into nitrate, which (although not proven to be harmful to fish) may inhibit growth.

Plants can use nitrate as a food source and nitrate levels can be further reduced (by dilution) as a result of partial water changes.

Biological filtration has several advantages over other filtration systems, the main ones being that it is unobtrusive, does not take up excessive room in the tank, and does not require any physical allowances (such as cutting the tank hood) made for it. The majority of U.S. aquarists have proved that it is not the demon it is often thought to be.

Choice of filtration systems

The use of any filtration system will greatly alleviate any deteriorating conditions in the aquarium, but the fishes' requirements and their everyday activity must be considered when choosing a filtration system.

Many cichlid fishes — particularly those of African origin — will nullify the use of biological filtration once the filter plates are uncovered by the fishes' digging actions, unless the gravel above the filter has a protective mesh fitted a few inches above the filter plates.

A filter's actions should also be considered during any fish's breeding period. A powerful, high water-flow rate filter causing much surface turbulence will be very frustrating for a Dwarf Gourami (*Colisa lalia*) trying to build a bubble-nest only to find it constantly disintegrating. Internal box filters need regular 'wool' changes and it can almost be guaranteed that a pair of cichlid fishes will choose to spawn on the very day such maintenance has been planned by the aquarist. Any intrusion into their tank at this stage will cause them to panic and eat their eggs or newly hatched fry. Filtration systems used in breeding tanks should be either external or of a type that is unlikely to disturb the fishes during maintenance operations.

Aeration

The use of air has already been discussed as a motive power for filtration systems, which incidentally fulfill an 'aeration' purpose while they operate. If filters are not used, what does straightforward aeration do? Aeration has the effect of enlarging the tank's fish-holding capacity. By agitating the water surface it exposes oxygen-depleted water to the air-water interface, thus allowing oxygen from the oxygen-concentrated atmosphere to enter into solution. Similarly, air bubbles from a submerged airstone contain more oxygen than the water surrounding them and lose oxygen by diffusion into the water as they rise to the surface. Aeration also drives free carbon dioxide from the water more rapidly by bringing greater amounts of respired water (containing carbon dioxide) to the water surface.

'More oxygen, less carbon dioxide = more fishes' is an equation that holds good only if the aeration system is kept running. Should the air supply fail, there will be a rapid build-up of carbon dioxide and the fishes may asphyxiate. Sheer numbers of fishes is not generally a problem.

Compressed air is provided by the air pump, whose usual form is of a small electric vibrator operating a diaphragm that pumps air through a one-way valve to the aquarium equipment.

Once the compressed air reaches the aquarium (by way of neoprene tubing) it passes through an airstone, which breaks up the air flow into tiny bubbles. The amount of air may be controlled either by a clamp on the air-carrying tube or by a control on the air pump itself. Although a vibrator air pump can have its output controlled by a clamp, excessive air from a piston pump should not be restricted in this way but bled away to the atmosphere.

Compressed air can also be used to operate an aquarium 'vacuum cleaner' — a device that sucks up detritus.

Below: Regular renewal of filter media in outside box filters is easy because of their accessibility.

Below: Some types of electrically driven 'power filters' can be used inside (left) or outside (right) the aquarium. It is a simple matter to attach the necessary extra tubing for this purpose but all water hose connections must be secure. When used internally, the water flow may be too powerful for a small tank; a spray bar will help to reduce excessive turbulence.

Above left: The stream of bubbles from an airstone helps to aerate the water in the tank directly as well as by constantly agitating the water surface.

AQUATIC PLANTS

A highly contrasting planting arrangement.

*I*n addition to their obvious visual impact, aquarium plants provide the following services: (1) They reduce the carbon dioxide in the water (during the aquarium's illuminated period only). (2) They provide shelter, shade, and sanctuary for the fishes. (3) They give a natural look to the aquarium. (4) They provide spawning sites or food for certain fishes. Many plants are anchored in the gravel by roots but not all draw nourishment through them. Salts are also absorbed from the water through their leaves. Plants suitable for the aquarium can be classified for convenience into three groups: Rooted plants, floating plants, and cuttings. Of course, plants may be classified in other ways, but the categories above coincide with how the plants are grouped when shown competitively at fish shows, and the newcomer may find this easier than trying to remember the scientific names.

Rooted plants form the major proportion of aquarium plants, and there are many diverse leaf forms from which to choose. Rates of growth vary from genus to genus. Some plants require less light than others. There are many shades of green to blend or provide contrast.

The various genera of aquarium plants are generally recognizable by their leaf shapes and colors, but some species readily hybridize to produce confusing varieties. In one genus, the only positive way to identify the species accurately is to allow the plant to grow in shallow water and then to study the flower structure above the surface.

It is not necessary to pre-cultivate the gravel to any great extent in order for the plants to flourish. After the introduction of the fishes, the aquarium plants will be provided with food by the action of bac-

Microsorium pteropus
Java Fern
India to Far East. Leaves up to 12in (30cm) long. Rootstock clings to logs and rocks. Young plants form on leaves. Does well in any light conditions.

Riccia fluitans
Crystalwort
Worldwide. Multibranched floating plant forms dense mats. Ideal refuge for fry and for shading the aquarium. Light requirement not critical.

Acorus gramineus var **pusillus**
Dwarf Japanese Rush
Eastern Asia. A 4in (10cm) foreground plant. A slow grower in the aquarium. Best suited for the cooler aquarium.

Vallisneria natans
Eelgrass
Throughout tropics. Up to 36in (90cm). Favorite background plant. Several varieties (one with tightly spiraled leaves). Propagation by runners.

Najas guadelupensis
Central America. Brittle, multistemmed plant with 1in (2.5cm) leaves. Forms dense clumps. Ideal spawning medium. Propagation by stem division. Synonym – *N. microdon*.

teria on the fecal material excreted by the fishes. Some aquarists provide a layer of peat or loam beneath the gravel when setting up the aquarium, placing the additional 'soil' in nylon bags to prevent it being stirred up by fishes digging in the gravel. However, you may wish to use only aquarium gravel for a first tank and use the special liquid or tablet fertilizers and foods for aquarium plants that can be purchased from an aquatic dealer, should the urge towards underwater gardening become overwhelming. Alternatively, if you are convinced that certain plants require extra nourishment, they can be planted in shallow pots (which contain clay or loam-enriched gravel) sunk in the aquarium gravel. Looking on

Right: An imaginative plant layout that gives not only color contrasts but also, by using plants of different heights, a sense of spaciousness.

Below: A planting stick may be useful in rooting plants in inaccessible locations or for stirring the gravel. The reverse end of many planting sticks has provision for mounting razorblades; they can then be used as algaescrapers to clean the aquarium glass.

Aponogeton crispus
Sri Lanka. Has a rhizome rather than roots. Leaves up to 12in (30cm); variable in color, may be reddish. Suited to bright light. Requires cool rest period in winter.

Hygrophila polysperma
Far East. The 1 to 2in (2.5 to 5cm) leaves are alternate on stem. Fast growing; forms bush when cuttings taken. Propagation easy; cuttings root quickly. Ideal aquarium filler.

Nomaphila stricta
Thailand. Larger, woodier version of *H. polysperma*. Its 4in (10cm) leaves may be eaten by snails. Propagation by cuttings. Prefers hard water. Purple flowers above water.

Salvinia natans
Asia. Floating leaves up to 1in (2.5cm) long. Roots provide shelter for fry. Often grows abundantly, covering the entire surface. Use cover glass to avoid lamp-scorching.

Aponogeton madagascariensis
Madagascar Laceplant Malagasy. The 8 to 12in (20 to 30cm) leaves are skeletal. Needs bright light, water changes, enriched gravel, and a rest period.

the pessimistic side, if things then do not turn out right, only the pots will need removing and a total aquarium stripping and rebuilding is avoided. On the optimistic side, specimen plants that do flourish in their pots will continue to do so undisturbed by any other aquarium rearrangement and the plants can even be transferred, still undisturbed, to new aquatic locations.

The gravel supplied by an aquatic dealer is usually adequate, the only stipulation being that it should be neither too coarse nor too fine—a particle size of about 0.125in (3mm) is suitable. This particle size is also suitable when using biological filtration.

Fast-growing, tall, grasslike plants such as *Vallisneria* and *Sagittaria* are ideal for masking the rear and sides of the aquarium. Bushy plants should be used to fill the corners (in front of the taller plants); Water Wisteria (*Synnema,* now also known as *Hygrophila difformis*) is an excellent choice along with other species of *Hygrophila, Ludwigia,* and *Ceratopteris.*

Foreground plants, visually very effective when placed in front of a rocky outcrop, may be of shorter stature and slower growing. Hairgrass (*Eleocharis*) and Dwarf Japanese Rush (*Acorus*) are often used in this position.

No aquarium scene would be complete without one or two featured 'specimen' plants. The Amazon Swordplant (*Echinodorus*) fills this role admirably, while dense, low clumps of members of the *Cryptocoryne* genus carpet the open swimming area. The sturdy broad leaves of these two genera provide excellent spawning sites for fishes that deposit their eggs on vertical surfaces. The Amazon Swordplant is a natural choice for its piscean companion, the Angelfish (*Pterophyllum* sp.); the Asian *Cryptocoryne* plays an unconscious host to the eggs of the Harlequin Fish (*Rasbora heteromorpha*), which deposits its eggs on the undersides of the leaves.

It will not matter if *Cryptocoryne* plants are shaded from the light by larger plants, because they are quite happy with low light levels.

Mention must be made of the splendid genus *Aponogeton* from Africa and Malagasy, carrying wide, ruffle-edged leaves; the famous Lace Plant (*A. madagascariensis*) has skeletal leaves, completely devoid of tissue between the veins. *Aponogeton* species do not have roots in the literal sense but have a rhizome. It is normal aquarium practice to rest these

Sagittaria subulata
Arrowhead
North America. Leaves 12in (30cm) long. Aquarium favorite similar to *Vallisneria*. Tolerates hard water. Propagation by runners.

Pistia stratiotes
Water Lettuce
Tropical areas. Wedge-shaped leaves are 4in (10cm) long and velvety. Long trailing roots. Grows very large in nature, smaller in the aquarium.

Hygrophila difformis
Water Wisteria
Far East. Light green leaves, up to 4in (10cm) spread, may vary in shape depending on the lighting. Roots easily. Synonym— *Synnema triflorum.*

Echinodorus bleheri
Brazil. Up to 20in (50cm). A popular Amazon Swordplant. Often featured as a specimen plant in the aquarium. Plantlets form on long runners sent out from the main plant.

Cabomba caroliniana
North America. Up to 1.5in (3.75cm) across whorls. A popular plant and spawning medium. Needs clean water, otherwise sediment will clog leaves. Roots easily.

Left: The fishes and plants in this aquarium have been very carefully chosen to contrast and complement each other. Note how the red of the fishes (center) keys in with the color of the plants (left). The silvery shapes of the other fishes add brilliance and movement. The aquarium lights may be adjusted, in both direction and intensity, to favor specific groups of plants, creating patches of light and shade to further the illusion of space and depth. In order to maintain such luxuriant plant growth, as in this Dutch aquarium, a great amount of light is needed—at least 40 watts (fluorescent) per sq. foot (900cm²) of water surface area.

flowering, seed-setting species during the winter months by transplanting them into a shallower, cooler aquarium until the following spring, when they regain their former glory once more.

It is a little difficult to classify *Microsorium;* it does have hairlike roots emerging from a creeping rhizome, but it is not anchored in the gravel, preferring to cling to rocks and tree roots, which it soon overgrows. Another plant that adopts a surface to cling to is Java Moss (*Vesicularia*); along with the coldwater Willow Moss (*Fontinalis*), its tangled mass of tiny leaves provides an excellent spawning medium for egg-scattering fishes, whose eggs are soon caught in these plants and well-protected from the hungry adult fishes.

Being totally submerged, plants in the aquarium tend to reproduce vegetatively

Echinodorus magdalenensis
Dwarf Amazon Swordplant
Tropical America. Up to 8in (20cm). Used as a foreground plant. Sends out many runners with young plants.

Azolla caroliniana
Fairy Moss
America. Velvety leaves up to 0.5in (1.25cm) may also be reddish in color. Provides shade and a haven for young fishes. Shown raised for detail.

Ceratophyllum demersum
Hornwort
Worldwide. Up to 1in (2.5cm) across whorls. Shown rooted, but mostly floats freely. Propagation by cuttings. Temperate species die in warm water.

Ludwigia repens
North America. Leaves up to 1.5in (3.75cm) long have reddish undersides. Needs good light. Propagation by cuttings. Popular plant used in terrariums. A bog plant in the wild.

Eleocharis acicularis
Hairgrass, Needlegrass
Worldwide. Up to 8in (20cm) tall. Common name most apt, different in form from any other plant. Needs good light. Propagates by root runner.

by sending out runners from which new plants develop, or new daughter plants may emerge on the leaves of certain species. One group of plants, the Aponogetons, actually flowers above the water surface and can be pollinated by the aquarist to produce seed pods. The seeds can then be sown in shallow water and will grow into new plants.

Floating plants

Although regarded as pests by some aquarists, these floating species do serve a useful purpose in the aquarium. They offer shade for the fishes from the almost perpetual glare of the lights, and provide a sanctuary for newly born young fish, which find safe refuge in the trailing roots hanging down into the water. Members of the Gourami family, notably *Colisa* species, utilize fragments of these plants in the construction of their bubble-nests, the plant's texture helping to prevent the nest from disintegrating.

The size of floating plants ranges from the diminutive *Lemna, Salvinia,* and brightly colored red and green *Azolla,* through the brittle strands of *Riccia* and *Najas,* to the massive velvety bulk of *Pistia*—which can almost push the aquarium hood off!

Referring back to lighting, another need for cover glasses becomes apparent here; they prevent the leaves of floating plants from being scorched by the heat from the lamps hanging low over the water surface.

Cuttings

This is an artificially created group, because plants within this category do root in gravel, but they are more usually propagated by means of cuttings. The top section of a plant is cut off and planted in the gravel, where it soon roots and forms a new plant. One effect of this pruning is to encourage the donor plant to take on a more bushy shape, as side replacement shoots develop.

Plants in this group (also known as 'bunch' plants in the U.S.) include the fine-leaved species such as the tropical *Cabomba, Limnophila,* and coldwater *Ceratophyllum* and *Myriophyllum.* Members of the *Hygrophila* genus may also be propagated by cuttings, and a severed leaf left floating in the aquarium will usually develop roots of its own accord.

Replicas of aquarium plants, modeled in some form of plastic, are also commercially available, and these will be discussed in the section dealing with decorative materials. (See page 22.)

Egeria densa
South America. One inch (2.5cm) opposite leaves on long stem. Receives nourishment through leaves, roots serving merely as an anchorage. Prefers hard water.

Cryptocoryne balansae
Far East. Up to 24in (60cm) tall. Long, narrow leaves make this plant ideal for a deep tank. Propagation by runners. Flowers above surface when grown in shallow water.

Cryptocoryne willisii
Sri Lanka. Variable in size, up to 8in (20cm) tall. Useful foreground plant shown pot-planted. This avoids any disturbance when transplanting to another aquarium.

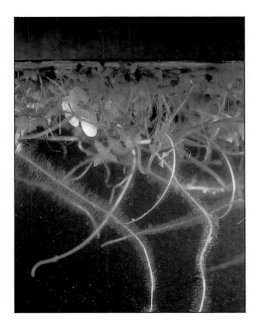

Left: Floating plants (here including *Lemna* sp.) offer shade from the aquarium lights and also provide safe hiding-places for newly born fishes.

Right: Increased plant stocks can be achieved by severing young plants from the parent and re-rooting. Some plants will develop roots from cuttings readily; the top portion is cut off and left to float until roots emerge. Alternatively, the cut portion can be rooted in the gravel immediately and it is usual practice to remove existing leaves from the bottom inch or so of the cutting's stem before planting so that roots are encouraged to form.

Ceratopteris thalictroides
Indian Fern
Southeast Asia. Up to 20in (50cm) tall. Grown rooted or floating. Roots from floating example very long. Leaves flat on water surface. Growth vigorous, propaga- tion by daughter plants appearing on leaves. Often attacked by snails. Requires good light and warmth. Floating plants provide shade but must be kept in check.

Cryptocoryne wendtii
Sri Lanka. 4 to 12in (10 to 30cm). Leaf color variable from specimen to specimen. Identification of *Cryptocoryne* species only positive through study of flower above shallow water.

Vesicularia dubyana
Java Moss
Southeast Asia. Leaves 0.1in (2.5mm) long on branched stems. A cling- ing moss needing a good light and protection from sediment and algae.

FURNISHING THE AQUARIUM

Correct gravel particle size is 0.125in (3mm).

*C*lumps of plants and avenues of tall grasses may be very artistic but for dramatic effect an outcrop of rocks cannot be topped. Rocks also provide shelter, territorial areas, and breeding sites. It is true that some fishes—such as those from the African Rift Valley Lakes—are more at home among rocks than among plants, and a tank especially created for these species (Pseudotropheus, Julidochromis, Labeotropheus etc.) should be furnished with plenty of terraced rocks, giving ample opportunity for each fish to find a cave of its own. Gravel is not only a medium in which the plants can root; it can also serve as a filtration bed and as a spawning site. In order to make the aquarium look even more natural, aquarists usually include roots and sunken branches in the aquarium's decor. There are many artificial decorations available, too.

The choice of rock should be made keeping in mind the shape, texture, stratum detail, color (matched to the gravel, ideally), and chemical composition. Although most rocks will be chosen mainly for their appearance, it must be appreciated that the fishes will live in close proximity to the rocks. There should be no sharp edges, nor should the rocks be erected in precarious, overhanging piles.

By far the most important consideration is the effect the rocks will have on the water's chemical composition. Rocks that are at all soluble, particularly those of a calcareous nature, should not be used in the freshwater aquarium where a soft water condition is required. However, water-hardening rocks may be valuable in aquariums containing fishes that tolerate hard water, such as the Rift Valley Lake species. Calcareous rocks are beneficial in saltwater aquariums, where they help to maintain the required high pH reading. (See section on water, page 24.)

Many newcomers to the hobby are tempted to add branches of dead coral as decoration, assuming that this normally submerged material is relevant to the aquarium. Although some fishes may enjoy amusing themselves among the coral, it should be barred from use in a freshwater aquarium since coral's high calcium content may adversely affect the water chemistry. Coral is also extremely sharp and will cut and scratch freshwater fishes. Of course, there are no such restrictions about its use in a marine aquarium.

Examples of suitable rocks for aquarium use are granite, basalt, quartz, and slate. Crumbly sandstone, limestone, and rocks carrying any metal ore should not be used.

Gravel

Much of what has been said about the selection of rocks also applies when choosing gravel for the aquarium. Very often, gravel dredged up off-shore will contain many fragments of calcium-rich seashells, which will again harden the water over a period of time. Some aquatic dealers stock lime-free gravel, and although it will invariably be more expen-

sive, it will be a worthwhile investment if softwater fishes are to be kept.

The particle size of the gravel is important. Coarse gravel is unsuitable for two reasons: Food will quickly fall beyond the reach of the fishes and will decay, beginning a pollution risk; and if biological filtration is used, coarse gravel will not provide enough surface area for the bacteria to colonize, and the water flow through the gravel will be too fast.

If the gravel is too fine, it will pack down too tightly. Under these conditions, the plant roots will have difficulty penetrating the gravel, and the water flow rate through a biological filter will be severely impeded.

A medium-size gravel must be found and, as mentioned earlier, a particle size of 0.125 (3mm) is ideal. So much for size; what about the color and the amount needed to furnish your aquarium?

A dark gravel is best from several standpoints. In the wild, a fish swimming over a light-colored river bed would be easily seen by any predator—fish, bird, or even man. Freshwater fishes normally have a dark-colored back or top (dorsal) surface, which camouflages them as they swim over a dark river bed. In the aquarium, light from above will be reflected back up from any light-colored gravel, washing out the colors of the fish, which will then appear faded to the viewing aquarist. (The exception to this might seem to be in marine aquariums, where the bright colors of the fishes are apparently not affected as they swim above brilliant white coral sand. As we shall learn later, only coloration due to reflective material is affected, and the marine fishes' pigmented colors are not diluted.) For this reason, exhibition tanks at fish shows usually have the bottom glass painted black (on the outside!).

Some aquatic dealers stock colored gravel, but there is something slightly unnerving about a bed of yellow, green, or even mottled red and white gravel. There is also a danger that the colors used to dye the gravel may leach out into the water and release toxic substances.

If the color of the rockwork does not blend with the color of the gravel, there is an easy trick to match the two colors—some of the rock can be smashed up into small pieces that are then scattered on the surface of the gravel. Wrap the rock in a piece of cloth before smashing it, to stop flying splinters and to collect the pieces all in one operation.

The amount of gravel needed for any one tank may surprise you. The plants must have an adequate depth in which to root, and if biological filtration is to be used, at least 2 to 3in (5 to 7.5cm) of gravel must be placed over the filter plate to avoid any adverse effects on plant growth. (Incidentally, plants grown in pots will not suffer from biological filtration, being isolated from water flow

In practical terms this means approximately a 2 gallon (7.6 liter) bucketful for every 1ft² (900cm²) of tank floor area; if the gravel is to be landscaped, considerably more will be needed.

Other tank decorations

Wood is a favorite material for furnishing the aquarium naturally. Sunken logs and twisted roots are notable features in a well-appointed aquarium. Such material can be collected from rivers, marshes, and forests, the only reservation being that any wood obtained this way must be long dead, with no traces of rotting.

Wood intended for aquarium use must be boiled in several changes of water and immersed in water for several weeks until completely waterlogged, then it may be considered fit for use. There should be no sign of discoloration of the water from the tannins in the wood. Alternatively, dead wood can be sealed with several coats of polyurethane varnish. Florists sometimes sell pieces of petrified wood for flower arrangements and this can also be used, after sealing, in an aquarium. Aquatic dealers will also stock this wood occasionally.

Another suitable natural material is cork bark, often used as a backdrop or to form terracing. The color is most pleasing, and it is easily cut to shape.

Modern technology has provided a synthetic substitute for natural wood decoration, and very realistic molded-resin 'logs' and 'tree roots' are commercially available. Modeled on real-life branches, after a few weeks in the aquarium they soon become coated with algae and it is difficult to tell them from the real thing.

Imitation plants are also a result of modern technology and, thanks to patient development in design tools and processing methods, it is now possible to purchase extremely lifelike replicas of the more popular aquarium plants—even down to the wet, floppy feel when taken out of water.

Of course, these artificial substitutes will not perform the same chemical and biological processes as their living counterparts, but they can provide shelter and spawning sites. Soon disguised by a covering of natural algae, artificial plants bring a touch of greenery to any aquarium in which boisterous fishes or those with vegetarian dietary habits are to be kept.

Several other objects of an artificial nature sometimes find their way into aquariums under the guise of being 'decorative'; these range from miniature, precast brick walls to sunken galleons, divers, treasure chests, and even mermaids. Usually out of scale, such ornaments are really quite out of place in the aquarium, and often the materials will emit color or poisonous substances into the water and endanger the fishes.

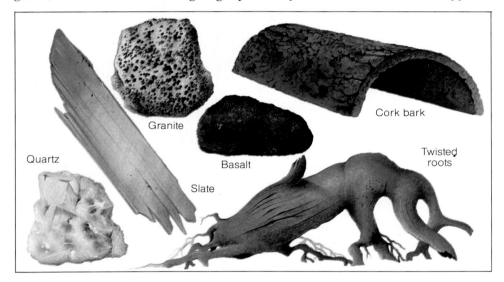

Quartz
Granite
Slate
Basalt
Cork bark
Twisted roots

Above: It is important to use only those rocks that will not adversely affect the water chemistry. Wood and cork bark should be sealed.
Left: A tank furnished to suit these rock-dwelling Malawi Blue Cichlids *(Pseudotropheus zebra)*.

Below: Plastic plants will provide decorative 'greenery' and shelter in tanks with herbivorous fishes. Algae will soon cover them and make them look more natural. The gray 'rock' and 'log' in this tank are also artificial.

WATER: THE VITAL INGREDIENT

The Discus Fishes need soft water.

We now come to the main ingredient of the aquarium, without which it would be unable to function—water. Water is the fishes' atmosphere and serious consideration must be given to its supply and condition. The fishes we keep in our freshwater aquarium can come from several different types of water depending upon location. It says much for our fishes' tolerance that, generally, it is not too difficult to maintain quite successfully a truly cosmopolitan collection of fishes (from all manner of natural waters) in one common type of water, usually tap water. This may be called 'fishkeeping', whereas 'fish-breeding' may well require a deeper knowledge of the water qualities needed to bring about the successful reproduction of a particular species of fish. There are still many fishes that have not been bred in an aquarium and water management is probably the key to success.

The water of all streams, rivers, and lakes begins ultimately as rain. The water then collects and drains across the land until it eventually reaches the sea, from which the evaporation and condensation cycle starts again. As rain falls through the atmosphere, it collects dust and minerals and absorbs gases, so that the water in rainfall is no longer pure. According to where the rain falls, the run-off is also affected by rocks and vegetation. Water falling on granite and flowing across moorland will be different from water that seeps through chalk hills. Lakes formed in rocky basins are again different in mineral composition from jungle streams. Yet we blithely expect to keep fishes from all these locations in water that probably resembles none of their natural habitats.

Above: The waters of the vast Amazon rain forest—whether they are rivers, streams, or lakes—are very soft and have an acidic reaction (pH value below 7) due to the large amounts of decaying vegetation present in the water.

Water quality

Tap water is supplied for one purpose—human consumption. It is carefully screened, cleaned, treated with prophylactic chemicals, and pumped into our homes for our use. It does not however carry a guarantee that it is suitable for fishkeeping!

Before you put it in an aquarium, tap water should be left standing for a day or two and, if possible, subjected to strong aeration to remove the chlorine in the water. Alternatively, a dechlorinating agent can be used. This can be obtained in liquid form from your aquatic dealer and is just mixed into the water. The amount to be used will be stated in the accompanying instructions.

Water drawn through copper piping can be toxic to fish (especially if the pipework or storage tank is new). So the first batch of water that flows through the tap, which may have been standing in the system for some time, should not be used.

Normally there is not too much to worry about, for any fish that is purchased locally will have been kept by the dealer in water similar to your supply while awaiting sale. If you are likely to buy the more exotic species (perhaps requiring special water conditions) or to bring fishes back from other areas, it might be wise to inquire about the water

conditions they are used to, in case these are different from yours.

Many aquatic publications deal in great depth with water chemistry, and the newcomer to fishkeeping is likely to be confused about the mystery surrounding such a normally taken-for-granted commodity.

There are two yardsticks used when describing water quality, and although they do bear some relationship to each

other, it is suggested that the hobbyist treat them as separate entities right from the start to avoid any confusion. The properties of water are classified under two main headings: pH (acidity or alkalinity), and hardness.

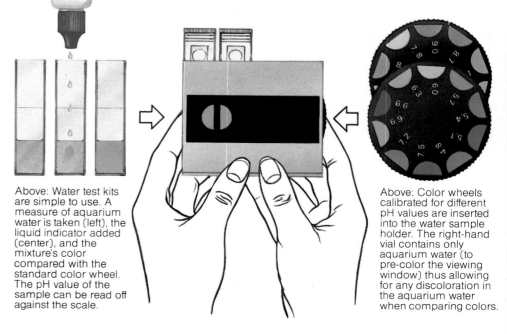

Above: Water test kits are simple to use. A measure of aquarium water is taken (left), the liquid indicator added (center), and the mixture's color compared with the standard color wheel. The pH value of the sample can be read off against the scale.

Above: Color wheels calibrated for different pH values are inserted into the water sample holder. The right-hand vial contains only aquarium water (to pre-color the viewing window) thus allowing for any discoloration in the aquarium water when comparing colors.

Above: The Rift Valley Lakes in Africa are gigantic clefts in the rocky basin, filled with water. Some fishes are endemic to their own lake, not being found elsewhere. The high mineral content of the water makes it hard and alkaline.

Right: *Labeotropheus trewavasae*, a cichlid found in Lake Malawi.

The pH scale

The pH scale is a logarithmic measurement denoting the strength of acidity or alkalinity. Ranging from 0 to 14 (strongest acid to strongest alkali), the pH scale concerns the aquarist over only a very narrow band. Water used in the aquarium should lie between 6.5 and 7.5 for freshwater and 7.9 and 8.5 for saltwater tanks. On the pH scale neutral is 7.

pH values	0 1 2 3 4 5 6 7 8 9 10 11 12 13 14
	←——Acid —— | ——Alkaline——→
	Neutral

The pH of any sample of water can be tested with inexpensive test-kits. These may employ sensitized papers or test liquids, and are quite accurate enough for the beginner. Much more accurate (and therefore expensive) electronic test apparatus exists, but this is usually well beyond the financial means and actual requirements of the average hobbyist.

To give an example of the practical use of pH: Freshwater fishes from jungle streams and rivers are usually found in waters with a pH below 7, whereas fishes from African rocky basins with waters of a high mineral content will require a pH above 7.

Much of the theory of pH and the fishes' needs is nullified by the fact that many fishes are bred commercially in water not always corresponding to that of their original natural habitat. Following their export to the aquarium markets of the world, they are then restocked into whatever water is convenient to the dealer, before finally ending up in a domestic aquarium.

Should it be necessary to stabilize the aquarium water around a definite pH value (for instance when trying to breed a species that requires very precise water conditions) a great deal of thought has to be given to everything that will be put into the tank (in the way of decoration and gravel), to avoid altering the pH. This is not generally necessary in the running of a cosmopolitan community collection of fishes, and it is only when the hobbyist decides to specialize with the more delicate species that water chemistry technology becomes important.

For those readers who are naturally curious, the pH of tap water in the U.S. is around 7.8 to 8.2. In most European domestic water supplies it is around 7.2. Both are a convenient average for the aquarium.

Water hardness

Probably a better-known property of water, hardness is also an important factor in the fishes' comfort and general well-being. Hardness is due to dissolved salts, usually of calcium and magnesium, and is one of two types—temporary or permanent. Temporary hardness can be removed by boiling the water, but permanent hardness can be removed or reduced only by chemical means or by distillations. A quick method of reducing hardness is by simple dilution—adding known soft water such as rainwater to hard tap water.

Most egg-laying fishes prefer soft water since any excessive hardness may prevent the development of the fertilized eggs. Live-bearing fishes and some African cichlids require hard water. Similarly, plants also have their preferences: *Echinodorus* will tolerate soft to medium-hard water, but *Cabomba* prefers soft and *Vallisneria* hard. (Many aquarists feel that certain plants are incompatible in each other's company; this may be so, but it also follows that the water composition could be wrong for some of the plants and not for others.)

There are several ways that hardness may be described: °DH (Germany), °hardness (English, Clark Scale), or ppm (parts per million, of either calcium carbonate $CaCO_3$ or calcium oxide CaO).

1°DH is 17.9ppm CaO.

1°hardness (1°H) is 14.3ppm $CaCO_3$. The factor of 56/100 is used to convert °DH into °H and 100/56 to convert °H into °DH.

To avoid confusion, examples of soft, hard, and very hard waters will be given in °DH only; these are, respectively, up to 5°DH, 20 to 30°DH and over 30°DH.

Usually, soft waters have an acidic reaction (lower than pH7) and hard water is usually alkaline (above pH7).

The hardness of the domestic water supply varies from region to region, depending upon the original source of water catchment. Water pumped from reservoirs in mountainous areas will generally be soft, whereas water collected from chalk soils will be very hard.

The newcomer should not feel intimidated by these brief notes on the technicalities of water management since, it should be stressed, thousands of hobbyists pursue a successful interest in fishkeeping without knowing the slightest thing about water chemistry. A simple way to ensure good healthy aquarium water is to undertake regular partial water changes, say 20 to 25% every three to four weeks, ensuring that the replacement water is of the same temperature and quality as that removed. In the marine aquarium, evaporation losses should be replaced not with salt but with fresh water, since none of the dissolved salts will have been lost during evaporation.

In every instance, fishes should not be subjected to drastic changes in water temperature or quality, and methods of ensuring this will be discussed in a later section. (See page 37.)

SETTING UP THE AQUARIUM

Keep the final design in mind during setting up.

Now that you understand the equipment and furnishings for the aquarium, you are ready to begin. There are three points to remember. First, the aquarium must be set up well in advance of the purchase of the livestock, for reasons that will become clear in the following chapter. Second, although the emphasis throughout this book has been concentrated upon tropical aquarium fishkeeping, much of the foregoing information (with the obvious exception of the section on heating) will also be applicable to the setting up of a coldwater aquarium. Finally, the photographs and diagrams in this section are from a studio performance carefully prepared to show the greatest detail. You may not be blessed with as much elbow room and things may be a little more cramped. But any variations, particularly in tank layout and design, are your prerogative.

Setting up an aquarium can be an inconvenient, and sometimes messy, operation. Usually the source of water (and the place to dispose of it) is nowhere near the proposed site for the aquarium. If this is the case, as much preparatory work as possible should be done before moving to the actual aquarium site. Repeated journeys with dripping buckets, to and from the kitchen sink by way of the carpeted hall, are not guaranteed to endear the fishkeeper to the rest of the family. A certain amount of setting up can be done, if necessary, at the sink—gravel and rocks can be installed in tanks up to 24in (60cm) in length and then carried into position. But for demonstration purposes in this book everything will be put into the tank in one location.

A small table next to the tank's position is very useful; on it you can keep all the

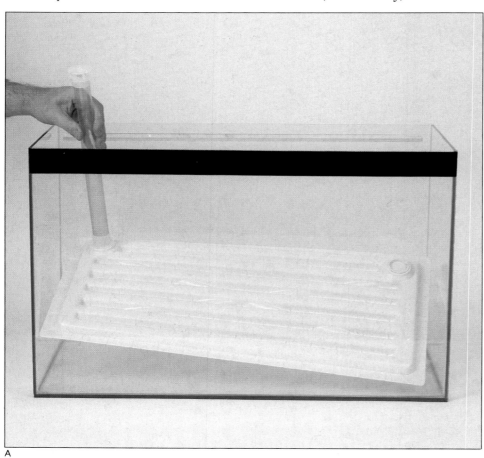

The biological filter is fitted first (A). The gravel placed over it (B) should be deep enough for plant roots, and slope from back to front (C).

Air-operated filters: The simple sponge filter (1) and internal box filter (2) are ideal for fry-raising, unplanted tanks. External box types (3,4) are more suitable for furnished tanks, where their regular maintenance will cause little disturbance to the plant arrangements inside the tank. Both filter wool and carbon can be accommodated within the filter body, and an airstone gives a good rate of water flow.

Power filters: Water flow rates can be increased by the use of electric pumps fitted to a biological system (5), or to an outside box type (6) that also uses cartridge filter medium. Internal or external cannister-type filters (7,8) are suitable for large tanks and care must be taken to ensure that all water connections are secure. The cleaned water is generally redistributed by a spray bar to reduce water pressure.

necessary equipment close at hand. Tools required will be a small screwdriver, pliers, scissors, a pair of metal shears, a glasscutter, a small hammer, and a tube of aquarium sealant. Although this sounds a formidable line-up, every tool may not be needed in every setting-up situation, but without all of these, you can almost guarantee that the very thing you want will not be there when it is required.

Advance preparation
Certain tasks, such as washing the gravel and selecting the rocks and plants, can be carried out in advance. The gravel is best washed out of doors, half a bucketful at a time, under a running hose until the water runs clear from the bucket. Rocks can be worked to the correct proportions with a few well-directed blows from a

hammer (protect your eyes!) and pieces can be glued together with sealant into preformed grottoes and caves ready for placing in the tank. At this stage a rocky backdrop can be constructed and glued directly onto the rear wall of the tank, or a decorative background can be fixed to the outside of the tank. The plants should be laid out in groups of species between sheets of very wet newspaper to prevent them from drying out as they await their turn to be placed in the tank.

It will be assumed that the site chosen for the tank fulfills all the requirements stated earlier, and that the empty tank is in position on its polystyrene base awaiting our attention.

Setting up
Before beginning to furnish an aquarium, make a plan of the desired layout. In this

way, you will have a clear picture and you will not waste time in trying (and rejecting) many ideas. While following this plan it is also wise to keep looking through the front panel of the aquarium to see how things are progressing!

The decision to use a biological filter or not has to be made at the outset because, if such a filter is to be used, it goes into the tank before anything else.

Gravel is then added to a depth of 2 to 3in (5 to 7.5cm) and contoured to suit; vertical slabs of rocks (resting on the tank base) are used to form terracing, and other rocks and items such as wood branches are firmly fixed in position. Note that the gravel should slope from back to front to give a more pleasing appearance. When 'rock-scaping' remember to allow room for the plants and for the extra visual effect they will give.

The combined heater/thermostat unit may be mounted across the back of the tank as shown (D), or vertically in one corner if the depth of water permits. Heaters controlled by separate thermostats of either internal (E) or external (F) design must be mounted clear of the aquarium gravel to ensure adequate water circulation around them; otherwise uneven internal temperatures will be generated, which are likely to shorten the heater's useful life.

D

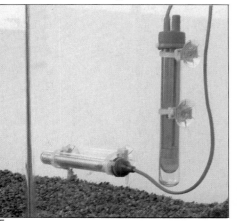

E

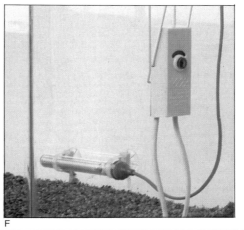

F

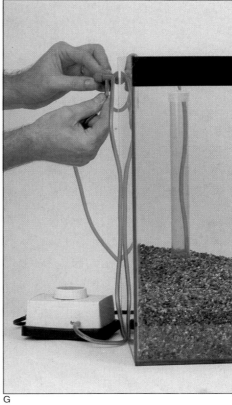

G

The air supply from the air pump is distributed via a ganged valve (G), allowing independent control of air to each piece of equipment.

5

6

7

8

While the aquarium is dry, and so far reasonably uncluttered, is the best time to fit the filtration system (unless a biological system is already in position), heating system, air supply tubing, and airstones.

Generally, heater/thermostat combined units have mounting clips provided, but otherwise heaters and thermostats should be fixed in position by non-metallic clips. Two heaters should be used for large tanks. All wiring connections must be made outside the tank.

Filter boxes are fitted to one end of the tank or to the rear wall, ensuring that the water flow is reasonably unimpeded to the inlet siphon tube. Do not obstruct the water flow with a huge rock. If possible, the returned cleaned water from the filter should be directed away from the inlet siphon by fitting an extension tube to the

filter's outlet pipe or, in the case of filters with provision of a separate return pipe, by fitting the return pipe at the opposite end of the tank. The return and inlet tubes to external power filters must be securely fastened to the side or rear walls of the tank and special care must be taken to ensure that the holes in the return tube spray bar face across the tank, preferably downwards!

Airstones can be located behind rocks for good visual effect and the connecting air tubing may be buried under the gravel and held down by a piece of rock. Provision must be made for an anti-siphon loop in the air tubing, or the air pump itself should be situated above the eventual water level. The air supply to the filters can be connected at this stage.

For the moment, all wires from filters, air pumps, heaters, and thermostats are

left unconnected to avoid the risk of accidental switching on at this time.

Planting the aquarium

The aquarium may be planted dry or wet. The wet method is generally preferable, as the plants instantly take up their natural positions in the water and the hobbyist can see at a glance if the planting plan is working out to his liking. So the tank must now be filled with water.

To avoid overflowing when the planter's arms and hands are in the tank, it should be filled only three-quarters full at the planting stage. Water must be added in such a manner as not to disturb the carefully contoured gravel and terracing. It is best done by means of a hose pipe running first into a saucer or other container sitting on the aquarium floor. The overflow from this container will then

H

I

K

J

Rockwork: The slope of the gravel can be maintained by the insertion of pieces of flat rock or slate at an angle into the gravel bank (H,I). Large rocks (or synthetic logs in this instance) can be embedded in the gravel to prevent toppling (J,K). Gravel is added (L) behind to form terracing where plants may be rooted. The biological filter's airlift tube and the heater/thermostat, although in plain view here, will be hidden by the plants later.

Water has to be added gently, to avoid disturbing the 'landscaped' gravel. A jar acts as a cushioning overflow (M) and the rock can also act as a water jet deflector (N). To avoid overflows, plant the tank when only three-quarters full of water (O). Plant the back corners first (P) and gauge their effect (Q) before putting the foreground plants in. Notice how the 'hardware' is being hidden. After planting, the tank can be completely filled.

L

Water capacities, weights and recommended heater sizes

Tank size	Volume			Weight of water		Heater size
	US Gallons	Imp Gallons	Liters	Lbs	Kg	
12 x 8 x 8in (30 x 20 x 20cm)	3.0	2.5	11.4	25	11.3	75W
18 x 10 x 10in (45 x 25 x 25cm)	6.0	5.0	22.7	50	22.7	100W
24 x 12 x 12in (60 x 30 x 30cm)	14.4	12.0	54.5	120	54.3	150W
24 x 15 x 12in (60 x 38 x 30cm)	18.0	15.0	68.2	150	67.9	150W
36 x 15 x 12in (90 x 38 x 30cm)	27.6	23.0	104.5	230	104.1	2 x 100W
48 x 15 x 12in (120 x 38 x 30cm)	36.0	30.0	136.4	300	135.7	2 x 150W

Above: An alternative to undergravel nutrients for plants is to plant individual specimens in a pre-formed plant-plug, which is then buried in the gravel. Ideal for tanks with an undergravel filter, and to give plants a little extra care.

M

N

O

P

Q

gently fill the aquarium without any undue disturbance. Cold water can be brought to approximately the correct temperature by adding some hot water.

Planting is done working from the edges of the tank towards the center. The tall plants go around the sides and back, with the bushy plants behind and between the rocks. Shorter plants look effective immediately in front of rocks, and 'specimen' plants are best planted away from groups of other plants. Remember that the crown (base) of a plant should be level with, or just above, the surface of the gravel. In cold-water aquariums, it is recommended that plant crowns are protected by a few small pebbles to prevent uprooting by fishes.

Most of the plants will take up their final positions almost immediately, but others may take some time to respond to the aquarium light, delaying your evaluation of the full effect of the planting.

Final preparations

Once planting has been completed, the aquarium can be filled with water and it is time to get the whole thing operating. The filter box should be filled with filter medium and activated carbon, and the filter siphon started. The filter will then fill with water and stop, until air is supplied. External, cannister-type power filters are filled by temporarily removing the return tube (at the filter end) and sucking air through the filter, thus drawing water from the aquarium into the filter container (previously filled with the filter medium). As soon as water emerges from the filter outlet, the return tube should be securely replaced. The filter will not work until power is supplied to the motor, ideally via a switched circuit.

The wires from the heater/thermostat, power filter (if fitted), air pump, and lamps can now be connected to their respective supplies; the lamps' supply needs to be switchable. Use can be made of a 'cable tidy', a proprietary piece of aquarium equipment that serves as an electrical connection box and switching center and is fixed to the outside of the aquarium by adhesive pads. An aquarium thermometer should be fixed in place, depending on the type used, so it can easily be seen by the hobbyist. Similarly, a row of airline valves may usefully be stuck to the aquarium outside, and the airline connections from the pump to the filter and airstone made secure.

The cover glass should now be fitted, and the aquarium hood put into place. Finally, a suitable plug is fitted to the

The temperature of the aquarium water can be conveniently monitored by easy-to-read thermometers. Floating types (R) may be anchored to the front glass by a rubber sucker to prevent them drifting around the tank. The dial type (S) can be stuck to the glass in such a way that the desired temperature reading is at '12 o'clock'; any deviation is then easy to see. External liquid crystal thermometers (T) are becoming very popular nowadays.

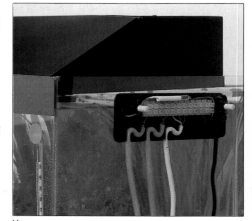

supply cable to the cable tidy and the connection can be made to the electrical supply. The switches can now be operated and the aquarium is in action.

At this stage, several things will happen, and just as likely, several other things will not. Expected occurrences, such as the lights coming on and the air-pump and filter motors starting, usually function the first time. A glow from the neon indicator on the thermostat indicates that electrical power is reaching the heating system, but until the thermometer indicates a change in temperature there will be no visible reassuring evidence of heat emerging from the heater—don't be tempted to take the heater out of the water to feel it.

One possible annoyance may be that air-operated filters and airstones seem to refuse to work in harmony with each other. This problem is easily overcome by adjusting the air flow to each, by means of the air flow valve, until the water pours from the filter return tube together with a satisfactory column of bubbles from the airstone and/or the biological filter system.

Running in

It is understandable that now that the aquarium is to all intents and purposes ready for livestock, the hobbyist will want to lose no time in acquiring the fishes. Ideally, the aquarium should be functioning as a wholly complete unit (biologically speaking) when the fishes are introduced.

Modern thinking and aquarium practices have done away with the necessity of letting the aquarium 'mature' itself for a few weeks before adding the livestock.

Water conditioners are available that neutralize the chlorine from tap water and that will precipitate heavy metals almost immediately.

The biological filter will not function unless the bacteria in the gravel have something to work upon and, as we have seen previously, this means a source of ammonia. It is often suggested that some gravel from an established aquarium is used to 'seed' the new gravel bed, or that a piece of food (meat, for example) is allowed to rot away in the new, uninhabited aquarium. It is now normal practice to let the fishes themselves provide the ammonia, although the newcomer is advised not to risk very expensive fishes at this initial stage—a few hardy species will do just as good a job.

During this initial period, some plants may shed their leaves or become uprooted

A cover glass (U) protects the electrical light fittings from damage by condensation and also prevents the leaves from being scorched. Cover glasses must be kept clean so that none of the light is blocked off from reaching the aquarium, although some ultra-violet rays will be. A neat, safe way to connect the electricity supply to the aquarium's equipment is by means of a proprietary junction box known as a 'cable tidy' (V). It has switched circuits for lighting and air pump, but the heating circuits are continuous. The wires have to be threaded through a mazelike track before connection to anchor them. A neon lamp glows through the cover (W) when the heating circuit is working. The two illustrations (X,Y) show different arrangements of lighting. The top hood has provision for tungsten lamps only (the aquarium is 24in/60cm long) and two 60watt lamps were used in this photograph. The lower hood (slightly smaller, but fitted to the same tank) is fitted with both tungsten and fluorescent lighting. The starter equipment for the fluorescent tube is housed in the recess immediately behind the tungsten lamps. If both types of lighting are used, each should be independently controlled by a separate switch, to allow the hobbyist to alter the lighting levels as required. In both hoods the use of waterproofed electrical fittings is recommended.

X

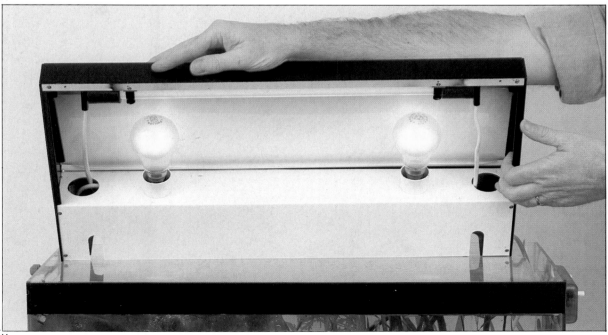

Y

Above: Floating the newly purchased fishes for a few minutes in the aquarium will equalize the water temperatures before release and the aquarium will soon be a living picture (right).

until enough roots develop to anchor the plants more firmly. Additionally, the presence of fishes in the tank from the beginning will mean that food will be available for the plants too, as they will utilize nitrates as a food source. This period is also a convenient time to assess the lighting requirements of the aquarium. The duration and/or brightness of the illumination can be adjusted accordingly, although the final evaluation cannot be made until the plants are at their full growth rate.

Another task that is best accomplished during the running in of the aquarium is getting to know as much as you can about the fishes before you purchase them. As you become acquainted with your developing aquarium you can mentally picture fishes inhabiting the aquatic landscape of your creation. Using the following pages to learn of the fishes' widely varied characteristics and how to look after them and the aquarium in the future will provide you with a basic knowledge. Then, armed with Dr. Vevers' information on the selection of the colorful fishes themselves, you can go ahead and complete the living picture that is the aquarium with all its fascinations. We wish you well.

BASIC FISH ANATOMY

The Swordtail's 'sword' is purely decorative.

Since fishes play the major role in an aquarium, it is recommended that the hobbyist becomes familiar with the animal and its general physiological characteristics as early as possible. In every book about fishes, the author invariably describes the fishes' appearance and habits using words that are unfamiliar to the novice fishkeeper. To avoid this common problem, this section of our book explains the structure of the fish's body, and its more general characteristics are noted. But it is a hypothetical fish that is described; there may well be several slight variations between this fundamental 'blueprint' and the widely varied living specimens in your own aquarium, because each of the many worldwide fish species has evolved different physical characteristics to suit its natural environmental conditions, in order to give that species the best chance of surviving and flourishing.

Not every fish conforms to the traditional torpedo shape since body shape reflects individual living and feeding habits. Ultra-streamlined bodies indicate fast-swimming, open-water predators whose large tail fins are often complemented at the other end by a large tooth-filled mouth. Laterally compressed fishes such as the Angelfish (*Pterophyllum* sp.) inhabit slower flowing, reed-filled waters and vertically compressed specimens live on the river-bed itself.

The position of the mouth often indicates in what level of the water the fish generally lives. An upturned mouth indicates a swimmer just below the surface, whose mouth is structured ideally for capturing insects floating on top of the water. These fishes usually have a straight, uncurved dorsal surface. Fishes whose mouths are located at the very tip of the head, on a horizontal line through the middle of the body, are mid-water feeders taking food as it falls through the water, although they can feed equally well from the surface or from the river-bed, should the mood take them. Many other fishes have underslung mouths. This, coupled with a flat ventral surface, clearly shows a bottom-dwelling species. A slight variation on this development is those fishes whose underslung mouths are used for rasping algae from rock surfaces (and the sides of the aquarium), in which case the fishes may not be entirely bottom-dwelling. Some bottom-dwellers have whiskerlike barbels around the mouth, which are often equipped with taste buds, so the fish can more easily locate its food as it forages.

The scales
A fish's scales provide not only protection for the body but also aerodynamic streamlining. A variation from a scale covering is found in the Armored Catfish group (Callichthyidae), whose bodies are covered with two or three rows of overlapping bony scutes. Some catfishes, particularly those of the Mochokidae and the Pimelodidae, are covered in neither scales nor scutes.

The fins
The fish uses its fins for locomotion and

stability, and in some cases as spawning aids either during courtship or in the hatching period of the eggs. Fins may be either single or paired. The caudal fin provides the final impetus to thrust the fish through the water—fast swimmers have a deeply forked caudal fin. The Swordtail (*Xiphophorus* sp.) has an elongated lower edge to the caudal fin.

The dorsal fin may be erectile (as in the Sailfin Mollies—*Poecilia velifera, P. latipinna*) and will often consist of hard and soft rays. In some species two dorsal fins may be present, but these should not be confused with the adipose fin, a small fin (usually of a fatty tissue) that is found in some species, notably the Characoid group, between the main dorsal fin and the caudal fin.

The anal fin is another single fin mounted under the body just forward of the caudal fin. Mostly used as a stabilizer, in the male live-bearing fishes it has become adapted to serve as a reproductive organ. In some Characoid fishes the anal fin of the male carries tiny hooks that help to hold the two fishes together during spawning.

The pelvic, or ventral, fins are paired and are carried forward of the anal fin. In many of the Anabantid fishes (Gouramies) these fins are filamentous and are often used to explore the fish's surroundings. The Angelfish also has narrow, elongated pelvic fins, but these are not so maneuverable, nor are they equipped with tasting cells. The Armored Catfishes in the *Corydoras* genus use their pelvic fins to transport their eggs to the spawning site.

Pelvic fins in some species of Gobies are often fused together to form a suction cup that anchors the fish to the river-bed and prevents it from being swept away by the water currents.

Pectoral fins emerge from just behind the gill cover or operculum. Primarily used for maneuvering, pectoral fins have also been adapted for other uses. The Hatchetfishes emulate the marine Flying Fishes as they skim across the water surface by means of their well-developed pectoral fins. The marine Gurnard literally walks across the seabed on 'legs' formed by rays of its pectoral fins.

Many aquarium fishes have overlong, decorative fins. Fish breeders developed these exaggerated fins through deliberate breeding programs and such fin developments are not found in fishes in the wild.

The fish's senses
The fish has the same five senses that a person enjoys—sight, touch, taste, smell, and hearing. Of these, the last two are more highly developed than those of humans. Many fishes detect food through

Basic fish anatomy
Knowledge of the fish's anatomy will help the aquarist to understand how a fish works and to use information found in aquatic books.

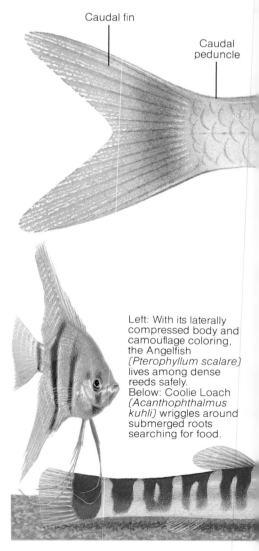

Caudal fin

Caudal peduncle

Left: With its laterally compressed body and camouflage coloring, the Angelfish (*Pterophyllum scalare*) lives among dense reeds safely.
Below: Coolie Loach (*Acanthophthalmus kuhli*) wriggles around submerged roots searching for food.

smell, often over great distances. A fish's nostrils are not used for breathing, only for smelling. It is debatable where the sense of actual hearing ceases and the detection of low frequency vibrations begins in the fish world. This is because fishes are equipped with a sixth sense — the lateral line system. Through perforations in a row of scales, the fish's nervous system can detect minute vibrations in the surrounding water. This warns of other fishes or obstacles nearby. The Blind Cave Characin (*Astyanax mexicanus*) copes quite easily with life in an aquarium, navigating by means of its lateral line system.

Some fishes have developed sophisticated aids to help them cope in darkness or in murky waters, and these include the ability to generate a weak electromagnetic field. The Electric Catfish (*Malapterurus electricus* sp.), although scaleless, needs little protection against predators, because it packs a hefty electric shock. It is thought that it uses this shock to stun smaller fishes.

The swim-bladder

A feature exclusive to fishes is a hydrostatic buoyancy organ known as a swimbladder. This enables the fish to position itself at any level in the water, automatically giving the fish neutral density. Some fishes, notably the marine sharks, lack this organ.

Color

Apart from attracting fishkeepers color plays an important role in the fish world. It serves to identify the species in general

Above: The Three-banded Pencilfish (*Nannostomus trifasciatus*) is seen here displaying its daytime colors; like related species, it has a different color pattern at night.

and the sexes in particular. It camouflages a fish from predators or gives clear visual warning that a species may be poisonous. Color presents false targets to an attacker and gives some clue to a fish's disposition, for instance frightened or angry.

Color is determined by two methods — by reflection of light and by pigmentation. Those silvery, iridescent hues seen on the flanks of many freshwater species are due to reflective layers of guanin. Guanin is a waste product that is not excreted from the kidneys and body, but stored just beneath the skin. The color seen depends upon the angle at which light hits and is reflected from these crystals. Many fishes, when lit by light coming through the front glass of the aquarium, seem to be colored differently than when lit by light coming directly overhead. This also explains why a light-colored gravel appears to wash out the fishes' coloring.

Fishes with deeper colors have pigment cells in their bodies, and some species are able to control the amount of color they display. This can be seen quite easily in those species that tend to rest on the gravel surface or on rocks, where their colors are adapted to suit the background. Other fishes take on nocturnal colorations. The popular Pencilfishes (*Nannostomus* sp.) are notable examples and the hobbyist may be initially surprised at finding these fishes a different color pattern each morning. Fishes effect such color changes by contracting or expanding the pigmented cells (chromatophores) to intensify or dilute the color.

Color intensity is likely to be heightened in the male fish during the breeding period in order to attract a mate, and some female fishes within the Cichlid group may also have their colors exaggerated in order to be recognized by their subsequent offspring. A good example of this is seen in the *Pelvicachromis* genus, where the females are often more colorful during breeding than the males.

It is possible to intensify fishes' colors by feeding them so-called 'color foods'. These contain additives, such as carotin, that will accentuate colors. The Tiger Barb (*Barbus tetrazona*) is a favourite fish that responds quite startlingly to color feeding, each scale becoming edged with black, giving a netted appearance. Unfortunately, in fish competitions the judges are quick to notice such artificial practices, and color-fed fishes are likely to be down-graded for not complying with the natural colors of their species. The use of color-enhancing lamps will also give the impression of more brightly colored fishes, but naturally the fishes will regain their normal colors when removed to more normally lit environments using standard lamps.

Dorsal fin

Swim-bladder

Adipose fin

Scales

Lateral line system

Liver

Gills (Gill cover, or Operculum, cut away to show detail.)

Kidney

Eye

Nostril

Mouth

Barbels

Heart

Vent (Anus and Urinogenital opening)

Ovary

Esophagus, leading to Stomach (hidden behind Ovary)

Anal fin

Intestine

Pectoral fin (paired)

Pelvic, or Ventral, fin (paired)

Left: The upturned mouth of the Siamese Fighter (*Betta splendens*) indicates a surface feeder. It is also useful for breathing atmospheric air, which then passes into the labyrinth organ.
Right, top: The terminally located teeth of the Piranha (*Serrasalmus nattereri*) are conveniently placed for biting anything!
Right: Barbels around the mouth of the *Corydoras* catfish are equipped with taste cells to assist in the search for food.

FISHES: MAKING THE RIGHT CHOICE

The voracious Piranha is its own best company.

The choosing of the fishes for your collection should not be rushed. The success of keeping fishes in captivity depends upon the selection of healthy, suitable stock, followed by proper handling and a careful introduction into the aquarium. The treatment your fishes receive at this stage of their progression from the dealer's tanks to your aquarium is yet another traumatic experience for them to survive. Remember, they may already have traveled halfway around the world, perhaps under extremely trying conditions, and a stress-free introduction into your aquarium will be appreciated and rewarded. A fish that is under considerable stress is likely to contract disease much more readily than a contented one, so get your fishes off to a good start by caring right from the beginning. Any failure to apply a few commonsense rules at this stage is certain to mean disappointment.

In order to make full use of the available aquarium space a selection of fishes that will occupy all levels in the water should be chosen, by studying their physical forms as described earlier.

Another factor to be considered is the size that any fish will eventually attain. Most of the fishes offered for sale are juveniles and it is likely that in the aquarium their size will at least double. In practical terms, it would be foolish to buy a number of 1in (2.5cm) fishes of different species, if some of them grow to 5in (13cm) and the remainder mature at 1.5in (3.75cm), since the law of the wild is often 'eat, or be eaten'. The hobbyist will not want this law demonstrated in his fish tank. Your aquatic dealer should be able to advise you on the likely adult sizes of his fishes.

Some fishes, although seen quite clearly in the shop's brightly lit but barely furnished tanks, may well be nocturnal by nature, so don't be surprised if they display this habit, hiding in the plants by day and swimming at night, when settled into your comfortable aquarium. Herbivorous fishes have been known to strip a lushly planted aquarium bare of vegetation—obviously a case for rocks and artificial plants!

Slow-moving fishes with exaggerated fins are often discomforted by the presence of faster-moving species, but this can be alleviated by providing retreats and refuges for the slower species. Gregarious fishes should not be purchased in ones or twos: A shoal of six or more will not only look more attractive, but the fishes will feel happier too. In addition, some male fishes are ardent suitors and it is then better to buy trios of a species (two females to one male) to ensure that one female is not harassed.

We now come to the situation where we have mentally chosen our fish and are faced with the actual moment of selection in the aquatic shop. Look for a healthy fish. The majority of freshwater fishes will swim with the dorsal fin erect. A folded-down dorsal fin usually indicates an ailing fish. The fish's body should be well-filled, with no 'knife-edge' dorsal or ventral surfaces. Colors should be dense and any color patterns clearly defined

with no smudging between different color areas. The act of swimming should be effortless, with no undue wobbling, and the fish should be able to remain at any depth in the water without bobbing to the surface or sinking to the floor.

Do not purchase fishes with obvious defects such as deformed bodies or missing fins; similarly, fishes with spots or open wounds should also be passed over.

Determining the sex of the fishes is not difficult. The live-bearing species are

easily distinguished by the obvious difference between the shapes of the anal fins. The general rule for egg-laying species is that the male fish is usually slimmer and more brightly colored, and often has more developed and pronounced finnage. Purchasing a number of specimens is more likely to provide both males and females than if you purchased only two or three.

Although the more exotic specimens are certainly appealing, they should be

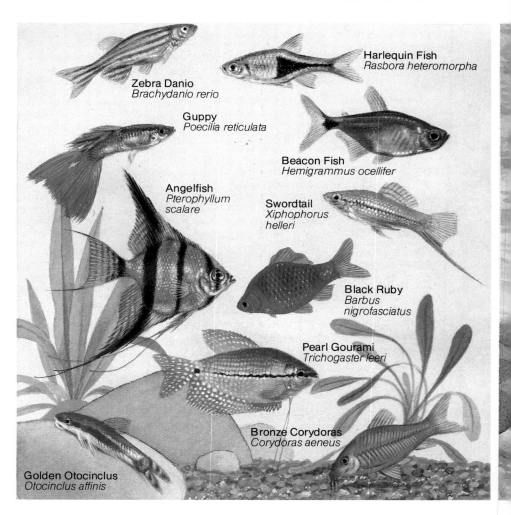

Fishes for a community aquarium

Fishes for the community tank should be chosen to make full use of all swimming space and water levels in the aquarium; additionally, the many various shapes, colors, and swimming habits of the fishes are automatically included in such a cosmopolitan collection. Similarly, it is quite usual to find aquatic plants from worldwide locations sharing the same aquarium. Avoid mixing boisterous species with the more timid fishes, and those of a vegetarian nature should not be included in a well-planted tank. Live-bearing fishes will interbreed within the same species regardless of color pattern; do not mix colors if you want pure strains.

Above: Fishes exhibiting severe wasting symptoms such as hollow bellies and emaciated bodies are not necessarily in need of a good meal. They may be suffering from fish diseases.

Above: When buying live-bearers, such as these Sailfin Mollies *(Poecilia velifera)*, it is easy to select pairs since sex differences are obvious; the male has a taller dorsal fin and a modified anal fin.

ignored (even if they are within your financial grasp) when you choose the original stock, and left until practical experience has been gained.

Transport and introduction into the aquarium

Fishes are usually transported in a plastic bag. Should the homeward journey be lengthy, however, there is a risk that tropical species may become chilled. It is advisable to wrap the plastic bag in a layer or two of newspaper or, better still, place the bag in an insulated box.

Despite such precautions, there will still be a temperature difference between the water in the transportation bag and in the prepared aquarium. To avoid any thermal shock to the fishes, the water temperatures must be equalized before the fishes are released into the aquarium. This is easily achieved by floating the plastic bag in the aquarium for several minutes. To accustom the fishes to the water quality of the aquarium, some hobbyists introduce increasing amounts of the aquarium water into the plastic bag during this temperature equalization. It may also be advisable to carry out the introduction of the fishes with the aquarium lighting off, so that they can accustom themselves to their new home under subdued lighting, and thus be protected from any shock brought on by environmental changes.

The introduction of fishes into an aquarium should always be made as calm an operation as possible. When adding new fishes to an already stocked aquarium, it can be a useful ploy to give the existing fishes some food to divert their attention away from the newcomers; in any case, make sure that there are always adequate retreats and refuges available for the more timid ones to take advantage of during their settling-in.

Trewava's Cichlid
Labeotropheus trewavasae

Malawi Golden Cichlid
Pseudotropheus auratus

Malawi Blue Cichlid
Pseudotropheus zebra

Golden Julie
Julidochromis ornatus

Blue Discus
Symphysodon aequifasciata haraldi

Lyretail
Aphyosemion australe

Oscar
Astronotus ocellatus

Clown Loach
Botia macracantha

Fishes for a rocky aquarium

These very territorial fishes are all originally from the hard waters of the African Rift Valley Lakes, and the rocky background should provide at least one retreat per fish. Many browse upon algae and plants, so the aquarist may wish to use artificial plants to decorate the otherwise barren tank, since natural plants may suffer.

Fishes for a species aquarium

These fishes may adapt to community life but their individual requirements (or anti-social behavior) are better provided for (or guarded against) in separate aquariums. Some may need special care or be of nocturnal habits; others may be your favorite shoaling fishes that you may prefer to keep on their own.

FEEDING AND MAINTENANCE

A floating worm dispenser for surface feeders.

We have seen how fishes have become adapted to suit their varying environments by evolving different body shapes, mouth positions, finnage, and so on. Similarly, we have learned that the aquarium water needs to be kept in good condition by means of filtration systems and aquatic plants. But things in the aquarium are not the same as in nature and many of the fishes' needs must be supplied, or carried out, by the hobbyist. The attention of the hobbyist is particularly drawn to the provision of a varied and nourishing diet for the fishes, together with a good service record in maintaining the aquarium's hygiene. Whenever it is impossible to recreate exact conditions any substitute must be as near the fishes' natural norm as possible. Again, in order to protect the fishes from any undue stress, changes to new conditions must be made gradually.

Having read about the fishes' natural diet (insects, smaller fishes, amphibians, water crustacea, etc.) the newcomer may be concerned as to how to keep his fishes from starving. Fortunately, fish nutrition has been the subject of research and production for many years and now vast industries keep the market well stocked with fish foods.

Modern fish food is far removed from the old-fashioned 'ants' eggs' approach. It is now possible to buy food to suit any fish's particular requirement, whether carnivorous or herbivorous. Nor is the choice limited to food content, for foods can be of various forms—flake, liquid, tablet, paste, powder, or freeze-dried lumps. These have been developed not only to suit the different feeding habits of fishes, but also to suit a fish throughout its whole life—from tiny, newborn fry (when microscopic-sized food is necessary) right up to adulthood (when a large chunk is taken without effort).

Despite the undoubted excellence of manufactured foods, which can provide a complete and varied diet, feeding exclusively with one type of food can have its drawbacks. The fishes can become bored with an unchanging diet and go off their food, but the main danger when feeding 'artificial' foods is that of overfeeding. No, the fishes will not develop a weight problem—unlike humans, they do not over-indulge. The problem arises from the food that is not eaten. These leftovers will decay in the aquarium and pollute it sooner or later, requiring a complete dismantling and refurnishing.

The rule is to feed 'little but often'. The fishes should be able to clear up all the food you give them in a matter of a few minutes. If you share the responsibility of looking after the aquarium with other members of the family, do tell them when you have fed the fishes. This will prevent someone else doing it again a few minutes later, with the result that overfeeding becomes a risk. A feed for the fishes morning, noon and night is quite acceptable, provided that only small amounts are given at any one time. The feed just before 'lights out' at night is important, as those fishes with nocturnal habits are then not neglected.

Above left: A selection of dried foods. (1) Multiflavored flake, (2) floating pellets, (3) freeze-dried *Tubifex* cubes, (4) flour-fine fry food, (5) stick-on tablet food, (6) granulated high protein food, (7) freeze-dried shrimp, and (8) green (vegetable formula) flake food. Tubed liquid fry food is also available.

Above right: Live foods. Water fleas and mosquito larvae can be caught in ponds. Eggs of brine shrimps hatch in warm salt water.

Water fleas

Mosquito larvae

Eggs

Brine shrimp

Bloodworms

In addition to the modern, protein-filled dried foods that are available, fishes can be given live foods. Such foods can be captured from ponds, or cultured.

Water fleas (*Daphnia pulex*), *Tubifex* worms, mosquito larvae, bloodworms, etc. are all excellent foods. Fishes benefit from the chase after the wriggling foods almost as much as from eating them.

There is an element of risk in the use of wild-caught foods, of introducing disease or predators into the aquarium. *Tubifex* worms are usually found in sufficiently large numbers to be of commercial interest only in river mud near sewage outfalls. The worms should be kept under running water until used. Turn them regularly to allow the muddy effluent to be washed away.

Small earthworms may also be given (do not use worms from ground that has been treated with weedkillers), and many fishes relish household scraps. Lean raw beef, ox heart, peas, lettuce, spinach, and wheat germ are quite common extras to the fishes' menu. However they may need to be trained to accept the new foods over a period of time.

Water crustacea should not be collected from fish-carrying waters (they are unlikely to be there in worthwhile numbers anyway), so as not to introduce any fish diseases into the aquarium. An even greater danger is that the catch will also contain predators that will attack small fishes. Such predators include the larval forms of the great diving beetle (*Dytiscus marginalis*), water boatman (*Notonecta*), whirligig beetle (*Gyrinus*) and dragonflies (*Aeshna, Libellula, Sympetrum*). It is also possible to introduce *Hydra*, leeches, and snails together with other waterborne creatures when netting foods from natural waters, so all collected foods should be carefully screened.

Mosquito and gnat larvae may be collected in any garden rain-barrel, and

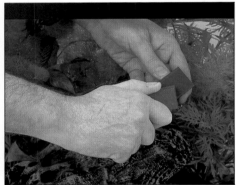

The removal of algae from the front glass of the tank is made easy by abrasive pads, either mounted on a long handle (above left) or on self-parking magnetic blocks (left). Detritus from the floor of the aquarium can be sucked up by a useful air-operated 'vacuum cleaner', the detritus automatically collecting inside the cloth bag (above) and the water returning to the tank.

these wriggling foods are much relished by aquarium fishes.

Live foods that can be cultured by the hobbyist include micro-worms, grindal worms and white worms; these are listed in ascending order of size. Micro-worms are very tiny and white worms not much thicker than a heavy thread. Such worms are fed on cereal foods and need to be grown in progressive cultures — as one culture becomes exhausted (or turns sour), a portion of it is used to start a new one.

A live food that plays a most important role in feeding aquarium fishes (particularly young newborn specimens) is the brine shrimp (*Artemia salina*). The eggs of this marine crustacean may be stored indefinitely, and hatched when required by immersing them in salt water. The resulting newly hatched shrimps, or nauplii, are an ideal first food for fry. They are highly nutritious and completely disease-free, unlike pond-caught food, which may carry fish diseases. Again, it is recommended that cultures of brine shrimp are started in rotation to ensure a continuing supply of the food. Brine

shrimp eggs are available in two forms — with and without shells — the latter form being produced commercially; the shells are already dissolved away and a higher hatch yield is expected.

Routine maintenance

Commonsense checks and chores need take no more than a few minutes a day, or perhaps an hour or two each month. Many of the checks will be made automatically while the hobbyist is watching his fishes, and it really is true that fishkeeping offers rewards far in excess of the necessary effort put into it.

A daily check easily carried out at feeding time is to see if all the fishes are well and present. Any missing fish should be located at the earliest opportunity, since a decomposing body (if it is dead) will pollute the tank or spread disease. A quick look at the thermometer will indicate if all is well with the heating system, and the filtration and aeration systems have readily visible proof of working. Faulty lamps should be replaced.

Depending upon the dirtiness of the tank (or the habits of the fishes) the filter

medium can be changed as needed, probably about every two to four weeks. When maintaining power filters, remember to check the tightness of all pipe unions and connections. Dead leaves should be removed from the aquarium; any rampant plants can be pruned, and the cuttings planted elsewhere. Algae should be scraped from the front glass, but may be left undisturbed on side and rear walls of the aquarium for the benefit of vegetarian species.

Each month or so, 20 to 25% of the aquarium water should be removed and replaced with fresh water of the correct temperature. During this process any detritus should be siphoned from the floor of the aquarium. Cover glasses should be cleaned at this time, too. Over a period of time, airstones become clogged; this may not be due to algae forming on the airstone's surface, nor due to the hardness of the water. Most airstones clog up from the inside through drawing poorly filtered air into the aquarium via the air pump. The better models of air pump are fitted with filter pads (usually in the base, where they are conveniently forgotten). Regular cleaning or replacement of air pump filters is recommended. Where biological filtration is used, there may be a tendency for the gravel to bed down; it is good practice to rake over the gravel periodically to ensure a continued water flow through the system.

Vacation worries

Unlike other pets, fishes do not present many problems when the annual vacation looms. Although fishes cannot be left at a neighbor's house, they can easily be looked after by a friend, provided that exact feeding instructions are given. The danger is that people without fishkeeping experience disbelieve the amount of food stated in any instructions and nearly always over-feed, with dire results. It is not unusual for a whole tin of fish food to be used by well-meaning 'fish-sitters' over a two-week vacation.

If the fishes have been well fed during the weeks running up to the holiday, they are quite able to endure a week or two without food or light. Of necessity, a hungry fish will search for food, and the aquarium will be well scoured by the time the owner returns. The plants, too, may have lost their covering of algae during the period of darkness, and another noticeable effect will be that the plants will have tilted themselves towards the front glass in their efforts to receive any available light.

Automatic feeders and time switches will keep an aquarium in full operation during absence. It may be a bit extravagant (or just impossible) to go to these lengths for the sake of a few weeks in the year when they will be needed.

DISEASES: PREVENTION AND TREATMENT

Parasitic anchor worm (*Lernaea* sp.) on the host.

Most of the illnesses to which fishes succumb may be regarded as nothing more serious than the occasional colds and influenza attacks that affect human beings. Without doubt, fish diseases will strike at your fishes at one time or another. "It won't happen to my fish," is a cry all too frequently heard from aquarists who, in truth, do not really care. Although the following information is broadly based, due to the diversities of proprietary brands of treatments available worldwide, the hobbyist must be prepared to face the occasional setback in his fishes' health. Nearly all ailments are curable, and more often than not the hobbyist puts his fishes at more risk from poor aquarium management than they are facing from disease. In addition, disease may be introduced into the aquarium through ignorance or laziness, when simple quarantine measures would avoid such occurrences.

With the exception of the initial furnishing and stocking of an aquarium (the settling down period may be regarded as a quarantine process), any further addition—be it fish or plant—should be well screened for potential disease before its introduction into the aquarium.

A separate small tank should be set up for quarantine purposes. It need not be fully furnished, but one or two rocks can be provided to give the new fish a sense of security. A period of two to three weeks should be enought time for latent diseases (if any are present) to manifest themselves. During this time, a careful watch should be kept on the fish for any spots, pimples etc. Should an ailment become noticed, the quarantine tank can immediately be converted into a hospital tank in which the fish can be treated.

Although plants may not develop such visible signs of disease as do fishes, they should be carefully prepared for use in an aquarium. The plant should be searched for unwanted 'passengers', particularly snails' eggs, which could result in an infestation of snails in a very short time. To make more sure of safety, some aquarists advocate that new plants be given a rinse in a weak solution of potassium permanganate to destroy any minute animal life that might otherwise be introduced with the plants.

Very often an outbreak of disease follows the addition of new stock, which is consequently blamed, as is the dealer from whom the new fish was purchased. The reason for this coincidence is that the new fish is often placed under stress due to the change in its environment, and it is thus more prone to those diseases to which the existing fishes of the aquarium may have built up some degree of immunity. It may therefore be unfair to blame the dealer for unhealthy stock. A good dealer will quarantine his stock before offering it for sale. If you want to buy a new fish from a dealer, inquire whether it can be quarantined and reserved for purchase at a later date.

Should the aquarist progress to multiple tanks, a risk of infection can occur by using a single net between all the tanks. Each tank should have its own

net, disinfected after every use. It should be unnecessary to warn against the transfer of water from an infected tank to a healthy one.

Aquarium water can become contaminated by such things as cigarette smoke, aerosols, fumes from paint or furniture polish, industrial smells, etc, all of which are pumped into the aquarium by the air pump. Metals and cement are also liable to contaminate the water, and nitrogenous compounds (ammonia, nitrite and—less harmful—nitrate) should be kept to a minimum by biological filtration

and regular partial water changes.

Despite the excellent quality of prepared foods, a full varied diet should be given to avoid any vitamin deficiencies, and live food will greatly improve a fish's health and breeding potential.

Treatments

In order for any disease or disorder to be treated successfully, an accurate diagnosis must first be made. Fortunately, the most common (but curable) ailments are all easily recognizable and, thanks to modern research, the necessary treat-

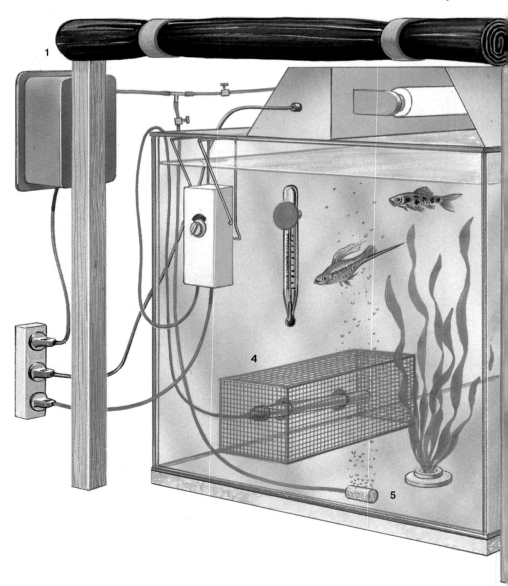

ENVIRONMENT: Don't overcrowd —stresses are set up, and any outbreak of disease spreads quickly. Don't keep large fishes with small ones, and provide plenty of retreats. Don't overfeed—uneaten food will cause pollution.
Don't underfeed—a starving fish has less resistance to disease.
Feed a varied diet—a fixed diet may not provide a correct balance of vitamins and may cause digestive disorders.
Avoid possible toxins entering the aquarium—tobacco smoke, paint fumes, aerosols, etc.
Keep filters clean, and make regular partial water changes.
Avoid stressing the fishes—don't change water conditions suddenly.

LIVESTOCK: Always buy healthy stock. Quarantine all new additions before introducing them to the main collection. Check plants for snail eggs and other unwanted aquatic animals; disinfect with a rinse in potassium permanganate. Remove any sick fishes as soon as possible.

TREATMENTS: Follow medication instructions as closely as possible in order to avoid overdosing.
Some medications adversely affect plants, or are affected by light—treat sick fishes away from the main aquarium if possible.
Some medications reduce oxygen levels, so increase aeration during treatment.
Remove activated carbon from filters during any course of medication.
Some chemicals (such as snail-killers) may adversely affect biological filtration, and may cause pollution problems if used to destroy snails that burrow in the gravel, whose dead bodies then decompose.

ment is usually easily available and administered. It is natural that a new-comer to the hobby will hope that any such ailments will not occur in his aquarium, but nevertheless he should be able to recognize the symptoms early.

Over-production of mucus by the fish is an indication that something is wrong. Mucus is a protective slime produced by the fish. It can immediately coat a wound, but it can be deceiving because it can also hide parasites from view.

A brief outline of the more common ailments and disorders follows on the next two pages. Suspected problems that are beyond the scope of this chapter should be referred to the nearest knowledgeable source, such as an experienced aquarist, your local aquatic dealer, or even a veterinarian, although the number of veterinarians qualified (or even interested) in aquatic problems is very limited, particularly in the U.S.

Treatments vary in method of application from individual baths to the dosing of the complete aquarium. Individual baths are generally only for short periods of time (a matter of minutes) while the treating of a complete aquarium is classified as a 'long-term' bath (until the medication ceases to be effective or the treatment is complete) and is carried out at a much lower concentration level of medication. Occasionally, a fish may need to be treated 'out of water', when dealing with a wound, for instance, or a parasitic infection that is large enough to be treated in this way.

It is important that doses of medication are calculated as accurately as possible because overdosing can be dangerous. Medications should always be dissolved into liquid form and prepared in basic stock solution strengths before being used. In some cases, medication can be administered internally to a fish by the simple method of soaking the fish's food in the medication before feeding. This method is a little uncertain, as no definite dosage can be proved to have been taken.

During the treatment of the whole aquarium, carbon should be removed from any filters to prevent it absorbing the medication (thus reducing its effect), but the filter should be left running to assist water movement. Medications often reduce the level of oxygen in the water and extra aeration can usefully be employed during the period of treatment. Some aquarium plants may be adversely affected by the addition of medication to the aquarium; usually the fine-leaved specimens are the worst affected. At the end of any long-term bath of medicated treatments, the fish should be gradually acclimatized to fresh, clean water again by the replacement with clean water over a period of days.

(1) The blinds may be lowered, if necessary, to cut off light reaching the aquarium and affecting the medication; the light in the hood would be switched off, too.

(2) The simple internal box filter contains no activated carbon, only filter wool.

(3) A few flowerpots and plastic plants give the fishes a feeling of security; plastic plants are used because some medications will cause damage to live specimens. It is unnecessary to have gravel on the aquarium floor; biological filtration may not be possible, as the bacteria may be affected by medications.

(4) The heater, controlled by an easily adjusted external thermostat, is guarded by a grid to prevent fishes sheltering near it being burnt.

(5) Bubbles from the airstone help to circulate warmth and keep the oxygen level in the water high.

The hospital aquarium
The hospital aquarium may lack the every comfort and visual appeal of the main aquarium, but it is designed to be a comprehensive treatment center. Following any course of treatment, the water in the hospital aquarium should be changed (gradually over a period of a few days) for fresh water similar to that of the fishes' normal aquarium, before they are returned.

White spot disease (*Ichthyophthiriasis*) This is the most common parasitic ailment and probably the easiest to diagnose. The fish's body is covered with tiny white spots, which extend to cover the fins. The disease is of a cyclic nature. The parasite leaves the fish's body to form cysts on the aquarium floor and upon hatching the parasite is then free-swimming, seeking a new host. It can be attacked by treatment at this stage. As the disease is likely to affect all the fishes in an aquarium, the whole tank should be treated. Proprietary cures are readily available, simple to administer, and extremely effective.

Fungus (*Saprolegnia*) In this disease, outbreaks of cotton-woollike tufts appear on the fish's body, or it may be covered completely with a fine layer of cobwebby or dusty fungus. An effective treatment for this is to immerse the suffering fish in a salt bath. This can be made by dissolving natural (not cooking) salt in fresh water. The strength for a short bath (15-30 mins) is 2 to 4oz/U.S. gallon, 2.5 to 5oz/Imp. gallon (15 to 30g/liter). The amount for long-term treatment is 0.8oz/U.S. gallon, 1oz/Imp. gallon (7g/liter). Proprietary treatments also prove effective.

Often confused with body fungus is mouth fungus. As its name implies, it affects a fish around the mouth; however, it is caused by a slime bacterium and will not be affected by normal fungus treatments. Antibiotics will be required and these are best obtained from a qualified veterinarian.

'Shimmying' The symptoms are aptly described, since the fish just makes rapid undulating movements without any forward movement occurring. One cause of this ailment is a drop in water temperature, so that the fish becomes chilled. The obvious remedy is to check the aquarium's heating system for any malfunction and to raise the temperature to the correct level. One species in particular seems prone to 'shimmying', the very popular Black Molly (*Poecilia* hybrid).

'Dropsy' Occasionally a fish's body becomes bloated to such a degree that the scales protrude outwards. This is due to the body cavities filling with liquid. There is some confusion as to what exactly causes this to happen, but the majority of hobbyists refer to the condition as 'dropsy'. It is difficult to cure, although some alleviation can be given by draining the liquid from the fish by means of a hypodermic syringe. Since dropsy can be contagious, it is best to isolate the affected fish until it recovers or has to be destroyed.

'Finrot' The degeneration of the tissue between individual rays of the fins is caused by a bacterial infection that is often encouraged by poor water conditions. The fins may have become damaged by bad handling techniques, or by a bullying fish. This allows the bacterial infection to gain a hold on the injured fins. A general clean-up of the aquarium water will be required, together with better aquarium management in the future. Proprietary cures will assist rapid recovery to full fin health, but these medicines cannot overcome neglect by the hobbyist.

Gill flukes Fishes are sometimes seen scratching themselves on rocks or plants, accompanied by an increased respiration rate with the gills gaping and obviously inflamed. Such fishes are infected with *Dactylogyrus* or *Gyrodactylus* parasites, which burrow into the skin or collect on the delicate gill membranes. The para-

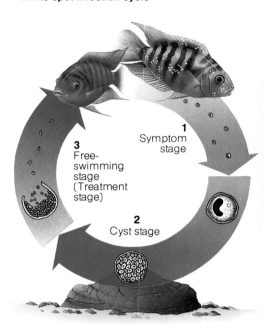

White spot infection cycle

1 Symptom stage

2 Cyst stage

3 Free-swimming stage (Treatment stage)

Fish diseases
Illustrated below are some of the more common ailments that befall fishes in the aquarium. Some are due to parasites introduced into the aquarium with live food or plants from other waters; others are bacterial infections brought about by poor aquarium hygiene and lack of proper maintenance.

Tailrot/Finrot
The very obvious symptoms appear on fishes of poor health. Low temperatures, physical damage, and unhygienic conditions all encourage the harmful bacterial action. Should tailrot reach the body of the fish, a satisfactory cure is unlikely. Treatment using acriflavine and phenoxethol have now replaced surgical methods.

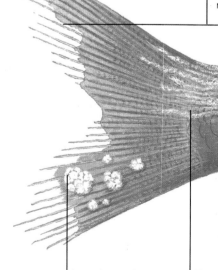

Lymphocystis
Causes cauliflowerlike growths on the fins and skin, together with a decrease in weight. Individual cell growth rapid. Rare in freshwater fish.

Fungus
Fungus (*Saprolegnia*) attacks fishes already weakened by physical damage, parasitic attacks, or poor conditions. Also liable to affect fishes if they are transferred to differing aquarium waters. As healthy fish will not be infected, it is only necessary to remove the infected fish for treatment.

Pox
White spots join to form large patches. Fish is emaciated and often left twisted. Faulty diet, lack of vitamins likely causes. May heal itself under good conditions.

Left: Infection cycle for white spot disease. (**1**) The symptoms appear. (**2**) Parasites leave fish and form cysts. (**3**) The cysts produce new free-swimming parasites to re-infect fish. Treatment is effective during this stage only.

Right: A Neon Tetra (*Paracheirodon innesi*) suffering from abdominal dropsy, where excess fluid has accumulated within the body. It is difficult to see the protruding scales that typify the condition in larger fishes.

White spot disease
Ichthyophthiriasis is a common ailment and well described. Many aquarists believe it lies dormant in every tank waiting to strike any weakened fish. Responds to treatment.

Velvet disease
Infected fishes have a dusty look. Caused by *Oodinium*, which undergoes an encystment stage. Treatment similar to white spot disease.

Skin flukes
Gyrodactylus make fish feeble and cause colors to fade; they rest frequently near surface. Gills may be attacked, too. Responds to treatment.

Eye infections
Cloudy eyes (below) are often due to eye fungus or to worm cataract, *Proalaria*. Protruding eyes (main illustration) suggest that other diseases are present.

Slimy skin
Thin gray film covers the body. Parasites *Cyclochaeta* and *Costia* (below left, right) cause the fish to produce excessive slime.

Dropsy
Protrusion of scales due to accumulated liquid in body. Fluid from infected fish may infect others. Remove sick fish at once.

Gill flukes
Caused by *Dactylogyrus*, a flatworm that hooks onto the fish's gills.

Mouth 'fungus'
Unrelated to body fungus and unaffected by similar treatments. Caused by slime bacterium *Chondrococcus*.

sites may be removed by bathing the fish in well-aerated solutions of methylene blue, formalin or acriflavine. Great care must be taken when using formalin as it is a poison. The strengths of the various baths for each substance are as follows:

Methylene Blue Stock solution 1%
    Long-term bath
    1.7 to 3.4cc per U.S. gallon
    2 to 4cc per Imp. gallon
    0.4 to 0.8cc per liter

Acriflavine   Stock solution
    10mg per liter
    Long-term bath
    8cc per U.S. gallon
    10cc per Imp. gallon
    2.2cc per liter

Formalin   Stock solution
    47% formaldehyde
    Short bath (45-50 mins)
    1cc per U.S. gallon
    1.2cc per Imp. gallon
    0.25cc per liter
    Long-term bath
    0.25cc per U.S. gallon
    0.3cc per Imp. gallon
    0.066cc per liter

Note: Concentrations of stock solutions available vary from country to country.

The parasites cannot survive without a fish host, so if the aquarium is left uninhabited for a few days while the fishes are being treated with methylene blue the parasites will be eliminated from the tank.

It is often easy to jump to wrong conclusions. Fishes panting at the surface may not be afflicted by parasites at all — they may be gasping for oxygen because of an excess of carbon dioxide in the water. Immediate relief can be provided by extra aeration, but better aquarium management is the real answer.

Serious diseases

More serious ailments result from internal causes such as tuberculosis, threadworms and tapeworms, which are unseen by the fishkeeper. Usually when the symptoms become apparent it is too late to effect a cure. Diagnosis of these conditions can be done only by examination of the organs of the diseased fish (which in practical terms means a post-mortem) and this aspect of disease is beyond the capability of the beginning aquarist.

There are several diagnostic services available by mail order, but as these will only reveal the cause of death (from examination of the corpse), this course of action, which can be rather expensive, may be regarded as a little too retrospective, to say the least!

BREEDING FISHES IN THE AQUARIUM

Spraying Characins spawning out of the water.

*O*ne of the attractions of fishkeeping is that the fishes may multiply in captivity. But, because of the confined space within an aquarium, it is often impossible for fishes to find enough seclusion or safe territory in which to raise a family, and any fry that are born soon get eaten by larger fishes. These difficulties are easily solved by providing a separate aquarium in which prospective breeders can be kept. That second tank kept for quarantine can be used. Fish-breeding can be divided into two phases: Events leading up to spawning, and the care of the young fry. In both phases the aquarist can have a fair measure of control: Selecting and conditioning the adult fishes; preparing the breeding aquarium; supervising spawning; and raising the fry. Add to these the challenge of producing a new variety and you will understand why this aspect of the hobby is so popular.

The egg-laying fishes spawn in a variety of ways: Egg-scattering, egg-burying, egg-depositing, nest-building, or mouth-brooding. Faced with these, the aquarist needs to prepare the breeding aquarium accordingly. Egg-scattering fishes are not protective towards their eggs and will eat them, given the chance. Various methods are used by aquarists to ensure that the eggs survive. The main principle is to separate the eggs and adult fishes as soon as possible after the eggs are released and fertilized. A layer of marbles on the aquarium floor provides fish-proof crevices into which the fertilized eggs fall. Thick bunches of plants also trap the adhesive eggs and effectively hide them from the adults or, alternatively, the fishes may be spawned above a net or grid submerged in the water through which the eggs fall.

Egg-burying species require the floor of the aquarium to have a deep layer of peat placed on top of the gravel into which the fish can dive and bury the eggs. The egg-depositors are very protective towards their eggs and young fry, but the aquarium needs to be furnished with suitable rocks or caves to provide a choice of spawning sites for these fishes. Nest-builders won't need extra material to help construct their nests; the fishes will collect fragments of plants. Their aquarium should be well planted to provide shelter for the female after spawning.

The incubation of the mouth-brooders takes place within the mouth and buccal cavity of the female fish, and all that she will appreciate is peace and quiet while this occurs—she won't even take food!

At birth, the young fry born to live-bearing fishes are free-swimming miniatures of their parents, but a well-planted nursery tank with a layer of floating plants will allow them to escape any cannibalistic tendencies on the part of their parents.

The breeding aquarium will have a low stocking level, and so a powerful filter will not be needed; even an undergravel filter may draw young fry into the gravel if driven by a too powerful air pump. A simple sponge filter is best in breeding aquariums, as this presents no danger at all to the young fishes.

The breeding aquarium should have the same water temperature and quality as the main aquarium. Should the breeding fishes require different water conditions (to induce spawning, for instance) they should be acclimatized to these over a conditioning period. This must be lengthened if necessary to allow the alterations to the water quality without shocking or stressing the fishes.

The breeding aquarium for live-bearing fishes will act as nursery accommodation for the gravid (pregnant) female fish only and she should be placed into it early in her 30-day gestation period. Breeding traps can have a quite traumatic effort on the female fish, who is very likely to give birth prematurely (to non-fully-developed fry) as a result of this confinement.

Selection and conditioning

Whether your choice of fishes to breed belongs to the egg-laying or the live-bearing group of fishes, the first task is to find a true pair—one male and one female. Referring to the notes on the fish's fins (page 34) indicates that determining the sex of live-bearing fishes does not raise too much of a problem, since males have a modified anal fin. Such obvious differences do not occur between the sexes of egg-laying species, but there are some rough guidelines that may help. Usually the male fish is slimmer and more colorful, and may have more pronounced finnage than the female. Fishes

Egg-scatterers
Above: The problem of Zebra Danios *(Brachydanio rerio)* eating their own eggs can be solved by placing a layer or two of pebbles or glass marbles on the aquarium floor. The eggs quickly fall between the crevices beyond the reach of the fishes, which should be removed after spawning is completed.

Egg-buriers
Above: The egg-burying Argentine Pearlfish *(Cynolebias bellotti)* needs a deep layer of peat on the aquarium floor. After spawning, the peat (complete with fertilized eggs) can be removed and stored almost dry for a few months. The hatching process is activated by immersing the peat in the aquarium water again.

from the Cichlid group select partners themselves, and any two fishes that keep together (often excluding others from their area of the aquarium) are likely to be a true pair.

Fishes selected for breeding should be healthy and free from disease and deformities. They should be chosen for good points like strong coloration, fin development, and so on. This is particularly the case when attempting to breed a definite color strain or more exaggerated finnage into the young. Live-bearing fishes are so ready to interbreed with any of their own species, regardless of color variety, that a very controlled breeding program has to be maintained in order to keep the strain pure.

'Absence makes the heart grow fonder' is one ploy to ensure more success when putting egg-laying fishes together to breed. It is usual to separate the sexes for a few weeks before introducing the fishes to each other in the breeding aquarium. During this period the isolated fishes are fed intensively with high quality foods, with live food predominating. This ensures that the female will be full of roe when spawning time approaches. If she is considered unready by the male fish, he will often attack her. For this reason the female is best introduced into the breeding aquarium first; it then becomes her territory and the male has to court

Left: The female live-bearer's anal fin is fan-shaped; the male's is modified (fully or partly, depending on genus) into a reproductive organ.
Right: Jewel Cichlids *(Hemichromis bimaculatus)* spawning on a piece of wood. Both parents guard the eggs.

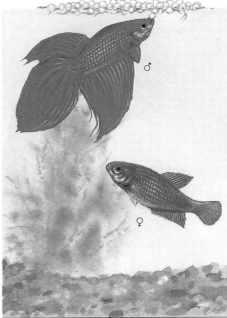

Egg-depositors
Above: 'Kribs' *(Pelvicachromis pulcher)* are secretive spawners and prefer the privacy of a flowerpot or rocky cave in which to spawn. Unfortunately, this often means that the hobbyist is not aware of spawning taking place until the proud parents bring their free-swimming youngsters out into the open.

Bubble-nest builders
Above: Siamese Fighters *(Betta splendens)* use fragments of plants in the construction of their bubble-nest. The female is often attacked by the male if he considers her not ready for spawning. For this reason the female should be put into the breeding aquarium before the male, so that he has to court her in her own territory.

Mouth-brooders
Above: Egyptian Mouth-brooders *(Hemi-haplochromis multicolor)* need no special breeding quarters. During the incubation period the female, who assumes full responsibility for this task, takes no nourishment and becomes very thin. The free-swimming fry seek shelter in their mother's mouth when danger threatens.

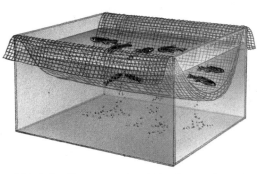

Left: Separating the male and female for two or three weeks and feeding them with high-quality and live foods ensures that both fishes are at peak condition for spawning and are keen to do so. They may be reunited by simply removing the partition.

Left, below: A layer or two of marbles on the bottom of the tank provides a fish-proof egg trap and prevents the adult fishes — in this case Tiger Barbs (*Barbus tetrazona*) — from eating the eggs. The shallow water level reduces the time that the falling eggs are at risk.

Right: The four photographs show a spawning of Rosy Barbs (*Barbus conchonius*). The more highly colored male nudges and butts the female (1-3) until they take up a side-by-side attitude (4); eggs are then released and fertilized.

Above: Another egg-saving device is a net draped in the water, through which the eggs fall. Zebra Danios may also be spawned as a shoal.

Above: Tetras lay adhesive eggs that may be trapped in a dense clump of plants where the female has been driven by the male to spawn.

Above: Live-bearers can give birth in breeding traps, the fry escaping to safety. A heavily planted separate nursery tank is preferable for them.

her. To conserve space, a breeding pair can be conditioned in the breeding aquarium by the use of a tank-divider; this may be made of glass or of sheet plastic, and some aquarists believe that the sight of each other, although physically separated, stimulates the two fishes towards successful spawning. It is then simplicity itself at the desired spawning time to introduce the fishes to each other by withdrawing the partition.

The prolific live-bearing fishes hardly need any encouragement to breed, but in order to maintain a certain quality, their spawning activities should be controlled. A collection of the many colored varieties of one species will not prove to be a stable strain for long. It may be more rewarding to specialize in one color variety only.

Spawning and after
The spawning should be supervised. Some male fishes are very active drivers of the female and will continue to harass her even after spawning; other males may not always accept the female as a partner at the outset and will attack her.

In both cases, the aquarist, if on hand, can rescue the ladies in distress. Egg-scattering fishes of both sexes are best removed from the breeding tank after spawning to eliminate the risk of them eating their own eggs. In any case, the aquarist usually wants to see what is going on and may even wish to photograph the events, particularly when observing the more ritualistic spawnings of the cichlid fishes.

Despite their reputation for being good parents, occasionally the cichlids do not fulfill their responsibilities and may well ignore, or even eat, their carefully laid eggs. In these instances the aquarist must either remove one of the parents (letting the remaining fish do its parental duty), or remove both fishes and artificially hatch the eggs by placing an airstone near the eggs and allowing the water currents to act as a substitute for the parents' fin-fanning actions.

The eggs of the egg-laying Toothcarps (Cyprinodontidae) may be deposited in bunches of natural plants, mops of nylon wool, or the peat layer on the aquarium floor. Depending on the species, the eggs

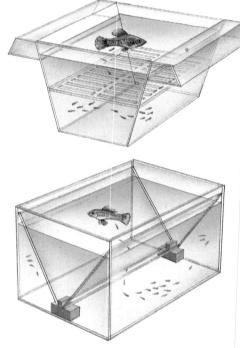

Top: A floating breeding trap that can be conveniently placed within the main aquarium. Above: Two pieces of glass quickly convert a spare tank into a live-bearer's nursery.

Left: A male American Flagfish (*Jordanella floridae*) is here guarding its eggs, which can be seen in the plants. This species is said to spawn and guard its eggs in a depression dug in the aquarium gravel but, unusually, this fish has spawned in among plants! Fishes obviously do not read the same books as aquarists. The female fish is best removed immediately after the spawning is completed, for her own safety.

Right: The Paradisefish (*Macropodus opercularis*), despite having a reputation for pugnacity, was probably the first tropical fish imported into Europe and has remained a firm favorite ever since. Here, the male inspects the bubble-nest as the female turns away after the spawning embrace. Again, the female should be removed after spawning.

Above: Some killifishes bury their eggs. There should be a deep layer of peat to accommodate such species as *Cynolebias,* shown here.

Above: Other killifishes *(Aphyosemion)* lay their eggs on artificial mops, from which they are collected and hatched in shallow dishes.

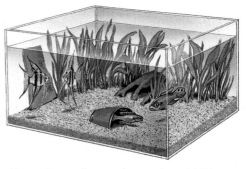

Above: Depending on the species, cichlids will require rocks, pieces of slate, flowerpots, or broad-leaved plants as spawning sites.

should be collected and either left in shallow water to hatch or kept in almost-dry peat for two or three months before re-immersing in water to activate hatching. Due to the vigor of the male fishes it is usual practice to spawn these fishes as trios, one male to two females. Female fishes of the bubble-nest building species are best removed after spawning: The male guards the nest and the fry quite fanatically.

After giving birth, female live-bearing fishes should, if possible, be allowed a further few days' rest before being returned to the main aquarium, otherwise they may be unable to cope with the renewed attentions of ardent males so soon after their confinement.

Care of the fry

As soon as any young fish begins swimming, it will require food, but until it actually swims it receives enough nourishment from its yolk-sac. It is pointless to give food before this time as the young fish cannot eat it and the added food will pollute the tank.

The first food for a fish depends upon the size of the fish. Not all fishes are the same size at birth. Generally fry from egg-scattering and nest-building species require smaller food than Cichlid and live-bearer fry.

Proprietary foods are available in liquid, paste, and fine powder forms, formulated to suit egg-laying or live-bearing species' requirements. Green water — cultures of infusorians — are very suitable for the smallest of fry. Micro-worms, screened *Daphnia*, and grindal worms are suitable for most young fishes, but the best food (as soon as the fry can cope with it) is brine shrimp. Soon the growing fry can be given white worms, crushed flake foods, and any other foods suitably reduced in size.

With the Anabantid fishes, such as the Siamese Fighting Fish (*Betta splendens*) and the Gourami families, the fry are susceptible to cold drafts, which may enter the aquarium hood; many aquarists drape the hood with a towel to minimize this risk.

Young fishes should feed continually and a low-power light should be left burning over the aquarium to encourage

this. As the fish mature, partial water changes should be made, the aeration rate increased, and the filtration system upgraded. This increase in water movement and the effect of the water changes will stimulate healthy growth. As the fishes grow and take on the familiar shapes and colors of their parents, the slow developers or stunted ones should be culled. At this time, a careful watch should be kept on live-bearer fry and the sexes separated as early as possible; again, fry not conforming to the required color or finnage pattern should be discarded. Although it may appear a callous act, unwanted fish fry make excellent food for other adult fishes. It is not good practice to raise large numbers of mediocre fishes out of soft-heartedness; if such specimens are introduced either back into your main collection or into the hobby (via friends or a retailer) the outcome will be a general lowering of fish quality.

A final note: Do keep written records of spawning attempts, particularly with the more difficult species. You may be the first hobbyist to get it right!

EXPANDING THE INTEREST

"Will it win?" thinks this young competitor.

It has been estimated that about one household in every ten either keeps an aquarium or has a garden pond. It is also probable that the majority of these fishkeepers are perfectly content with their decorative pets and have no desire to expand the number of their aquariums or to become involved with the organized side of the hobby. However, there are a number of advantages in joining an aquarist society, particularly if you want more from your hobby than just a pleasant 'living picture' in your home. Even the single aquarium has a good deal to offer within itself by way of information and education. Geography, biology, chemistry, physics, and mathematics are all skills that need to be exercised by the aquarist in the pursuit of fishkeeping. As a teaching aid, the aquarium may be far larger on the inside than we outsiders think! But was there ever a more enjoyable way of learning?

Aquarist societies—usually meeting monthly—offer regular lectures by visiting speakers, competitive Bowl Shows, inter-society quizzes and shows, trips to public aquariums, conventions, etc. Within these societies aquarium hobbyists can find all the latest information on recently imported species, plus all the practical hints to be had by the newcomer —from initial problems to how to cope with the more exotic species. In addition to local societies there are aquatic groups specializing in certain species of fishes including Catfishes, Cichlids, Goldfish, Koi, Live-bearers, and Marine Fishes.

Most local societies are affiliated with larger national bodies. In the U.S. the largest is the Federation of American Aquarium Societies (F.A.A.S.). Canada has the Canadian Association of Aquarium Clubs (C.A.A.C.), and Britain has the Federation of British Aquatic Societies (F.B.A.S.). European aquarists can affiliate as individuals (rather than by societies) with their respective countries' aquatic governing bodies: Germany — Verband Deutscher ver Aquarien (V.D.A.); France—Fédération Français des Associations Aquaphile et Terrariophile (F.F.A.A.T.); Belgium—Belgique Bond Aquaria et Terraria (B.B.A.T.); Netherlands—Nederlands Bond Aquaria et Terraria (N.B.A.T.); Denmark—Dansk Akvarie (D.K.A.); Norway—Norsk Akvarieforbund (N.A.F.); Poland—Polski Zwiazeke Akwarystow (P.Z.A.); Luxemburg—Federation Luxembourg Aquariophile et Terrariophile (F.L.A.T.); and Sweden—Sveriges Akvarietföreningars Riksförbund (S.A.R.F.). All these organizations are in turn members of the Aquarium Terrarium International (A.T.I.).

The aquarium hobby may not appear to be quite so tightly knit in Australia, where the large distances between societies is a contributory factor, but New Zealand aquarists enjoy the services of the Federation of New Zealand Aquatic Societies.

These national bodies lay down rules that are used by the local societies which organize open competitive shows and also publish much valuable information on nomenclature and the sizes attained by aquarium fishes.

During the show season there is a fish show somewhere every weekend. Even if the newcomer is not particularly competitive, a visit to an open show will reveal a whole selection of fishes suited to aquariums, together with superbly set-up, furnished tanks and aquatic plants. It is an excellent showcase for products and a meeting place for anyone interested in keeping fishes.

It is natural for a newcomer to look for assistance with issues that seem important to him. Aquarist magazines, with their advisory columns, are a good source of information; and most fish food and aquatic equipment manufacturers operate an advisory service or issue information packs that can be helpful.

Above: The fishkeeper often has a well-developed eye for beauty and an artistic appreciation. The way that the aquarium has been incorporated into this room amply illustrates this design sense to stunning effect.

Showing

As with other organized competitive pet shows, aquarium shows in the U.S., Canada, and Britain revolve around the animals on display. They are generally divided into classes based roughly on broad family groups—Cyprinids, Characins, Cichlids, Catfishes, Anabantids, Live-bearers, etc. Fishes are shown singly (except for pairs and breeders, classes) in bare tanks. Each fish may earn up to a maximum of 100 points (under one system), divided into five groups of 20 points each. Points are awarded for size, body, fins, color, and condition and deportment. Speciality clubs may differ in their allocation of points. Each entry is judged individually (about five judges evaluating approximately 500 entries in two hours) and the results are displayed for the benefit of exhibiting owners and for visitors to the show. In addition to single fish classes, there may be opportunities to see furnished aquariums, aquatic plants, pairs and breeders' teams —a group of four or six fishes of the same species bred by the owner. The main interests of the day's show are to see which fish is going to be 'Best in Show' and whether the host society can win the trophy for gaining the most winning places.

The show scene on the continent of Europe is slightly different; there, the show may not be so competition-orientated and the accent is more likely to be upon informative (and extremely decorative) furnished aquariums for display purposes only, coupled with lectures and seminars during the exhibition. Another type of competition (shared by many aquarist societies the world over) is where the hobbyists' home-furnished

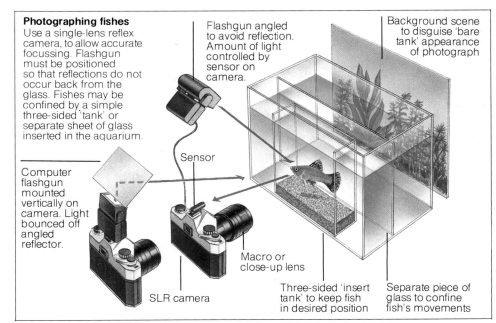

Photographing fishes
Use a single-lens reflex camera, to allow accurate focussing. Flashgun must be positioned so that reflections do not occur back from the glass. Fishes may be confined by a simple three-sided 'tank' or separate sheet of glass inserted in the aquarium.

Flashgun angled to avoid reflection. Amount of light controlled by sensor on camera.

Background scene to disguise 'bare tank' appearance of photograph

Sensor

Computer flashgun mounted vertically on camera. Light bounced off angled reflector.

SLR camera

Macro or close-up lens

Three-sided 'insert tank' to keep fish in desired position

Separate piece of glass to confine fish's movements

aquariums compete against each other and are evaluated by a visiting panel of judges.

Often, the competitive aspect of the hobby is frowned upon by non-competitors but aquarium shows do provide the main impetus for further interest in serious fishkeeping and breeding, bringing more and more new species to the attention of the aquarist, together with vital information as to how they may be successfully kept in the aquarium.

International connections
Many aquarists subscribe to specialist societies that have evolved into international groups. The fact that Killifishes' eggs can be directly mailed to aquarist acquaintances around the world certainly strengthens the ties between hobbyists who are interested in these fishes. With air travel becoming more convenient and vacations taking people further from home than ever, contacting fishkeepers and societies wherever you travel can be a fun and friendly way to meet people in foreign places.

Photography
If an aquarist also is a competent photographer, here is an ideal parallel interest. With modern high-speed color-correct films allied to electronic flash photography, it is not too difficult to capture some of your favorite fishes and aquascapes on permanent film.

With the advent of macro-lenses and the now ubiquitous single lens reflex (SLR) camera, even spawning sequences can be recorded. Should you see an unfamiliar fish at a fish show, a photograph of it, together with its scientific name from the show's judging sheets on display, will provide you with perhaps another new aquatic interest.

The video-recorder provides the aquarist with yet another means of capturing live aquatic action in pictorial form, with the extra benefit of 'action-replays' whenever desired. From here you can add commentary on a synchronized soundtrack and thus provide a fully documented visual record of your living hobby.

Above: Judging fishes is a skilled job. Each fish (in this case a coldwater goldfish) is accurately measured for size.
Below: A magnifying glass reveals any scale damage or split fins. An essential show check.

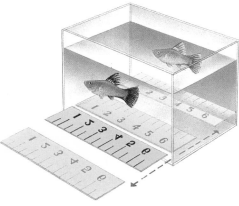

Above: Rulers with mirror-image markings help to measure fishes easily; watch the reflection of the ruler in the glass. Move the ruler *away* from the tank to measure a fish at rear of tank—the image follows the fish.

PART TWO

SPECIES GUIDE

Two hundred tropical freshwater fishes are featured here, with details on their shape and coloration, their diet and breeding habits, and—most important—the conditions under which each species can be kept.

The vast majority of the world's freshwater fishes live in warm-water lakes and rivers, particularly in tropical America, Africa, and Asia. It is these fishes that provide the aquarist with such a galaxy of different shapes, sizes, and colors.

Most aquarium fishes belong to a small number of large groups, each with quite distinctive characteristics. These are the Characins, the Carps and Barbs, the Catfishes, the Toothcarps, the Cichlids, and the Labyrinth Fishes. The remainder are members of a large number of small families.

Every kind of fish—indeed, every kind of animal—is given a scientific name consisting of two words, the genus or generic name and the species or specific name. These scientific names are used internationally, whereas the common names are mostly confined to a limited area or language. There are a few fishes that have been given more than one scientific name and these have been indicated in the text. However, do not get too involved in the intricacies of fish nomenclature; it is better to spend time and energy on getting to know the habits and biological requirements of your fishes.

Left: The contrasting shapes of
Angelfishes (Pterophyllum scalare)
and Neon Tetras (Paracheirodon innesi).

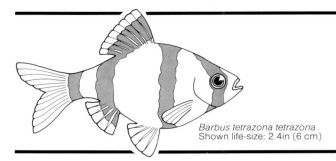

Barbus tetrazona tetrazona
Shown life-size: 2.4in (6 cm)

Family POLYPTERIDAE

This is a small group of fishes found only in tropical Africa. Characterized by the ability to swallow air at the surface and use it as an aid to respiration, these fishes are also distinguished by the dorsal fin, which is divided into a number of finlets.

Family POLYPTERIDAE

Calamoichthys calabaricus
Reedfish

● **Distribution:** Africa: Cameroon and Niger Delta at Calabar
● **Length:** Up to 14.6in (37cm), possibly more
● **Tank length:** 36in (90cm)
● **Diet:** Worms, crustaceans, insects
● **Water temperature:** 73 to 83°F (23 to 28°C)
● **Community tank:** Will eat small fish in the aquarium

Also known as *Erpetoichthys calabaricus,* this is a very elongated, cylindrical, eellike fish with seven to 13 small, well-separated dorsal fins. These fins are usually kept folded down. There are no ventral fins. The two nostrils are developed into tubular processes. The fan-shaped pectoral fins serve as paddles when swimming, and also as struts to support the body when the fish is resting on the bottom. The swim-bladder has an open connection with the esophagus, and functions as a lung; air swallowed at the surface passes into the swim-bladder where its oxygen content is absorbed into the blood system. The anal fin has 12 to 14 rays in the male and nine to 12 in the female. The back is a delicate olive-green; the flanks are a pale green and the underparts are yellow. There is a large black marking at the base of each pectoral fin.

This hardy fish should be kept in a tank with a good lid, and with rocks and roots arranged to provide hiding-places. This species must have access to air. The tank should not be too full so that there is a space between the water surface and the tank lid. It is mainly active at night, preferring to remain hidden during the day. The water can be soft or medium-hard. The species has not yet been bred in captivity.

This is the only species in its genus, but the family Polypteridae contains several species in the genus *Polypterus,* all from tropical waters of Africa. They are known colloquially as bichirs, and most are quarrelsome among themselves. Like the Reedfish, they are nocturnal, rather secretive fishes. Little is known about their reproductive habits. The young are known to have treelike external gills and are similar in appearance to newt larvae.

Left: **Calamoichthys calabaricus**
This is a rather shy fish that lurks among vegetation on the bottom, moving about like a snake.

Family NOTOPTERIDAE

This is a small family with representatives in tropical Africa and Southeast Asia. These active, nocturnal fishes have a swim-bladder that serves as an accessory respiratory organ.

Family NOTOPTERIDAE

Xenomystus nigri
African Knifefish

● **Distribution:** Africa: Nile westwards to Liberia
● **Length:** Up to 8in (20cm)
● **Tank length:** 36in (90cm)
● **Diet:** Worms, crustaceans, insects, snails, meat
● **Water temperature:** 75 to 83°F (24 to 28°C)
● **Species tank:** Or in a community of medium-sized, peaceful fishes such as Angelfish and Gouramis.

The African Knifefish is elongated and very laterally compressed. Its large mouth has two nasal tentacles. The anus is situated very far forward on the body. The dorsal fin is lacking, but the anal fin is very long, starting immediately behind the anus and extending to the rear tip of the body where it fuses with the caudal fin. This fringelike anal fin is the fish's main organ of propulsion, and its undulatory movements enable the fish to swim forward or backward. The general coloration is dark brown or dark gray with paler underparts. The flanks sometimes have one or more rather indistinct longitudinal stripes.

This is a shy, retiring fish, which comes to the surface from time to time to swallow air. The brief sounds emitted at intervals are due to the expulsion of air from the swim-bladder into the alimentary tract. A shoal of young individuals can be kept in a tank with subdued lighting, areas of dense vegetation, and a tangle of rocks and roots that will provide shelter. The fishes rest in a slightly oblique position with the head down. They come out at dusk and during the night to hunt for prey. The species has not yet been bred in captivity.

The related *Notopterus afer,* from Congo to the Gambia in Africa, reaches a length of about 24in (60cm), but is suitable for the home aquarium only when young.

Above: **Xenomystus nigri**
This is an interesting fish to watch as it moves to and fro using the long anal fin for propulsion.

A practical reminder
You will get maximum enjoyment from fishkeeping only if your fishes are provided with the very best conditions. Only then will they be able to repay you by looking their best and living the longest.

Family PANTODONTIDAE
This family, containing only one genus and one species, is found in tropical West Africa. The large pectoral fins allow the fish to glide over the surface of the water. It does not, however, beat its fins as do the the hatchetfishes. It is active mainly at night.

Family PANTODONTIDAE
Pantodon buchholzi
Butterflyfish
● **Distribution:** Africa: Niger Cameroon, Zaire
● **Length:** Up to 4in (10cm)
● **Tank length:** 24in (60cm)
● **Diet:** Crustaceans, insects, fish
● **Water temperature:** 75 to 84°F (24 to 29°C)
● **Community tank:** May swallow smaller specimens

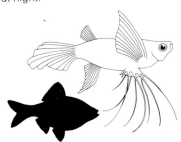

Right: **Pantodon buchholzi** ♀
Although it takes most of its food from the surface, this fish can also leap out to catch flying insects.

This fish is boat-shaped with a flat dorsal surface and rounded underparts. The large, winglike pectoral fins are held out from the body. The dorsal fin is quite small, rounded, and positioned far back on the body. The anal fin and the central rays of the caudal fin are elongated. The large mouth faces upward, and the nostrils are elongated and tubular. The upperparts and flanks are silvery or greenish and are marked with an irregular pattern of brown spots and streaks. The rays of all the fins show alternating dark and pale rings. A dark band runs from the forehead, across the eye, to the lower jaw.

This is a surface-living fish of standing waters. It is capable of leaping out of the water and gliding for short distances with the help of the outstretched pectoral fins, though the pectorals are not beaten or flapped. The Butterflyfish can be kept in a tank with floating plants to cover only a part of the surface and a few rooted plants with leaves that grow up to the water surface. There should, of course, be a well-fitting lid to prevent 'flying'. The water must be soft, slightly acid, and filtered through peat. The sexes are not difficult to distinguish since the rear edge of the anal fin is straight in the female, but concave in the male. Spawning is preceded by vigorous driving. Afterward the fishes coil around one another and the eggs and sperm are shed in batches. The eggs, which are brown or almost black, hatch in 36 to 48 hours. Spawning has been observed on many occasions, but successful rearing of the fry is very rare. Tiny nauplii can be offered, but the fry do not chase them, taking only those that drift past in the surface waters.

Family MORMYRIDAE
This is an exclusively African family. Some long-nosed species probe the substrate for food, while others hunt in midwater. Muscles at the rear of the body have developed to form an electric organ that serves mainly for orientation, for species recognition, and for delimiting territories. Most species in the family have poor eyesight.

Family MORMYRIDAE
Gnathonemus petersi
Elephant Nose
● **Distribution:** Africa: Congo, Cameroon to Niger
● **Length:** Up to 9in (23cm), possibly more
● **Tank length:** 24in (60cm)
● **Diet:** Worms, insects, dried food
● **Water temperature:** 75 to 83°F (24 to 28°C)
● **Community tank**

Right: **Gnathonemus petersi**
A peaceful fish that prefers to hide during the day, this species has a large brain in relation to body size.

This is an elongated and laterally compressed fish with a small round mouth. The lower jaw has a mobile, trunklike extension, hence the popular name. The caudal fin is deeply cleft, and the dorsal and anal fins are almost opposite one another. The brain is very large and—relative to body weight—is comparable to the brain of a human being. The slender caudal peduncle contains an electric organ that is not used for stunning prey as in the Electric Eel, but is used for finding its way about in turbid water. The organ emits about 20 electric pulses per minute, thus producing an electrical field. Objects in the vicinity will disturb this field and this is detected by sense organs in the head of the fish. The general coloration is blackish brown with violet iridescence when seen in reflected light. There are two irregular, yellowish-white transverse bars between the dorsal and anal fins. The dorsal, caudal, and anal fins have narrow white edges.

This is an active fish that lives close to the bottom where it probes (mostly at night) for food with the long snout. It is territorial and is usually rather aggressive towards members of its own species. However, it is quite peaceful with other fishes. It can be kept in a tank with dense vegetation, a soft substrate, and a number of rocks and roots arranged to form hiding-places. The lighting should be subdued or it can be installed so that some parts of the tank are dark. The composition of the water is not very critical, but it should preferably be mature, and about a quarter of it must be changed once a month or so. The Elephant Nose has not yet been bred in the aquarium.

THE CHARACINS

Above: *Poptella orbicularis,* a South American
member of the family Characidae.
Right: A peaceful stretch of water in tropical
Amazonia, a typical habitat for characins.

*T*his large group of fishes consists of several closely related
families with some 200 species in Africa and about 1,000
species in South America, Central America, and southern North
America. The body is typically scaled, but the head has no scales
and no barbels. There is usually, but not always, an adipose fin.
Many of the species live in shoals and are active during the day.
Brood protection occurs only rarely. The parent fishes show no
interest in their brood except that, at least in captivity, many species
chase and eat their own eggs. The suborder contains carnivores,
omnivores, and herbivores.

The group contains the following families.

The Characidae or true characins occur in Africa and more
numerously in Central and South America. Many are small or
very small fishes with a short dorsal fin, usually an adipose fin,
and a deeply cleft caudal fin. Most species spawn at random and
the eggs are adhesive.

The Serrasalmidae or piranhas of central and northern South
America are aggressive predators with powerful jaws and
numerous very sharp teeth. Only small individuals are suitable.

The Gasteropelecidae or hatchetfishes, restricted to tropical
America, are very compressed fishes with the pectoral fins forming
'wings' that can be beaten to propel the body out of the water.

The Lebiasinidae of South America are slender, elongated
fishes with a short dorsal fin; some species have an adipose fin.

The Anostomidae of tropical America are elongated, spindle-
shaped fishes with a wedge-shaped head and a small mouth. Only
a few species have been bred in the aquarium.

The Curimatidae of South America are very similar to the
Anostomidae. They have an elongated body, and an adipose fin is
usually present.

The Citharinidae are restricted to tropical Africa. Many are
medium-sized to large fishes that are suitable only when young.

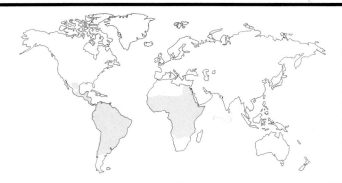

Left: Most species in this large group are typically shoaling fishes living in fresh waters. The numerous species in South America inhabit different types of water. In the Amazon region there are clear greenish waters and white water rivers, so-called because of their content of clay particles. Finally, there are 'black' waters, which are perfectly clear but colored dark brown by their content of organic compounds.

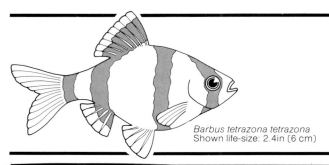

Barbus tetrazona tetrazona
Shown life-size: 2.4in (6 cm)

Family CHARACIDAE
Alestes longipinnis
Long-finned Characin
- **Distribution:** Tropical West Africa, from Sierra Leone to the Congo
- **Length:** Up to 5in (13cm)
- **Tank length:** 24in (60cm)
- **Diet:** Flies, beetles, small cockroaches
- **Water temperature:** 73 to 77°F (23 to 25°C)
- **Community tank**

The Long-finned Characin is a laterally compressed, olive-green to yellow-green fish with marked silvery iridescence and a broad black band on the caudal peduncle. In males the dorsal fin is much elongated and the anal fin has a white border. The eyes are bright golden-red.

This is an attractive fish for a large community tank, where it can be kept in a shoal. Take care to have a close-fitting lid, because this fish jumps very well. They mostly swim in the middle water layers and the tank should have groups of fine-leaved plants to provide shelter.

Above:
Alestes longipinnis ♂(t), ♀(b)
This is sometimes a shy, nervous fish and any disturbance in the aquarium should be avoided.

For breeding it is essential that the water should be soft and slightly acid. Spawning is preceded by vigorous driving among the plants. The female lays 300 or more eggs, which hatch after about six days. The fry can be fed at first on rotifers and very small nauplii.

The related Chaper's Characin (*A. chaperi*) from West Africa (Ghana to Nigeria) is a smaller fish (up to 2.8in/7cm) with grass-green flanks and red dorsal and anal fins with broad yellow borders. It requires similar conditions to *A. longipinnis,* but has probably not yet been bred successfully in captivity.

Family CHARACIDAE
Aphyocharax rubropinnis
Bloodfin
- **Distribution:** South America: Rio Paraná, Argentina
- **Length:** Up to 2.2in (5.5cm)
- **Tank length:** 12in (30cm)
- **Diet:** Worms, small insects and crustaceans, dried food
- **Water temperature:** 72 to 83°F (22 to 28°C)
- **Community tank**

Bloodfins are shoaling fishes which swim mainly in the upper and middle water layers. The elongated body is yellow to grayish green with a bluish sheen. The basal parts of the dorsal, caudal, anal, and ventral fins are blood-red, hence the popular name. Tiny hooklets on the anal fin of the male often become entangled with the meshes of the net when the fish is being caught. If this happens, the fish should not be pulled away from the net, because this may tear off the hooklets. The fish will survive this loss, but will not be able to mate since during mating, the hooklets of a male are briefly engaged with the anal fin of the female.

Spawning takes place usually in early morning, after a period of very active driving by the male. The water must be soft and slightly acid. The female lays a large number of glass-clear eggs, sometimes 700 to 800, which sink to the bottom of the tank. These must be protected from the parents, which will eat them if given the chance. The eggs hatch in about 20 to 25 hours, and after a day or two the fry can be fed on rotifers and small nauplii. Under favorable conditions they grow very rapidly.

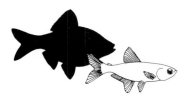

Right: **Aphyocharax rubropinnis**
This attractive shoaling fish is easy to breed in the aquarium. A fine mesh netting just above the bottom will safeguard the eggs.

A practical reminder
Select as large a tank as you can accommodate, with the largest water surface area, regardless of its total capacity. This makes for a stable environment and lessens changes in water temperature and conditions.

Family CHARACIDAE
Arnoldichthys spilopterus
Red-eyed Characin
- **Distribution:** Tropical West Atrica: Niger estuary to Lagos
- **Length:** Up to 4in (10cm)
- **Tank length:** 24in (60cm)
- **Diet:** Worms, small insects, crustaceans, dried food
- **Water temperature:** 75 to 81°F (24 to 27°C)
- **Community tank**

These are rather shy, shoaling fishes that require sufficient space for swimming and not too many plants. The body is elongated, with green or bluish green flanks and a yellowish belly. The dorsal fin has a prominent black marking. The scales on the upper half of the body are much enlarged, a characteristic that helps to distinguish this particular species—the only one in the genus *Arnoldichthys*—from related African characins, such as *Alestes*. The eye is bright red. Females show less green coloration.

This species requires soft,

Above: **Arnoldichthys spilopterus**
The color and pattern of this fish are variable; in some males the anal fin has a blood-red spot at the base. In hard water the species is susceptible to infection with fish turberculosis.

slightly acid water and preferably a diet of live insects, but will also take dried food. It is not an easy species to breed in the aquarium: In fact, this was not accomplished until 1967. After vigorous driving the female lays up to 1000 eggs, which hatch in 30 to 34 hours, depending upon the temperature. The fry are free swimming after six or seven days, and can then be fed on tiny nauplii and rotifers. When conditions are just right the young grow rapidly, but they are often difficult to rear.

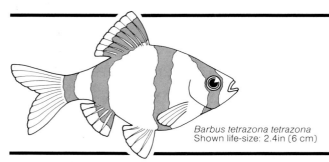

Barbus tetrazona tetrazona
Shown life-size: 2.4in (6 cm)

Family CHARACIDAE

Chalceus macrolepidotus

Pink-tailed Characin

- **Distribution:** South America, in Guyana
- **Length:** Up to about 9.5in (24cm)
- **Tank length:** 24in (60cm)
- **Diet:** Worms, insect larvae, and small fishes
- **Water temperature:** 75 to 81°F (24 to 27°C)
- **Community tank**

Sometimes classified in a separate family, the Chalceidae, these elegant shoaling fishes are predatory and require plenty of space for swimming. They mostly live near the surface and at times they jump out of the water. The body is elongated and laterally compressed, but the most striking and characteristic feature is the arrangement of the scales. The upper half of the body has three rows of very large scales, but the lower half has considerably smaller ones. There is a medium-sized adipose fin; the dorsal fin is set slightly behind the middle of the back; and in the caudal fin the lower lobe is larger than the upper lobe. The flanks are silvery with violet or greenish iridescence while the belly is shiny white and the back relatively dark. The anal fin is red or yellowish red. The dorsal, caudal, and ventral fins are usually wine-red, but may be more yellowish. There is a prominent dark brown marking just behind the gill cover.

In addition to live food, this fish can also be fed on chopped lean beef. The species is not often available to aquarists, and it has not yet been bred in captivity.

Right: **Chalceus macrolepidotus** ♂
An elegant fish best kept in a shoal in a tank with a good lid.

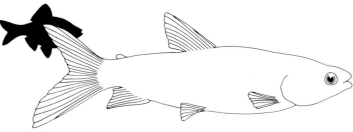

Family CHARACIDAE

Astyanax mexicanus

- **Distribution:** North and Central America, from Texas south to Panama
- **Length:** Up to 3.5in (9cm)
- **Tank length:** 24in (60cm)
- **Diet:** Insects, crustaceans, worms, dried food
- **Water temperature:** 66 to 77°F (19 to 25°C)
- **Species tank**

There are two forms of this species, the normal one and a blind form found in subterranean streams in the Mexican province of San Luis Potosi. The normal form is brassy or silvery in

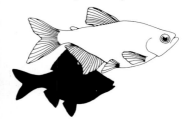

Left: **Astyanax mexicanus** ♂
This blind form comes from underground waters and shows an uncanny ability to navigate without functional eyes.

A practical reminder
Make sure the tank is standing on a firm and level foundation away from windows. It should be situated near an electrical power outlet, and in a place where regular maintenance is easy.

Cheirodon axelrodi
Cardinal Tetra
- **Distribution:** South America, in tributaries of the Orinoco and Rio Negro
- **Length:** 1.6 to 1.8in (4 to 4.5cm)
- **Tank length:** 12in (30cm)
- **Diet:** Worms, small crustaceans, dried food
- **Water temperature:** 73 to 79°F (23 to 26°C)
- **Community tank**

This is one of the most attractive and popular of the tropical American characins. It mostly lives in a shoal in the middle water layers. Females are usually a little larger than males. The body is elongated and laterally compressed, and there is an adipose fin. The most striking feature, however, is the coloration. A broad, iridescent blue-green longitudinal band extends from the tip of the snout, through the eye, to the caudal peduncle. Below this there is a bright red band also extending to the base of the tail. The fins are colorless, and the back is brownish-red.

Cardinal Tetras do best, and also look most attractive, when kept in subdued light in a tank with a dark substrate. The water should be soft and slightly acid. Under such conditions spawning may take place, often at night or at any rate in subdued light. The eggs hatch in 24 to 30 hours and the fry are free-swimming after three or four days. They can be fed on very small nauplii and rotifers, but they are not always easy to rear.

The related *C. meinkeni* from coastal areas of Brazil (Bahia to Rio de Janeiro) is a little larger, up to 2in (5cm) long, but less brilliantly colored. The flanks are silvery with an olive tinge and an iridescent longitudinal band.

coloration with an olive upper side. The caudal peduncle has a roundish dark marking with pale yellow borders in front and behind.

The blind form of *A. mexicanus*, known as the Blind Cave Characin, is an altogether more interesting fish. For many years it was called *Anoptichthys jordani*. The body is flesh-colored with silvery iridescence, the fins being colorless or reddish. The two forms can mate with one another, and the offspring may be intermediate.

Juveniles of the blind form often have normal vision in their early stages, but as they get older the eyes become covered with skin and are then non-functional. The fishes find their way about by their sense of smell and by the lateral line organs; they have no difficulty in finding food or avoiding obstacles.

Both forms of *A. mexicanus* breed quite readily in an aquarium. The eggs, which are laid at random, hatch in about 25 hours, and the fry are free-swimming after four or five days. They can then be fed on fine live and dried food, and they grow rapidly into healthy young fish.

Left: **Cheirodon axelrodi** ♀(t), ♂(b)
A larger and more brilliantly colored version of Paracheirodon innesi, *this species looks particularly attractive in a shoal in dim lighting conditions. Not easy to rear.*

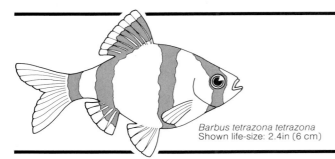

Barbus tetrazona tetrazona
Shown life-size: 2.4in (6 cm)

Family CHARACIDAE
Ctenobrycon spilurus
Silver Tetra
- **Distribution:** South America: coastal districts of Venezuela, Guyana and Surinam
- **Length:** Up to 3.5in (9cm)
- **Tank length:** 24in (60cm)
- **Diet:** Worms, crustaceans, insects, plant matter, dried food
- **Water temperature:** 68 to 81°F (20 to 27°C)
- **Community tank:** Sometimes aggressive

The Silver Tetra is a hardy characin with a very laterally compressed body that is almost lozenge-shaped when seen from the side. As in the related Disk Tetra *(Poptella orbicularis)* the anal fin is very long, an adipose fin is present, the dorsal fin is short and pointed, and the caudal fin is forked. The sexes are similarly colored. A large blue-black marking, just behind the iridescent green gill cover, is united to a similar marking on the caudal peduncle by a thin, greenish longitudinal band.

This is an active fish that should be kept as a shoal in a tank with other characins of similar size. There should be a few tough plants, bearing in mind that the species tends to nibble the leaves of soft-leaved plants. The composition of the water is not critical for the adults.

For breeding a well-fed and compatible pair should be placed in a separate tank, preferably with soft or medium-hard water. There is usually a vigorous courtship among the plants and the female lays about 1000 eggs, sometimes more, which must be protected from the parent fishes. At a temperature of 77°F (25°C) the eggs hatch in 24 hours. The fry should then be fed on *Paramecium,* rotifers and a plentiful supply of brine shrimp nauplii. Large broods should be divided up if they are growing rapidly.

This species has a reputation of nibbling the fins of Angelfishes.

Right: **Ctenobrycon spilurus**
A good shoaling fish for the community tank, although it may be aggressive to smaller species.

Family CHARACIDAE
Gymnocorymbus ternetzi
Black Tetra
- **Distribution:** South America: Mato Grosso area of Rio Paraguay and Rio Negro
- **Length:** Up to 2.4in (6cm)
- **Tank length:** 18in (45cm)
- **Diet:** Worms, small crusta-ceans, insects, dried food
- **Water temperature:** 73 to 79°F (23 to 26°C)
- **Community tank**

This is an excellent aquarium fish that is particularly attractive when young. In juveniles the flanks are black, but they become smoky-gray with increasing age. The

Left: **Gymnocorymbus ternetzi**
A good all-round fish, tolerant of others and generally easy to breed.

Family CHARACIDAE
Hemigrammus caudovittatus
Buenos Aires Tetra
- **Distribution:** South America, in the Rio de la Plata Basin
- **Length:** Up to 2.8in (7cm)
- **Tank length:** 18in (45cm)
- **Diet:** Worms, crustaceans, insects, plant matter, dried food
- **Water temperature:** 64 to 83°F (18 to 28°C)
- **Community tank**

This is a very undemanding fish, and particularly suitable for the beginner. The female is somewhat stouter than the male. The back is blackish brown or olive brown, the flanks are iridescent silvery, and the upper part of the iris is red. In males the dorsal, adipose, and anal fins and the lobes of the caudal fin are red or yellowish red. The ventral fins are reddish. Just behind the gill cover there is a comma-shaped dark marking, which is best seen in reflected light. However, the most characteristic marking is a black streak on the caudal peduncle, which extends back onto the center of the caudal fin with a yellowish white area above and below. There is a color variant in which the caudal fin lobes are lemon-yellow. The females are less colorful, with delicate pink or almost colorless fins and a more rounded body.

This is an easy fish to breed at a water temperature of about 75°F (24°C). Spawning takes place among plants, the eggs being laid at random. They hatch very quickly, usually in 20 to 24 hours, and after a few days the fry can be fed on tiny live food such as rotifers and nauplii.

This is one of the hardiest tropical fishes for the home aquarium, and it has been popular for almost 60 years. It has a tendency to eat delicate plants.

Below:
Hemigrammus caudovittatus
A hardy fish ideal for beginners.

back is olive-green and the belly whitish with a silvery sheen. Behind the gill cover there are two prominent black bands. The dorsal, anal, and adipose fins are black or blackish. The ventral and pectoral fins are more or less colorless. A selected form with longer fins is sometimes available. The female is a little larger at the rear than the male, with the body cavity rounded; this can be seen when the fish is observed against the light. In the male, the rear part of the body cavity is pointed, and the caudal fin has white spots, which do not occur in the female. This is a fish of the middle and upper water layers, which should preferably be kept as one of a small shoal.

Before mating the male swims around the female with fins spread out, sometimes in circles, or sometimes following a zigzag track. The tiny, transparent eggs are laid at random among plants, preferably those with feathery leaves; at this point the parent fishes should be removed to prevent them eating the spawn. The eggs usually hatch in 24 to 26 hours, and the fry are free-swimming three to five days later. They should then be fed on rotifers and tiny nauplii.

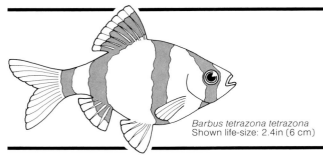

Barbus tetrazona tetrazona
Shown life-size: 2.4in (6 cm)

Family CHARACIDAE

Hemigrammus erythrozonus
Glowlight Tetra

- **Distribution:** Northeastern parts of South America
- **Length:** Up to 1.6in (4cm)
- **Tank length:** 18in (45cm)
- **Diet:** Worms, small crustaceans, plant matter, dried food
- **Water temperature:** 75 to 83°F (24 to 28°C)
- **Community tank**

This species is one of the most beautiful of the South American characins, and similar in shape to the Neon Tetra. It lives mostly in the lower water layers of the tank, which should have patches of dense vegetation and plenty of open water for swimming.

The background coloration of the body is gray-green, the back brownish olive, and the belly silvery. A broad ruby-red band extends back from the upper lip, through the upper part of the eye, and along each flank to the base of the caudal fin. At its rear this band widens into a gleaming spot, hence the popular name. The front of the dorsal fin is bright red, but all the other fins are a delicate pink or colorless, and more or less transparent. The tips of the dorsal, anal, and ventral fins are ivory-white.

This species thrives best in soft, slightly acid water, and this is essential for breeding; filtration through peat is also strongly recommended. At the moment of spawning the parent fishes swim in among the plants, which should preferably be those with feathery leaves. The eggs usually fall to the bottom of the tank, and must then be protected from the parents; the safest method is to remove the pair from the tank. The eggs hatch in 20 to 25 hours, and when free-swimming the fry can be fed on rotifers and very tiny nauplii.

Right: **Hemigrammus erythrozonus**
Popular in the aquarium world since the 1940s, this fish's common name refers to the bright spot of red at the base of the tail, which shines in a well-lit tank.

Family CHARACIDAE

Hemigrammus ocellifer
Beacon Fish

- **Distribution:** Northern South America
- **Length:** Up to 1.8in (4.5cm)
- **Tank length:** 12in (30cm)
- **Diet:** Worms, small insects, crustaceans, plant matter, dried food
- **Water temperature:** 72 to 81°F (22 to 27°C)
- **Community tank**

There are two subspecies of Beacon Fish and this has caused some confusion. The one usually seen is *H. ocellifer falsus,* which was introduced into the aquarium world around 1910. The other, *H. ocellifer ocellifer,* was not widely known until 1960.

In *H. ocellifer falsus* the flanks are brownish to greenish yellow with silvery iridescence. Behind the gill cover there is a rather indistinct dark marking within an area of iridescent green. At about the level of the dorsal fin there is the start of a narrow dark band, which extends back to the base of the tail. There, it is crossed by a dark transverse bar flanked by brilliant golden-yellow spots, which give this fish its popular name. The other subspecies is perhaps even more attractive. The marking behind the gill cover is black, with a golden area in front and behind, and there is red at the base of each caudal fin lobe.

Both subspecies have been

Right: **Hemigrammus ocellifer ocellifer**
This colorful fish is highly suitable for a community tank.

bred in the same way as the Buenos Aires Tetra. The swimbladder of the slimmer male can be clearly seen when the fish is viewed against the light, but it is usually masked in the more robust female.

A practical reminder
Choose the correct size heater. Allow 10 watts per gallon (3.8 liters). Large tanks need two heaters to spread heat evenly and quickly. Do not test heaters out of water. Always switch off the power before adjusting

Family CHARACIDAE
Hemigrammus pulcher
Pretty Tetra
- **Distribution:** South America: the Peruvian part of the Amazon, above Iquitos
- **Length:** Up to 1.8in (4.5cm)
- **Tank length:** 12in (30cm)
- **Diet:** Worms, small crustaceans, plant matter, dried food
- **Water temperature:** 73 to 81°F (23 to 27°C)
- **Community tank**

This is a deep-bodied, rather high-backed characin living in the middle water layers. Depending upon the angle of light the flanks are pale grayish green to coppery. The back is brownish green and the belly whitish. The head is dark green, becoming darker towards the black snout. The iris is bright purple above, blue-green below. Just behind the gill cover there is a shiny copper-red marking and the upper part of the caudal peduncle has a brilliant golden area. Below this there is an area of black, which extends forwards to below the dorsal fin. The dorsal, caudal, and anal fins are violet or reddish. In the male, which is more slender than the female, the swim-bladder is clearly visible when the fish is viewed against the light, but it is only partly visible in the female. The first four rays of the male's anal fin each end in a tiny hook.

This is not always an easy fish to breed. Some pairs do not succeed in spawning; if this happens, the male should be replaced. Once a pair have spawned successfully they will usually continue to do so. It is probably advisable to attempt breeding in a tank at least 18in (45cm) long, with a water temperature two to four degrees Fahrenheit (one or two degrees Centigrade) above the normal. The water should be soft, slightly acid and preferably filtered through peat. Spawning takes place in the same manner as *Hemigrammus caudovittatus*.

Left: **Hemigrammus pulcher**
Successful breeding of this fish depends upon finding a compatible pair. Once established such a pair is usually very prolific.

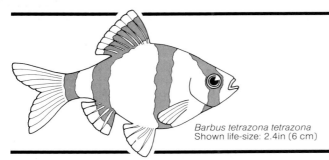

Barbus tetrazona tetrazona
Shown life-size: 2.4in (6 cm)

Family CHARACIDAE

Hyphessobrycon callistus
Blood Characin

- **Distribution:** South America, in the Basin of Rio Paraguay
- **Length:** Up to 1.6in (4cm)
- **Tank length:** 12in (30cm)
- **Diet:** Worms, crustaceans, insects, plant matter, dried food
- **Water temperature:** 73 to 79°F (23 to 26°C)
- **Community tank**

This deep-bodied characin is much compressed laterally, and is very suitable for the beginner. The ground coloration of the body is brownish red with silvery iridescence, the belly yellowish brown, becoming much rounded and blood-red in females that are ready to spawn. Just behind the gill cover there is a vertical black marking, which becomes less prominent with increasing age. The dorsal fin is black but its base is a transparent yellow or yellowish brown. An adipose fin is present but colorless. The anal fin is red, the rear part with a black border. The caudal, ventral, and pectoral fins are also red.

This is not a difficult fish to breed. Spawning is preceded by vigorous driving by the male during the early hours of the day. The brownish eggs mostly fall to the bottom, and must be protected, because the parents are notorious spawn-eaters. This can be done either by removing the parents or by installing a fine-mesh grating 1in (2.5cm) above the bottom—the eggs fall through this and are then beyond the reach of the parent fishes. The fry are darkly pigmented.

There is a blood-red fish, known as *Hyphessobrycon 'minor'*, which is now regarded as a variant of *H. callistus*; its fry are pale reddish. There are also several other very closely related species of *Hyphessobrycon*, including the well-known *H. serpae*, which has often been confused with *H. callistus* but is now regarded as a distinct species. Its eggs and newly hatched fry are almost colorless.

Right: **Hyphessobrycon callistus**
Striking in appearance and easy to breed, this species has several variants differing in coloration.

Family CHARACIDAE

Hyphessobrycon erythrostigma
Bleeding Heart Tetra

- **Distribution:** Northern South America: Colombia
- **Length:** Up to 2.8in (7cm)
- **Tank length:** 36in (90cm)
- **Diet:** Worms, crustaceans, plant matter, dried food
- **Water temperature:** 73 to 77°F (23 to 25°C)
- **Community tank**

Also known as *H. rubrostigma,* this is a hardy shoaling characin.

Left: **Hyphessobrycon erythrostigma** ♀(t), ♂(b)
Living up to four years, this fish is hardy but not easy to breed.

The body is very deep and almost lozenge-shaped, and an adipose fin is present. The back is brownish to grayish green, often with a reddish tinge, particularly when the fish is excited. The flanks are silvery and iridescent, and the underparts are orange. Just behind the gill cover there is a large red marking, which accounts for the popular name, and a red longitudinal band extends back from the middle of the body to the base of the tail. The dorsal fin is red, somewhat prolonged in the male, with a white border and with black rays at the front. In the female this fin is shorter with a black marking. The caudal fin is red with bluish white streaks in the male; the ventral fins are reddish; and the adipose fin is bluish white. In the male the anal fin is elongated, with a black edge and a bluish white base, but in the female it is reddish with a whitish area in the front.

Attempts at breeding this species have rarely been successful. The males often drive by swimming around the plants, but the females seldom react, even though they appear to be full of spawn. This is a pity, as the species is very handsome and lives often for two to four years.

Family CHARACIDAE

Hyphessobrycon flammeus
Flame Tetra

- **Distribution:** South America: Rio de Janeiro, Brazil
- **Length:** Up to 1.8in (4.5cm)
- **Tank length:** 18in (45cm)
- **Diet:** Worms, small crustaceans, plant matter, dried food
- **Water temperature:** 68 to 77°F (20 to 25°C)
- **Community tank**

This colorful old favorite was introduced into the aquarium world around 1920, and is a very good fish for a beginner. It is sometimes known as the Red Tetra from Rio. The shape of the body, but not the color pattern, is very similar to that of Griem's Tetra; an adipose fin is present. The back is grayish olive, and the belly silvery; the flanks are a brilliant brassy color. However, the characteristic feature is the rear part of the body, which is a particularly brilliant red, as are all the fins except the pectoral fins, which are colorless. In the male the tips of the ventral fins and the edge of the anal fin are black. These fins are not so brightly colored in the female and they lack the black edge.

Above:
Hyphessobrycon flammeus ♂
Ideal for a beginner, this peaceful characin will brighten a community tank with its red markings. It is easy to breed.

This is a peaceful shoaling fish, swimming mainly in the middle and lower water layers. The tank can have areas of dense vegetation, leaving sufficient open water for swimming. Although it probably does best in soft water, it will tolerate and even breed in medium-hard water. The female lays 200 to 300 eggs, which hatch in two to three days. The fry hang from fine-leaved plants for three more days and can then be fed on rotifers and small nauplii.

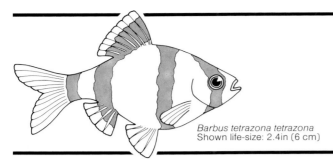

Barbus tetrazona tetrazona
Shown life-size: 2.4in (6 cm)

Family CHARACIDAE

Hyphessobrycon griemi

Griem's Tetra

● **Distribution:** South America: the Goyaz area of Brazil
● **Length:** Up to 1.2in (3cm)
● **Tank length:** 18in (45cm)
● **Diet:** Worms, crustaceans, plant matter, dried food
● **Water temperature:** 72 to 81°F (22 to 27°C)
● **Community tank**

Griem's Tetra is a very small, dainty characin, and a relative newcomer to the aquarium, being first introduced in 1956. The body is similar in form to that of the Flame Tetra, but significantly smaller. The background color is a delicate chestnut-brown or olive-brown, flushing to a shade of cinnabar-red when the fish becomes excited. There are two dark vertical markings behind the gill cover, surrounded by a zone of yellow; the first marking is often rather indistinct. The dorsal and anal fins have white tips; an adipose fin is present.

Griem's Tetra does well when kept in a small shoal in a tank with soft or even medium-hard water, where it swims about in the middle layers. It is not difficult to breed. The female is stouter than the male and usually a little longer. As in other related characins the eggs are laid at random, often among clumps of dense vegetation such as Milfoil *(Myriophyllum)*.

An even smaller relative is *Hyphessobrycon georgettae,* sometimes known as the Strawberry Tetra. The average length is 0.8in (2cm), the female a little longer, the male slightly shorter. In males the body and fins are blood-red or strawberry-red, in females yellowish red, and there is no dark marking behind the gill cover. Although quite easy to breed it is not very prolific.

Right: **Hyphessobrycon griemi**
Although small, this fish may be aggressive to others in the tank.

Family CHARACIDAE

Hyphessobrycon herbertaxelrodi
Black Neon
- **Distribution:** South America: Rio Taquari, Mato Grosso area of Brazil
- **Length:** Up to 1.4in (3.5cm)
- **Tank length:** 12in (30cm)
- **Diet:** Worms, small crustaceans, plant matter, dried food
- **Water temperature:** 75 to 81°F (24 to 27°C)
- **Community tank**

Named after the well-known American ichthyologist and aquarist Dr. Herbert Axelrod, this is a relatively recent arrival in the aquarium world. The general shape of the body is very similar to that of the Flag Tetra *(Hyphessobrycon heterorhabdus)*. The back is a delicate brownish color, and the scales have dark edges that give a reticulated appearance. The belly is silvery and an adipose fin is present. The characteristic feature, however, is the flank pattern: A broad, black longitudinal band extends back from the gill cover to the root of the tail. Parallel to and above this, there is a narrower brilliant iridescent green to yellowish green stripe. The iris is bright blood-red above, iridescent green below.

This is a typical shoaling fish of the upper and middle water layers. It is peaceful, and best kept in a tank with soft, slightly acid water, some patches of vegetation, and space for swimming. Spawning takes place in the open water, sometimes while the sexes are swimming along the side panes of the tank. The parent fishes should be removed immediately after egg-laying has ceased, or the eggs can be protected by a fine-mesh grating. The eggs hatch in 24 to 30 hours and the fry can be reared initially on very fine live food.

Hyphessobrycon heterorhabdus
Flag Tetra
- **Distribution:** South America: Rio Tocantins, lower Amazon
- **Length:** Up to 1.8in (4.5cm)
- **Tank length:** 12in (30cm)
- **Diet:** Worms, crustaceans, plant matter, dried food
- **Water temperature:** 73 to 77°F (23 to 25°C)
- **Community tank**

This species, introduced to the aquarium about 1910, is not as hardy as many of the other tetras described. The general shape of the body is similar to that of the Black Neon. The females appear bulkier, with the rear end of the body cavity rounded, whereas the males are more slender and the body cavity has a pointed rear end. There is an adipose fin.

The back is reddish brown and the belly silvery, sometimes with an olive-green tinge. The flanks are yellowish brown marked with a three-colored band extending from the gill cover back to the base of the tail. The central broad band is whitish or golden, the upper narrow band bright red, and the lowermost band black, with a rather indistinct lower border. The fins are colorless or a delicate yellowish color.

This is an active shoaling fish best kept in a tank with soft, slightly acid water, preferably filtered through peat. Clumps of plants should be arranged so as to leave sufficient open water for swimming. Spawning takes place in the same way as Black Neon, but the broods are sometimes relatively small and may fall prey to disease.

Below:
Hyphessobrycon heterorhabdus
This is a delicate characin and not easy to breed successfully.

Left:
Hyphessobrycon herbertaxelrodi
Distinctively striped, this species will swim peacefully in the middle and upper water layers of the tank. It is not a prolific breeder.

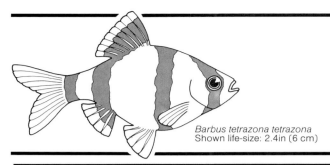

Barbus tetrazona tetrazona
Shown life-size: 2.4in (6 cm)

Family CHARACIDAE

Hyphessobrycon pulchripinnis

Lemon Tetra
- **Distribution:** South America, the precise area is unknown
- **Length:** Up to 1.6in (4cm)
- **Tank length:** 12in (30cm)
- **Diet:** Worms, crustaceans, plant matter, dried food
- **Water temperature:** 73 to 77°F (23 to 25°C)
- **Community tank**

Although this small tetra was introduced to the aquarium as long ago as about 1932, the exact place where the original stock was caught is still a mystery. It has sometimes been incorrectly known as *Hemigrammus erythrophthalmus*. The body is fairly deep and translucent with a tinge of yellow; an adipose fin is present. Behind the gill cover there is a rather indistinct marking. The eyes are large and the upper part of the iris is bright red, a point noted in the erroneous specific name *(erythrophthalmus* means 'red eye').

The flanks are silvery, with a scarcely visible longitudinal band

Above:
Hyphessobrycon pulchripinnis ♂♂
A small characin of beautiful color.

extending back from the rear edge of the gill cover to the root of the tail. In general, the fins are yellowish. The front rays of the anal fin are somewhat elongated and lemon-yellow, and the same color occurs at the tip of the dorsal fin. In the male the anal fin has a broad black edge, but in the female this is narrower and only blackish.

This is a quiet shoaling fish of the middle and lower water layers, and it thrives best in soft water. For successful breeding the females must be given a varied diet of live food. Even so, spawning may not take place as readily as in most other tetras. Sometimes, however, a female may be very productive.

Family CHARACIDAE

Hyphessobrycon scholzei

Black-line Tetra
- **Distribution:** South America, in the Pará region of Brazil
- **Length:** Up to 1.8in (4.5cm)
- **Tank length:** 24in (60cm)
- **Diet:** Worms, small crustaceans, plant matter, dried food
- **Water temperature:** 72 to 77°F 22-25°C
- **Community tank**

This is a hardy, shoaling species with the typical tetra body form. The back is greenish to brownish, the belly silvery; the flanks are iridescent bluish. The characteristic feature, however, is a narrow black longitudinal stripe extending back from the rear of the gill cover to the basal part of the caudal fin, where it widens out into a blackish area on the central caudal fin rays. The pectoral fins are colorless, but all the other fins have a reddish tinge, the tip of the anal fin being white. The iris is yellow.

This is a peaceful fish that is perfectly hardy and very suitable for a beginner. It is not difficult to

breed in a tank with soft to medium-hard water. Before spawning the male carries out a courtship display in front of the female. The female lays her eggs at random and these hatch in about 30 hours. The tiny fry are free-swiming a few days later and can then be fed on live food such as rotifers and very small nauplii. As they grow the young fishes can be gradually accustomed to taking some dried food.

There are several related groups in the large genus *Hyphessobrycon*, and the Black-Line Tetra is considered to be most closely related to *H. heterorhabdus, H. herbertaxelrodi* and *H. metae* (from the Rio Meta).

Right: **Hyphessobrycon scholzei**
Introduced into the aquarium in the 1930s, this fish is easy to breed.

A practical reminder
Heavily planted tanks require a lot of light—
40 watts (fluorescent) per square foot
(900cm²) of water surface area.
Illumination time should be 12 hours daily,
with reduced lighting for a pleasant
evening's viewing.

Left: **Megalamphodus megalopterus**
*Their large blackish fins identify
these fishes clearly as males of the
species. Females have reddish fins.*

Family CHARACIDAE

Megalamphodus megalopterus
Black Phantom Tetra
- **Distribution:** South America: Rio Guapore on the border between Bolivia and Brazil
- **Length:** Up to 1.8in (4.5cm)
- **Tank length:** 18in (45cm)
- **Diet:** Worms, small insects, crustaceans, dried food
- **Water temperature:** 73 to 79°F (23 to 26°C)
- **Community tank**

This peaceful shoaling fish has the typical body outline of the tetras. In general, the male is grayish with a blackish back and a paler belly. The flanks have a prominent black vertical marking situated behind the gill cover and surrounded by an iridescent turquoise-green area. The pectoral fins are colorless, but all the other fins are blackish; the dorsal fin is quite elongated. In the female the back is gray; the flanks are brownish-red and the vertical marking is similar to that of the male. The dorsal and caudal fins are grayish or blackish, the pectoral fins reddish, and the adipose and ventral fins bright red.

This is a species that should always be kept in a tank with soft, slightly acid water, whether for breeding or at other times. The lighting should be subdued and the planting generous, but leave plenty of space for swimming. This species is very susceptible to fish tuberculosis. Breeding is not always easy and it seems that older fishes cease to breed. Spawning behavior is similar to that in members of the genus *Hyphessobrycon*. Newly hatched fry can be fed on rotifers and very small nauplii.

Fishes belonging to the genus *Megalamphodus* are very similar to many other characin genera, but they are separated from these by differences in the dentition and in the structure of the skull.

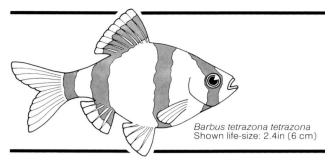

Barbus tetrazona tetrazona
Shown life-size: 2.4in (6 cm)

Family CHARACIDAE

Megalamphodus sweglesi

Red Phantom Tetra

- **Distribution:** South America: Orinoco region, Rio Muco and the upper reaches of the Rio Meta
- **Length:** Up to 1.6in (4cm)
- **Tank length:** 18in (45cm)
- **Diet:** Worms, small insects, crustaceans, dried food
- **Water temperature:** 73 to 79°F (23 to 26°C)
- **Community tank**

This relatively recent introduction to the aquarium has a body outline very similar to that of *M. megalopterus*. Both species are shoaling fishes, swimming mostly in the lower water layers. The general body coloration is yellowish red. There is a more or less rounded marking on the flanks just behind the gill cover. The belly has a faint shiny golden tinge. In the male the dorsal fin is considerably longer than in the female, with a tapering point. In the female the dorsal fin has a rounded tip and is marked with a conspicuous dark blotch. The dorsal, caudal, anal, and ventral fins are bright yellowish red.

On the whole this is a peaceful species; at times a couple of males may indulge in a sparring match with their fins, but they do not damage one another. Spawning behavior takes place as in members of the genus *Hyphessobrycon*. Some authorities recommend that peat should not be added to the tank, maintaining that although the embryos may develop normally the peat has a tanning action on the egg coverings that prevents the fry from breaking out, and they then die within the egg coverings.

This species is not as susceptible to disease as *M. megalopterus*.

Below:
Megalamphodus sweglesi ♂♀
This colorful shoaling fish will thrive in a community tank.

Family CHARACIDAE

Micralestes interruptus

Congo Tetra

- **Distribution:** Central Africa: Zaire region
- **Length:** Males up to 3.2in (8cm), females 2.4in (6cm)
- **Tank length:** 24in (60cm)
- **Diet:** Worms, small insects and crustaceans, plant matter, dried food
- **Water temperature:** 75 to 79°F (24 to 26°C)
- **Community tank**

Formerly known as *Phenacogrammus interruptus*, this is one of the most elegant of the medium-sized characins, with large eyes, a laterally compressed body, and large scales. In the male the dorsal fin is much elongated and so are the central rays of the caudal fin. In the rather smaller female these parts are scarcely elongated. In reflected light the flanks of the male are iridescent greenish blue with a tinge of reddish brown, yellow, or sometimes violet. The back is brownish, and the dorsal and caudal fins are gray; the anal and caudal fins have a white border.

This is not a difficult species to keep, but for the male's fins to develop fully the tank must have soft, slightly acid water filtered through peat, not too many plants, plenty of space for swimming, and preferably a dark substrate. Under these conditions spawning may occur during the hours of morning sunshine. After vigorous driving by the male, the female lays up to 300 eggs, sometimes more, which sink to the bottom. The eggs hatch after about six days, and the fry can be fed immediately on rotifers and very small nauplii.

Right: **Micralestes interruptus** ♂♂
Although it appears rather delicate, this species has proved perfectly hardy when kept in the soft, slightly acid water that it needs, and it breeds quite successfully. For the male fins to develop properly as shown here the fish should have a spacious tank.

A practical reminder
Use inside filters for unfurnished fry-raising tanks. Outside filters are much better for fully planted tanks, however, since you will not have to disturb the planting layout to carry out the necessary regular maintenance.

Left: **Moenkhausia pittieri** ♂
The beautifully developed dorsal and anal fins identify this as a male specimen of this hardy species.

Family CHARACIDAE
Moenkhausia pittieri
Diamond Tetra
- **Distribution:** Northern South America: Lake Valencia in Venezuela
- **Length:** Up to 2.4in (6cm)
- **Tank length:** 18in (45cm)
- **Diet:** Worms, crustaceans, insects, dried food
- **Water temperature:** 72 to 81°F (22 to 27°C)
- **Community tank**

This is a particularly active shoaling fish of the middle and upper water layers; it was introduced to the aquarium in the early 1930s. In the male the dorsal fin is quite elongated and the anal fin is also better developed than in the female. In males the body and fins are a delicate violet color with golden iridescence when seen in reflected light, and small iridescent greenish dots. Apart from the colorless pectoral fins all the other fins have white borders. The females are paler in coloration and usually yellowish with slight iridescence.

This is a hardy fish, best kept in soft, slightly acid water filtered through peat. Plant patches of vegetation, but leave sufficient water for swimming. In most cases spawning takes place quite readily and the female is usually very prolific. In fact, the species has been known to breed in quite small tanks (about 5 gallons/20 liters) and the parents do not normally eat the eggs. The young hatch after about 25 to 30 hours (possibly longer) and then hang for a few days from plants or sometimes the glass panes of the tank. They will then be free-swimming and can be fed at first on rotifers and tiny nauplii. When the water conditions are right the young feed voraciously and grow rapidly.

The related Glass Tetra (*Moenkhausia oligolepis*), up to 4.7in (12cm) in length, comes from the Amazon and Guyana regions, and can be kept in the same way as *M. pittieri*.

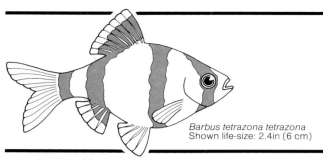

Barbus tetrazona tetrazona
Shown life-size: 2.4in (6 cm)

Family CHARACIDAE

Moenkhausia sanctaefilomenae

Red-eye Tetra

- **Distribution:** South America: Rio Paraguay and Rio Parnaiba
- **Length:** Up to 2.4in (6cm)
- **Tank length:** 24in (60cm)
- **Diet:** Worms, insects, crustaceans, plant matter, dried food
- **Water temperature:** 70 to 79°F (21 to 26°C)
- **Community tank**

This relatively deep-bodied characin, lives in small shoals, mainly in the middle water layers.

It was introduced to the aquarium in the middle 1950s. The females have a markedly rounded belly profile when ready to spawn.

In general the body is silvery, with the back pale greenish or brownish and iridescent. The scales, particularly those on the upper side, have dark edges. The caudal peduncle has a wide iridescent yellow area and the base of the tail carries a broad black transverse bar. The fins are colorless or more or less smoky-gray, except that the dorsal and anal fins have white tips. The upper half of the eye is a brilliant blood-red. The Red-eye Tetra resembles a smaller, more

colorful version of *M. oligolepis.*

Red-eye Tetras should be kept in a spacious tank with tough plants arranged to leave sufficient open water for swimming; members of this species have a tendency to nibble soft plants. They need some plant matter in their diet, and this can be conveniently supplied by having a small piece of lettuce in the tank. This must be removed, however, as soon as it shows signs of rotting in the warm water.

The tank water should be soft to medium-hard and there will be no difficulty in getting this species to spawn. The fry should be treated like those of the Diamond Tetra

Above:

Moenkhausia sanctaefilomenae
This is one of the best shoaling characins. It behaves peacefully in a community tank and breeds easily. Ideal for a beginner.

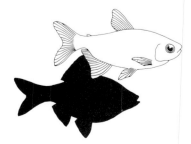

A practical reminder
Biological filtration relies on bacterial activity and must have a constant water flow through the gravel. Do not disconnect the air supply to such filters or the water flow will stop and all the bacteria will die.

Paracheirodon innesi
Neon Tetra
- **Distribution:** Northern South America: Upper Amazon
- **Length:** Up to 1.6in (4cm)
- **Tank length:** 12in (30cm)
- **Diet:** Worms, small insects and crustaceans, plant matter, dried food
- **Water temperature:** 70 to 79°F (21 to 26°C)
- **Community tank**

Originally described in 1936 as *Hyphessobrycon innesi,* after the American aquarist W.T. Innes, this brilliantly colored small characin is one of the most popular fishes for the home aquarium.

The body is slender, spindle shaped and only slightly laterally compressed, and has an adipose fin. The back is dark olive-green, the belly yellowish white. The flanks show a brilliant iridescent greenish blue stripe extending from the front of the eye back to the level of the adipose fin. Below this, but beginning only in the middle of the body, there is a broad, very bright red band that extends back to the root of the tail. (In the closely related Cardinal Tetra, the red band extends from the mouth to the tail base.)

Neon Tetras are active characins, swimming mostly in the lower and middle water layers, and thrive best in a tank with a dark substrate and subdued lighting. The adults can be acclimatized to medium-hard water, but for breeding it is essential that the water be soft and slightly acid. The breeding tank can be quite small (length 8in/ 20cm) with just one clump of vegetation. A pair introduced to such a tank may spawn the following morning. The female lays a relatively small number of eggs, which hatch in about 24 hours. The parent fishes should be removed after spawning. The fry are free-swimming four days after hatching and can then be fed on very small live food.

Family CHARACIDAE

Nematobrycon palmeri
Emperor Tetra
- **Distribution:** Northern South America: Colombia
- **Length:** Up to 2.2in (5.5cm)
- **Tank length:** 12in (30cm)
- **Diet:** Worms, crustaceans, finely chopped meat, dried food
- **Water temperature:** 73 to 79°F (23 to 26°C)
- **Community tank**

An active and very colorful fish, the Emperor Tetra swims mostly in the lower water layers. The body is relatively tall and there is no adipose fin. The male has an elongated dorsal fin and a conspicuously developed caudal fin, the central rays being very elongated. The anal fin is very long, with a narrow dark band along its outer edge. The female lacks the elongations of the dorsal and anal fins. In both sexes the back is olive-brown and the flanks have a broad, iridescent grass-green or sometimes blue-green longitudinal band that extends from the gill cover to the caudal peduncle. Below this runs a broad blackish band that extends onto the caudal fin. The iris is an iridescent blue-green.

This very attractive characin should be kept in a tank with a dark substrate, patches of dense vegetation, and sufficient space for swimming. The lighting should be subdued, and this can be best achieved by having some floating plants at the surface. These conditions help to enhance the Emperor Tetra's brilliant coloration. The water should be soft and slightly acid.

This is not always an easy fish to breed. Provided a compatible pair can be found, the male drives the female very actively. The eggs are laid among fine-leaved plants. Once they are free-swimming the fry can be fed on very small live food. They grow quickly.

Above: **Nematobrycon palmeri**
♂(t), ♀(b) *An active characin.*

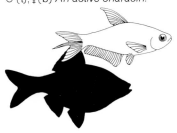

Left: **Paracheirodon innesi**
Widespread and universally popular in the aquarium world, this species is active, colorful, and hardy, and breeds readily in soft water.

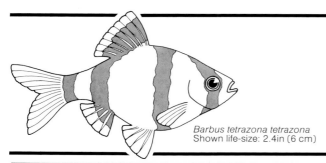

Barbus tetrazona tetrazona
Shown life-size: 2.4in (6 cm)

Petitella georgiae
False Rummy-nose
- **Distribution:** South America: the upper Amazon
- **Length:** Up to 2in (5cm)
- **Tank length:** 12in (30cm)
- **Diet:** Worms, small crustaceans, plant matter, dried food
- **Water temperature:** 75 to 79°F (24 to 26°C)
- **Community tank**

The False Rummy-nose is a peaceful shoaling fish. The body is silvery with blue-green iridescence and a dark longitudinal stripe that extends from the caudal fin forwards onto the caudal peduncle. This characin has been much confused with the very similar Red-nosed Tetra *(Hemigrammus rhodostomus)*, in which the flanks are silvery and iridescent, with a

Left: **Petitella georgiae**
This colorful fish is best kept in a small shoal, which will swim in the middle and lower water layers.

Family CHARACIDAE
Poptella orbicularis
Disk Tetra
- **Distribution:** South America: Amazon Basin, Guyana and Paraguay
- **Length:** Up to 4.7in (12cm)
- **Tank length:** 36in (90cm)
- **Diet:** Worms, insects, crustaceans, plant matter, dried food
- **Water temperature:** 77 to 81°F (25 to 27°C)
- **Community tank**

This species was formerly known as *Ephippicharax orbicularis*. It is a disk-shaped, laterally compressed, omnivorous fish that is perfectly hardy in an aquarium. The flanks are silvery with a greenish, yellowish, or bluish sheen, depending upon the lighting. The upper side is dark green and there are two curved dark markings just behind the gill cover. The scales are relatively large and the fins almost colorless except that the dorsal, anal, and caudal fins are marked with small dark dots. There is also an adipose fin. Although this species is not as colorful as many other characins, its more unusual shape adds variety to the tank.

This is a shoaling fish living mostly in the middle and lower water layers, which does best in a tank with plenty of space for swimming and a dark substrate. The light should be fairly subdued. For breeding the tank should have soft, slightly acid water. The eggs are laid at random and the females are normally very productive. The fry should be fed at first on tiny live food, such as rotifers and small nauplii.

Right: **Poptella orbicularis**
A handsome fish, first introduced into the aquarium in the 1930s.

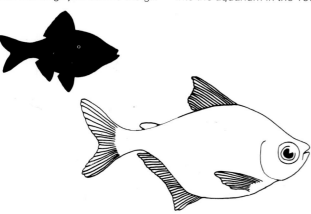

A practical reminder
The biological filter plate should cover the entire base of the tank. If it is sealed in place permanently, there is no possibility of water finding a path around it and the whole gravel bed becomes a colony of bacteria.

dark longitudinal stripe extending back from the center of the body to the caudal peduncle and onto the end of the caudal fin, where it becomes appreciably wider.

When the fish is in good condition the iris and the snout are blood-red, hence the popular name. The lobes of the caudal fin are whitish, sometimes yellowish white, each with a prominent black blotch. The other fins are colorless.

The False Rummy-nose does not produce a large number of eggs and the fry are evidently rather delicate. This species should be kept in soft, slightly acid water, but it is not an easy fish to breed. The fry grow slowly at first.

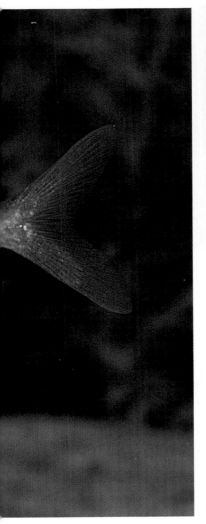

Family CHARACIDAE
Pristella riddlei
X-ray Fish, Water Goldfish
● **Distribution:** Northern South America and Lower Amazon
● **Length:** Up to 1.8in (4.5cm)
● **Tank length:** 18in (45cm)
● **Diet:** Worms, small crustaceans, insects, dried food
● **Water temperature:** 70 to 79°F (21 to 26°C)
● **Community tank**

This is an old favorite introduced into the aquarium world in the middle 1920s. The body is laterally compressed and fairly elongated, particularly in the males and juveniles, but females have a more rounded belly profile; the popular name refers to the remarkably translucent body. An adipose fin is present. The caudal fin is deeply cleft. In general, the translucent body has a pale yellowish or greenish tinge, and appears silvery in reflected light. The dorsal and anal fins have an area of lemon-yellow at the base, a black marking in the middle, and white tips. The caudal fin is red. Just behind the gill cover there is a distinct black blotch.

This is a hardy, shoaling characin that should be kept in a tank with a dark substrate and subdued light. The water can be soft to medium-hard, although the former is preferable.

Breeding is not all that easy. It seems that some pairs are not compatible. If two fishes have spawned successfully, they should be kept together and may then go

Above: **Pristella riddlei**
This lively fish should be kept in a shoal in subdued light. Breeding success needs a compatible pair.

on breeding for four years or so; the female will usually produce about 300 eggs at each spawning. These hatch in 24 hours, and the very tiny fry should be fed on fine live food as soon as they become free-swimming.

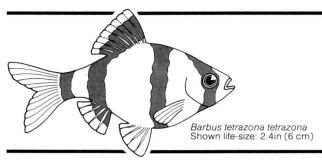

Barbus tetrazona tetrazona
Shown life-size: 2.4in (6 cm)

Family CHARACIDAE
Thayeria boehlkei
Boehlke's Penguin Fish
- **Distribution:** South America: Amazon Basin
- **Length:** Up to 2.4in (6cm)
- **Tank length:** 24in (60cm)
- **Diet:** Worms, small insects and crustaceans, dried food
- **Water temperature:** 73 to 79°F (23 to 26°C)
- **Community tank**

Boehlke's Penguin Fish is a hardy shoaling fish found mostly in the upper water layers. It swims in a characteristic oblique position with the head upward. The body is laterally compressed; an adipose fin is present. The back is brownish or olive. The main distinguishing feature is the prominent black longitudinal band on the flanks. This starts immediately behind the gill cover and extends back to the tail, where it bends downwards and ends at the tip of the caudal fin's lower lobe. Beneath and parallel to this band there is a greenish golden stripe. The fins are more or less colorless, except that the anal fin and the lower lobe of the caudal fin are yellowish white. As in most related characins the females are stouter when sexually mature, with a more rounded belly profile than the males.

These striking fishes do best in soft water, but will tolerate medium-hard water. For breeding the tank should have clumps of fine-leaved plants such as Milfoil (*Myriophyllum*), and the water must be soft and slightly acid. Before spawning takes place (usually at twilight) the pair indulge in vigorous driving and the female then lays a large number of eggs. These hatch in about 20 to 24 hours and the fry are free-swimming four or five days later.

There has been some confusion between this species and the very similar *Thayeria obliqua*. However, in the latter the dark longitudinal band starts just behind the dorsal fin (rather than behind the gill cover) and runs back to the lower lobe of the caudal fin.

Below: **Thayeria boehlkei**
An elegant, hardy fish that swims typically in an oblique position.

Family GASTEROPELECIDAE
Gasteropelecus sternicla
Common Hatchetfish
- **Distribution:** South America: middle Amazon, Guyana
- **Length:** Up to 2.6in (6.5cm)
- **Tank length:** 24in (60cm)
- **Diet:** Worms, crustaceans, insects, dried food
- **Water temperature:** 73 to 86°F (23 to 30°C)
- **Community tank**

This very tall, strongly compressed fish has an almost straight dorsal profile as far back as the dorsal fin, behind which it dips down to the caudal peduncle. But the throat and belly are very convex. This peculiar development of the underparts is due to the enlargement of the shoulder girdle and the powerful muscles attached to it. These give power to the pectoral fins, which the fish is able to beat rapidly. Thus it can fly over the water for distances of up to 16.5ft (5m).

There is a small adipose fin. In reflected light the fish shows silvery iridescence. The scales are actually gray and those on the upperparts have dark edges. The flanks are marked by a dark longitudinal band that extends from the edge of the gill cover to the root of the caudal fin. This band is bordered above and below by a paler line. In some individuals the front edge of the dorsal fin has dark markings, but otherwise the fins are almost colorless. Adult males appear thinner than adult females when viewed from above.

This is an active, peaceful fish that lives at the surface of the water. It is quite a hardy species when kept under suitable conditions. The tank must have a well-fitting cover to prevent the fish from 'flying' out and landing on the floor. The nature of the substrate is not important for the hatchetfishes and can be made suitable for any other occupants of the tank. A few floating plants and some roots will supply the

A practical reminder
Most air pumps have filter pads to clean the air. You should clean these regularly to keep the pump performing in peak condition. Air valves should also be kept clean and mechanical pumps well oiled.

Family SERRASALMIDAE
Serrasalmus nattereri
Red Piranha
● **Distribution:** South America: Amazon, Orinoco, Paraná
● **Length:** 12in (30cm)
● **Tank length:** 48in (120cm)
● **Diet:** Insects, worms, fish, meat
● **Water temperature:** 75 to 81°F (24 to 27°C)
● **Species tank**

Sometimes known as *Rooseveltiella nattereri,* the Red Piranha is an aggressive, predatory fish. The body is tall and very compressed laterally and an adipose fin is present. The back is bluish gray and the belly strikingly red. The flanks are pale brown to olive with numerous shiny spots, but the coloration varies somewhat, depending to a certain extent on the age of the fish. The dorsal and caudal fins are dark and the anal fin usually has a broad black border. The keel of

Left: **Serrasalmus nattereri**
Only young specimens are really suitable for a home aquarium.

the belly has a number of serrations.

Only young specimens are really suitable for the home aquarium. They need a tank with a few tough plants, and possibly some rocks and roots for decoration. The water should be soft, slightly acid, and filtered through peat.

The Red Piranha and related species have been bred in large public aquarium tanks. A single spawning may produce 4000 to 5000 large eggs, which adhere to the plants and are not attacked by the parent fishes. These hatch in nine or 10 days.

In general, the ferocity of the Red Piranha and its relatives has been overstated. They are aggressive but will usually attack only when they smell blood in the water. Their extremely sharp dentition and powerful jaws enable them to reduce even a large animal such as a tapir to a skeleton in a matter of minutes. The genus *Serrasalmus* and related fishes were formerly classified in the family Characidae.

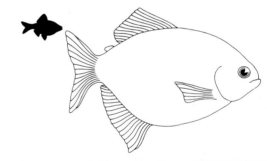

decoration. The water must be soft, slightly acid, and filtered through peat. This species has been bred on a few occasions, but the details are sketchy. Spawning has not been observed, but probably takes place at dusk. The eggs have been seen hanging from fine-leaved plants or lying on the substrate. The fry have been reared on rotifers and small nauplii.

Right: **Gasteropelecus sternicla**
This surface-dwelling fish is quite capable of leaping out of an uncovered tank. The species will thrive in soft water but has not been bred with great success.

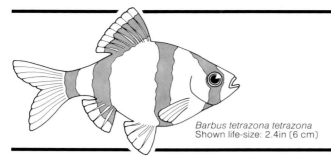

Barbus tetrazona tetrazona
Shown life-size: 2.4in (6 cm)

Family GASTEROPELECIDAE

Gasteropelecus levis
Silver Hatchetfish

● **Distribution:** South America: lower Amazon
● **Length:** Up to 2.4in (6cm)
● **Tank length:** 24in (60cm)
● **Diet:** Worms, crustaceans, insects, dried food
● **Water temperature:** 75 to 86°F (24 to 30°C)
● **Community tank**

The shape of this species is exactly the same as that of the Common Hatchetfish and the coloration is also similar. The dorsal profile is straight back to the dorsal fin with a short concave part in the region of the small adipose fin. The underparts are very convex. The body is more silvery, particularly on the lower half, than that of the Common Hatchetfish and there is a dark marking at the base of the dorsal fin. The longitudinal band is more pronounced and there is sometimes a thin black line along the base of the anal fin.

This is an active fish that lives at the surface of the water, where it also takes much of its food. In general, it is not as hardy as the Common Hatchetfish. The tank must have a well-fitting lid and a few floating plants, with sufficient open water available for swimming. Occasionally these fishes chase after food that is sinking to the bottom. The water must be soft, slightly acid, and filtered through peat. This species is not known to have been bred in captivity.

The related Spotted Hatchetfish, *Gasteropelecus maculatus,* comes from the area between western Colombia and Panama, and is up to 3.5in (9cm) in length. The flanks are gray-green with strong silvery iridescence and brownish spots arranged in transverse rows. A black longitudinal band extends from the gill cover to the base of the tail and it is bordered above by a shiny silver line. The fins are almost colorless, except for the dorsal fin, which has a dark edge. This species has not been bred successfully in an aquarium.

Right: **Gasteropelecus levis**
Sometimes rather delicate in an aquarium, this is a lively 'jumper'.

Family GASTEROPELECIDAE

Carnegiella marthae
Black-winged Hatchetfish

● **Distribution:** Venezuela, Peru, Amazon, Rio Negro, Rio Orinoco
● **Length:** Up to 1.4in (3.5cm)
● **Tank length:** 18in (45cm)
● **Diet:** Crustaceans, insects, dried food
● **Water temperature:** 73 to 84°F (23 to 29°C)
● **Community tank**

This is the dwarf among the hatchetfishes. The body is the same shape as in the other species except that there is no adipose fin. The flanks are silvery with a dark longitudinal line running from the gill cover to the base of the tail. This is bordered above by a delicate golden or silver line. The central part of the pectoral fins has a black marking, and the keel of the belly and breast has a black border. There are two black cheek markings.

This is a peaceful, surface-living fish that has usually been found to be rather delicate for an aquarium. It should be kept in a tank with a well-fitting cover to prevent jumping. A few roots and plants with fine leaves, as well as floating plants, will help to subdue the light. The other inmates of the tank should be peaceful fishes that live on or near the bottom. The Black-winged Hatchetfish feeds entirely at the surface and does not chase prey or other food that is sinking in the water. Hence, insects that are trapped at the surface of the water form a large portion of its diet in the wild. This habit can certainly be encouraged in the aquarium.

Spawning has been seen on a few occasions. It takes place among roots of floating plants, the male performing a fluttering dance and then swimming just below the female as spawning begins. The eggs adhere to plants and hatch in 24 to 36 hours. The fry remain hanging from the plants while they consume the contents of the yolk-sac and are free-swimming about five days after hatching. They are not difficult to rear and take infusorians as a first live food.

Left: **Carnegiella marthae**
This small species needs careful attention from the aquarist.

A practical reminder
Vibrator type pumps run quieter with back pressure applied; piston pumps must have any excess air bled away since back pressure due to clamping causes wear. Air from these pumps must be filtered to remove oil.

Family GASTEROPELECIDAE
Carnegiella strigata
Marbled Hatchetfish
- **Distribution:** South America: Amazon, Guyana
- **Length:** Up to 1.8in (4.5cm)
- **Tank length:** 18in (45cm)
- **Diet:** Crustaceans, insects, dried food
- **Water temperature:** 75 to 84°F (24 to 29°C)
- **Community tank**

This is an attractive fish with a belly profile that is almost semi-circular. The ventral fins are very small. Between these fins and the caudal fin the profile is almost straight. The dorsal fin is fairly short and positioned far back on the body. The winglike pectoral fins are almost half the length of the body. There is no adipose fin. The general coloration is silvery-green to silvery-violet. A longitudinal band that is pale above and dark below runs from the gill cover to the root of the tail. The marbled pattern is formed by three dark brown oblique bands on the belly which are irregularly toothed and partly broken up into separate spots. The back is dark brown, and the keel in the breast region is yellowish. The fins are all colorless. There are no external sex differences.

This is a peaceful fish that is mainly active at dusk. It can be kept in a tank with a good lid to prevent unwanted flights, and with some feathery-leaved plants. A few floating plants will provide shade; the colors of this species tend to fade if the light is too strong. The water must be soft, slightly acid, and filtered through peat. The species has been bred on a few occasions. After a preliminary period of courtship, during which the male flutters around the female, spawning takes place among the fine-leaved plants. The eggs adhere to these plants and will hatch in about 30 hours. The fry are swimming five days later. They feed at first on infusorians, and, at this period, they are not confined to the surface waters. They start to develop the typical adult form when they are about 20 days old.

Left: **Carnegiella strigata**
A peaceful, surface-dwelling fish that thrives in shady conditions.

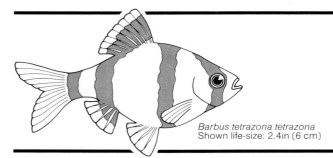

Barbus tetrazona tetrazona
Shown life-size: 2.4in (6 cm)

Family LEBIASINIDAE
Copeina guttata
Red-spotted Copeina
- **Distribution:** South America, in tributaries of the middle Amazon
- **Length:** Up to 3.2in (8cm)
- **Tank length:** 24in (60cm)
- **Diet:** Worms, insects, small crustaceans, dried food
- **Water temperature:** 75 to 81°F (24 to 27°C)
- **Community tank**

Nowadays this species and the following one, *Copella arnoldi,* are classified in the family Lebiasinidae, but they were formerly placed in the Characidae.

This is a hardy aquarium fish that shows some interesting biological features. The body is slender with small short fins, but lacks an adipose fin. The caudal fin is forked, and in males the upper lobe is rather larger than the lower one. In males the flanks are pale blue to greenish blue, the belly is white, and the back is brownish green. There are reddish dots at the base of each scale, giving the impression of longitudinal rows. The smaller females show paler coloration, with yellowish gray fins. The dorsal fin has a fairly prominent black marking.

For successful breeding the water should be soft and slightly acid. At spawning time the male, after some vigorous driving and prodding of the female, comes alongside and slightly below her. The male then pushes an open pocket (formed by his anal fin) below the genital opening of the female. She releases her eggs into this and the male fertilizes them and allows them to drop into a small pit in the sand that he has previously prepared. The male fans the eggs with his fins until they hatch, in about 25 hours, and he continues to protect the fry until they are free-swimming. The fry can be fed at first on tiny nauplii.

Below: **Copeina guttata** ♂♂
This attractively marked fish tends to jump, so the tank must have a close-fitting lid. Not difficult to breed, this species has an unusual spawning behavior. The male fans the eggs and protects the brood.

A practical reminder
The aeration rate should always be increased when you use the tank for sick fishes, because some medications reduce the level of oxygen in the water. Aeration also helps to drive carbon dioxide from the water.

Copella arnoldi
Spraying Characin
- **Distribution:** South America: lower Amazon and Rio Paru.
- **Length:** Male up to 3.2in (8cm), female up to 2.4in (6cm)
- **Tank length:** 18in (45cm)
- **Diet:** Worms, insects, crustaceans, dried food
- **Water temperature:** 73 to 81°F (23 to 27°C)
- **Community tank**

This fish, formerly known as *Copeina arnoldi,* has now been assigned to the genus *Copella* on the basis of certain rather small differences in jaw structure. However, there is still some doubt about its new classification, and the subject requires further detailed analysis by professional ichthyologists. The fish's real

Left: **Copella arnoldi** ♀
Of particular interest because it spawns above the water surface.

interest to aquarists lies in the unusual method of breeding.

In the male the flanks are yellowish, the scales have dark edges, and the gill cover has a greenish gold marking. When excited during courtship or fights, the male becomes black with silvery dots. The dorsal fin of the male is elongated and roughly triangular, red at the tip and marked with a black blotch that has a white base. The other fins of the male are yellowish red and elongated. The coloration of the female is more subdued, and the fins are not so well developed.

Spraying Characins spawn on the undersides of leaves growing above the surface of the water. The male and female swim vertically to the surface, flick their tails and leap up to a leaf, which may be 1.6 to 2.4in (4 to 6cm) above the surface. The female lays from five to eight eggs on the leaf and these are immediately fertilized by the male. This highly original spawning procedure is repeated many times, until some hundreds of eggs have been laid. The male then keeps the eggs damp by flicking his tail to spray them with water. As they hatch, the fry fall into the water. In an aquarium, the eggs are often laid on the underside of the tank lid.

Nannostomus beckfordi
Golden Pencilfish
- **Distribution:** South America: Guyana to Rio Negro
- **Length:** Up to 2.6in (6.5cm)
- **Tank length:** 12in (30cm)
- **Diet:** Worms, crustaceans, insects, dried food
- **Water temperature:** 75 to 81°F (24 to 27°C)
- **Community tank**

The Golden Pencilfish is elongated and torpedo-shaped with slight lateral compression. It has a symmetrical caudal fin but no adipose fin. The dorsal and ventral fins are immediately opposite one another. With such an extensive geographical distribution it is not surprising that the coloration varies and several color variants or subspecies have been discovered. The subspecies *N. beckfordi anomalus* is probably no longer on the aquarium market. On the other hand, *N. beckfordi aripirangensis,* from Aripiranga Island in the lower Amazon, is often available. In the male of this subspecies, the flanks and the bases of the dorsal, caudal, anal, and ventral fins are blood red—particularly when the fish is excited. There is a broad, blue-black longitudinal band running from the snout to the root of the tail, and this is accompanied above by a golden-yellow band. The female is not as brightly colored and only the fin bases are red.

The Golden Pencilfish should be kept in a tank well stocked with areas of dense vegetation, including plants with feathery leaves, and sufficient open water for swimming. The water must be soft, slightly acid, and filtered through peat. The lighting should be subdued. At spawning time the male and female swim alongside one another. Several batches of one to five eggs are laid among the fine-leaved plants, with a total of up to 200 eggs in some cases. The eggs hatch in 30 to 40 hours and the fry are free-swimming about six days later. They can then be fed on brine shrimp nauplii or other live food of the same size.

Left: **Nannostomus beckfordi**
Variable in color, this species should be kept in a shoal.

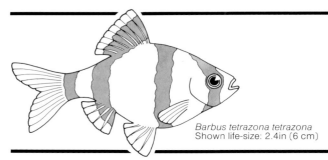

Barbus tetrazona tetrazona
Shown life-size: 2.4in (6 cm)

Family LEBIASINIDAE
Nannostomus eques
Tube-mouthed Pencilfish
- **Distribution:** South America: central Amazon
- **Length:** Up to 2in (5cm)
- **Tank length:** 12in (30cm)
- **Diet:** Worms, crustaceans, insects, dried food
- **Water temperature:** 72 to 79°F (22 to 26°C)
- **Community tank:** Best kept with other small, non-aggressive species

Also known as *Poecilobrycon eques,* this is a slender, spindle-shaped pencilfish with a pointed head. The lower lobe of the caudal fin is larger than the upper lobe. The adipose fin is very small or non-existent. The male is slender with an almost straight belly profile; the female is stouter with convex underparts. This species swims in an oblique position with the head up, becoming almost vertical when at rest. The back is pale brown to silvery-gray with five rows of dark dots. Below these dots there is a broad dark brown longitudinal band that extends from the tip of the snout to the lower lobe of the caudal fin. The upper lobe is colorless. The anal fin is black and red with a white border, but the dorsal fin is colorless. In the males the ventral fins have bluish-white

tips. In general, the females are less colorful than the males. During the night, two broad dark and somewhat oblique transverse bars appear on each flank.

This peaceful fish swims mostly near the surface and should be kept in a shoal in a tank with other small, non-aggressive species. There should be areas of dense vegetation interspersed with space for swimming. The water should be soft, slightly acid, and preferably filtered through peat. Spawning is preceded by active driving, during which the male may swim obliquely above the female. The actual spawning takes place on the underside of leaves; the eggs are laid in batches of about four. Most of them sink to the bottom and they may have to be protected from the parent fishes. They hatch in 25 to 30 hours and the fry are usually free-swimming about five days later. They can be fed on brine shrimp nauplii.

Below: **Nannostomus eques** ♂♂
A surface-dwelling, peaceful fish that swims in an oblique position.

Family LEBIASINIDAE
Nannostomus espei
Comma Pencilfish
- **Distribution:** South America: Rio Mazaruni, Guyana
- **Length:** Up to 1.4in (3.5cm)
- **Tank length:** 12in (30cm)
- **Diet:** Worms, crustaceans, insects, dried food
- **Water temperature:** 75 to 79°F (24 to 26°C)
- **Community tank**

This elongated, spindle-shaped fish has a pointed snout, a very small mouth, and an adipose fin. The caudal fin is deeply forked with both lobes pointed. The male is more slender than the female. It is characteristic of the species to swim in a slightly oblique position with the head up. The general coloration is pale gray-brown; the back is a delicate olive and the underparts are silvery. The flanks are marked by a golden longitudinal band that runs from the snout across the eye to the root of the caudal fin. In the head region this golden band is accompanied below by a shorter dark marking that runs over the gill cover to the pectoral fin area. However, the most striking features of the pattern are the four short, dark oblique bars on the

A practical reminder
Plants not only look nice, but also provide shelter and breeding sites for fishes. Many water plants can be easily propagated by cuttings, which root quickly when they are planted in the aquarium gravel.

Family LEBIASINIDAE

Nannostomus trifasciatus
Three-banded Pencilfish

- **Distribution:** South America: Guyana, central Amazon, Rio Negro
- **Length:** Up to 2.4in (6cm)
- **Tank length:** 12in (30cm)
- **Diet:** Worms, crustaceans, insects, dried food
- **Water temperature:** 72 to 79°F (22 to 26°C)
- **Community tank**

The Three-banded Pencilfish is an elongated, spindle-shaped fish with slight lateral compression. It has a pointed snout and a protruding upper jaw. The adipose fin is either very small or lacking. The male is slender with a rounded edge to the anal fin; the female has a more convex belly profile and a truncated or slightly concave edge to the anal fin. The back is olive and the flanks and

Left: **Nannostomus trifasciatus**
The three longitudinal stripes are replaced at night by broad bars.

underparts are silvery-white. There are three dark longitudinal markings. The first and uppermost mark is a narrow band from the upper edge of the eye to the caudal peduncle; the second and most prominent is a broad band running from the snout across the eye to the root of the caudal fin; and the third is a short band from the ventral fins to the anal fin. The dorsal, caudal, anal, and ventral fins are red at the base but otherwise colorless. At night these bands fade into scarcely visible blotches.

This rather delicate pencilfish swims in a horizontal position in the upper and middle water layers. It can be kept in a tank with a certain amount of dense vegetation, including fine-leaved plants, and sufficient space for swimming. The water should preferably be soft and slightly acid, possibly with peat filtration or with a little peat in the substrate. Spawning takes place among the plants. In some instances the eggs have been laid on fine-leaved plants such as Java Moss. However, this is not an easy species to breed and it is doubtful if there have been many successful rearings. The newly hatched fry should at first be fed on *Paramecium* and rotifers as they may not be able to take brine shrimp nauplii in the first few days.

lower half of the body and a similar bar on the caudal peduncle. The fins are translucent or very pale red-brown.

This peaceful fish of the upper and middle water layers should be kept in a small shoal with plenty of dense vegetation, leaving an adequate area of open water for swimming. The water must be soft, slightly acid, and possibly filtered through peat. The species has the reputation of being slightly delicate. A sexually mature pair introduced into a breeding tank will usually start to spawn among the plants within a few hours, often producing a total of 50 to 70 eggs. These hatch in 30 to 40 hours and the fry are free-swimming five or six days later. They can be fed initially on brine shrimp nauplii. Growth is rapid and it is not unusual for the fish to reach sexual maturity in six or seven months.

Right: **Nannostomus espei**
Possibly delicate in an aquarium.

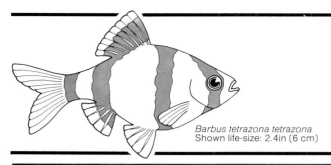

Barbus tetrazona tetrazona
Shown life-size: 2.4in (6 cm)

Right: **Pyrrhulina laeta**
The photograph shows a spawning pair. This species swims and takes most food in the upper layers.

Family LEBIASINIDAE

Pyrrhulina laeta
Half-banded Pyrrhulina
● **Distribution:** South America: Guyana and Middle Amazon
● **Length:** Up to 3.2in (8cm)
● **Tank length:** 24in (60cm)
● **Diet:** Worms, crustaceans, insects, dried food
● **Water temperature:** 70 to 83°F 21 to 28°C)
● **Community tank**

The body of the Half-banded Pyrrhulina is elongated and very slender, with only slight lateral compression. The back is dark gray or dark brown and the belly whitish or yellowish. The flanks are delicate gray-brown with pale bluish or violet iridescence. Some of the scales have dark edges. A blackish or dark brown band runs from the tip of the snout, across the eye, and obliquely back to end just above the anal fin; this is a characteristic feature of the species. The fins are delicate yellowish or reddish, the dorsal fin having a large dark marking in the middle. The upper lobe of the caudal fin is elongated in the male.

This very attractive fish should be kept in a tank with a dark substrate and a few broad-leaved plants, such as the Amazon Sword Plant (*Echinodorus sp.*). The water should be soft, slightly acid, and filtered through peat. Specimens kept in water that is too hard and lacking in peat may survive but they do not thrive. This species has evidently not yet been bred in an aquarium.

The related Striped Vittata (*Pyrrhulina vittata*) has obliquely positioned blackish markings on the flanks. This is not a particularly difficult fish to breed. The female spawns on the upper surface of a leaf and the eggs hatch in 26 to 30 hours. After a few days the very tiny fry will be free-swimming and can then be fed on rotifers. The female is not very prolific and usually lays about 90 to 100 eggs at a spawning.

Family LEBIASINIDAE

Nannostomus unifasciatus
One-lined Pencilfish
● **Distribution:** South America: middle and lower Amazon, Guyana
● **Length:** Up to 2.8in (7cm)
● **Tank length:** 18in (45cm)
● **Diet:** Worms, crustaceans, insects, dried food
● **Water temperature:** 73 to 81°F (23 to 27°C)
● **Community tank**

Also known as *Poecilobrycon unifasciatus,* this is a very elongated pencilfish with an adipose fin and symmetrical caudal fin lobes. There are two subspecies distinguished by a slightly different color pattern. The edge of the anal fin is rounded in the male but straight-cut in the female. The swimming position is slightly oblique, with the head upward. In *N. unifasciatus unifasciatus* the upperparts are a delicate beige color and the underparts are silvery-white. The yellow-brown or golden-brown flanks are prominently marked with a broad, black longitudinal band that extends from the tip of the snout across the eye to the caudal peduncle and ends in the lower lobe of the caudal fin. It is sometimes accompanied above by a narrow golden streak. The upper lobe of the caudal fin is transparent, and the other fins are all colorless. The front edge of the anal fin appears soft-white in both sexes, and the ventral fins have white tips in the male. The other subspecies, *N. unifasciatus ocellatus,* has the same general coloration and pattern but is distinguished by the lower lobe of the caudal fin. This lobe has a black eye-spot, bordered above with white and below with red. During the night the whole body becomes very dark and two broad transverse bars appear on the flanks.

This is a peaceful pencilfish, which should be kept in a small

Above: **Nannostomus unifasciatus**
This is the most slender pencilfish. When the fish is healthy the scales on the back have dark edges.

shoal in a tank with dense vegetation and sufficient space for swimming. The water should be soft, slightly acid, and preferably filtered through peat. There is still some confusion about the breeding of this species in captivity. Some authorities say that spawning takes place among plants, preferably *Hygrophila* and *Ludwigia*. Others suggest that the species has not yet been bred in the aquarium. It may well be that it has been bred, but only rarely.

A practical reminder
Fast-growing plants are best used for
background decoration and for corner-
fillers; more slow-growing plants are used
as foreground or feature plants. Fine-leaved
plants are often nibbled by herbivorous fishes.

Pyrrhulina metae
Rio Meta Pyrrhulina
- **Distribution:** South America,
  Peruvian Amazon, Rio Meta
- **Length:** 2.4in (6cm)
- **Tank length:** 24in (60cm)
- **Diet:** Worms, crustaceans,
  insects, dried food
- **Water temperature:** 70 to 83°F
  (21 to 28°C)
- **Community tank**

Also known as *Copella metae,* this
is a very slender species with only
slight lateral compression. The
mouth faces slightly upward. In
the males the back is chestnut-
brown and the underparts are
whitish. The brownish flanks are
marked with a broad, longitudinal
dark band that extends from the
tip of the snout to the caudal
peduncle; it is bordered above by
a cream-colored stripe. At times
the dark band becomes much
paler. Each scale on this part of
the body is marked with a blood-
red spot. The fins are reddish to
brownish, and somewhat
elongated. The females are
generally paler, with shorter fins.

This very elegant species
should be kept in a tank with a
dark substrate (preferably of peat)
and a number of plants with
broad leaves that grow up to the
water surface; these help to
subdue the light. If it is too bright
the fishes become scared and
their colors do not develop fully.
The water should be soft, slightly
acid, and filtered through peat.
The eggs are laid on the upper
surface of a large leaf, which has
been previously cleaned by the
male. Up to 300 eggs may be laid
and they are fanned by the male
until they hatch after 26 to 30
hours. The very tiny fry lie near the
water surface for a few days.
Once they are free-swimming they
can be fed on rotifers and very
small nauplii. Although spawning
may take place quite readily, the
fry grow rather slowly and they are
not easy to rear.

The genera *Pyrrhulina, Copeina,
Copella,* and *Nannostomus,*
now placed in the family
Lebiasinidae, were formerly
classified in the family Characidae.

Left: **Pyrrhulina metae**
*The photograph shows a
spawning pair. Some eggs have
already been laid on a leaf.*

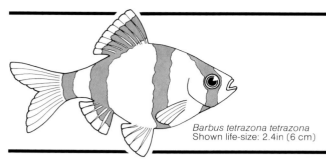

Barbus tetrazona tetrazona
Shown life-size: 2.4in (6 cm)

Family ANOSTOMIDAE

Anostomus anostomus
Striped Anostomus

- **Distribution:** South America: Amazon, Orinoco, Guyana
- **Length:** Up to 6.3in (16cm)
- **Tank length:** 36in (90cm)
- **Diet:** Worms, crustaceans, insects, plant matter, dried food
- **Water temperature:** 75 to 81°F (24 to 27°C)
- **Community tank:** Occasionally aggressive

Because of its interesting shape and striking markings, the Striped Anostomus is a favorite of aquarists. It is very elongated and spindle-shaped with a pointed head, a small mouth that faces upward, and an adipose fin. The body is mostly held obliquely with the head down. The general coloration is yellow with three dark longitudinal bands that have finely toothed edges. The upper band starts on the head and runs along the back; the middle band starts at the mouth, crosses the eye, and extends back along the flanks to the root of the tail; the bottom band runs from the throat, over the insertion of the pectoral fin, to the lower part of the caudal peduncle. The fins are reddish at the bases, and yellow or colorless towards the edges.

The tank for this handsome fish should have roots to give hiding-places and a few plants with long leaves, such as *Echinodorus*. There should be plenty of open water for swimming. The water must be soft, slightly acid, and filtered through peat — or the substrate can contain peat. The fishes are very adept at removing algae from leaves and the aquarium glass. The species is not known to have bred in an aquarium, but has probably been bred in a few commercial hatcheries.

The related Three-spot Anostomus, *Anostomus trimaculatus,* is not as slender as the Striped Anostomus. The body is olive-gray marked with three black blotches — one on the gill cover, the second in the middle of the flanks, and the third on the caudal peduncle.

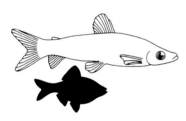

Below: **Anostomus anostomus**
This handsome fish feeds with the head pointing downward, often with the body held vertically. It has not been bred in an aquarium.

Family ANOSTOMIDAE

Abramites hypselonotus
Headstander

- **Distribution:** South America: lower Amazon, Guyana
- **Length:** Up to 5.5in (14cm)
- **Tank length:** 24in (60cm)
- **Diet:** Worms, crustaceans, insects, plant food, dried food
- **Water temperature:** 77 to 81°F (25 to 27°C)
- **Community tank:** Old individuals are often very quarrelsome

Sometimes known as *Abramites microcephalus,* the Headstander is an elongated, quite tall fish with strong lateral compression, a very small head, and a pointed snout. The height of the body increases with age and is greatest in old females. The body is held obliquely with head downward — a striking characteristic of the family. Coloration varies but it is usually pale to dark brown and marked with seven to nine broad dark transverse bars that are irregular in shape. There is a bright yellow area in the forehead region. The adipose fin is bright yellow in the middle and has a

A practical reminder
The plant's crown—the junction between stem and root system—should not be buried when planting. It should be level with, or just above, the surface of the gravel; otherwise the plant will rot away.

Family ANOSTOMIDAE

Leporinus fasciatus
Banded Leporinus

● **Distribution:** Northern and central South America
● **Length:** Up to 12in (30cm)
● **Tank length:** 36in (90cm)
● **Diet:** Worms, crustaceans, insects, plant matter, dried food
● **Water temperature:** 75 to 79°F (24 to 26°C)
● **Community tank:** Sometimes aggressive, particularly in small tanks

The Banded Leporinus is an elegant, elongated and laterally compressed fish. It has large eyes, a cleft upper lip, a small mouth, and an adipose fin. The caudal fin is deeply cleft, the upper lobe

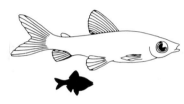

Left: **Leporinus fasciatus**
The pattern is sometimes variable in this species, but the dark vertical bars are characteristic. The related species Leporinus striatus *has longitudinal stripes.*

being slightly larger than the lower lobe. The general coloration is yellow, lemon-yellow, or almost golden. It is marked with nine or 10 broad dark transverse bars that gradually fade away towards the underparts. The first bar runs over the forehead and ends at each eye, the second crosses the edge of the gill cover, and the last is immediately in front of the caudal fin. The fins are colorless or delicate gray. Adult males are more slender than females and often have an orange-red or blood-red throat. There are, however, several color varieties, which is not surprising in view of the very wide geographical distribution (Rio Orinoco to Rio de la Plata).

This peaceful fish lives mainly in the lower water layers and has a taste for soft vegetation. In an aquarium the vegetarian part of its diet can include lettuce, boiled spinach, and soaked oat flakes. Like other members of the family Anostomidae, it swims in an oblique, head down position. This fish is a keen jumper so it should be kept in a tank with a good lid. Some rocks and roots and a few plants with tough leaves should also be included. The water must be soft, slightly acid, and filtered through peat. This species, like many other members of the genus *Leporinus,* has not yet been bred in captivity.

broad black border. The fins are generally yellow, the bases of the dorsal and anal fins being dark. The iris of the eye is blood-red above, golden-yellow below.

This rather timid fish dwells in the middle and lower water layers. It comes from shallow water along the banks of rivers, where it moves about in shoals among the vegetation. It should be kept in a tank with a good lid (it is a jumper) with some rocks and roots to provide shelter, a few scattered plants, and a dark substrate. The water must be soft, slightly acid, and preferably filtered through peat. The Headstander relishes plant matter, and in an aquarium this can be provided by lettuce and boiled spinach.

This species has not yet been bred in captivity.

Right: **Abramites hypselonotus**
A shy species that swims with the head held obliquely downward.

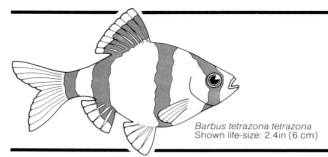
Barbus tetrazona tetrazona
Shown life-size: 2.4in (6 cm)

Family ANOSTOMIDAE

Leporinus striatus
Striped Leporinus

- **Distribution:** South America: Upper Amazon, Mato Grosso in Brazil
- **Length:** Up to 10in (25cm)
- **Tank length:** 36in (90cm)
- **Diet:** Worms, crustaceans, insects, plant matter, dried food
- **Water temperature:** 75 to 79°F (24 to 26°C)
- **Community tank**

The Striped Leporinus is an elongated, spindle-shaped fish with little lateral compression, a tapering pointed head and a small mouth. The genus *Leporinus* is characterized by the cleft upper lip or hare-lip (*Leporinus* means 'of a hare'). The eyes are relatively large. The upperparts and flanks are brown and the underparts are yellow. There are four longitudinal stripes. The central dark brown one is always the most prominent and the other stripes are pale brown. The fins are almost colorless and translucent. The anal fin, however, may have a brownish base and the adipose fin is also brown. The sexes show no external differences.

This is an active but peaceful fish that swims mainly in the lower water layers. It should be kept in a tank with a well-fitting lid to discourage jumping. Arrange rocks and roots to provide hiding-places, and scatter some tough-leaved plants since any plants with soft leaves will soon be consumed. The water must be soft, slightly acid, and filtered through peat, or the substrate can be peat. In addition to helping condition the water, a dark substrate of peat enhances both the color and pattern of the fish.

The related *Leporinus frederici* from Guyana to the Amazon is yellowish gray with slight silvery iridescence, and the flanks are marked with three dark blotches: One below the dorsal fin, one in front of the adipose fin, and the third at the rear end of the caudal peduncle.

Neither of these species has been bred in captivity.

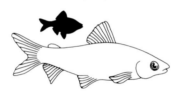

Right: **Leporinus striatus**
The two middle teeth of the upper jaw protrude, which accentuates the harelike expression of this fish.

Family CURIMATIDAE

Chilodus punctatus
Spotted Headstander

- **Distribution:** South America: Amazon, Guyana
- **Length:** Up to 4in (10cm)
- **Tank length:** 24in (60cm)
- **Diet:** Worms, crustaceans, insects, plant matter, dried food
- **Water temperature:** 70 to 83°F (21 to 28°C)
- **Community tank**

Formerly placed in the family Anostomidae, this is an elongated, spatulate fish with moderate lateral compression, a small head, and a small mouth with a thick upper lip. When swimming the body is held obliquely, head down. The female is larger than the male. The general coloration is gray or brown with a slightly darker back and silvery-white underparts. Each scale on the flanks has a dark base, giving it a spotted appearance. From the upper lip the spots fuse to form a short horizontal line that crosses the eye and ends just behind it. A narrow longitudinal line may run from below the dorsal fin, along the flanks, to the root of the tail. The fins are all colorless and translucent except for the dorsal fin, which is spotted with a dark brown front edge and tip.

This active fish inhabits the middle and lower water layers. It is peaceful towards other species but may quarrel with members of its own species. It should be kept in a tank with rocks and roots, a few plants (including some that float), and a dark substrate. The water must be soft, slightly acid, and peat-filtered. Spawning takes place on the bottom. The male curls his caudal peduncle under the female as the eggs and sperm are shed. The parent fishes should then be removed from the tank. The fertilized eggs swell to reach a diameter of 0.08in (2mm) and hatch in three or four days. The fry can be fed almost immediately on rotifers and brine shrimp nauplii, but they are not easy to rear.

Right: **Chilodus punctatus**
The characteristic oblique swimming position adopted by the headstanders may help them to hide among vegetation.

A practical reminder
Rocks form caves and territories for fishes
in addition to providing dramatic decoration.
Be careful to use only rocks that will not
affect the aquarium water chemistry.
Stand large rocks directly on the tank floor

Family CITHARINIDAE
Distichodus
sexfasciatus
Six-banded Distichodus
● **Distribution:** Central Africa:
middle and lower Congo
(Zaire)
● **Length:** Up to 10in (25cm)
● **Tank length:** 36in (90cm)
● **Diet:** Worms, crustaceans,
insects, plant matter, dried food
● **Water temperature:** 75 to 81°F
(24 to 27°C)
● **Community tank:** May be
aggressive. Their large size may
intimidate smaller species

This moderately elongated fish
with strong lateral compression
has large eyes, a relatively small
pointed head, an adipose fin, and
a forked tail. The fins are all well-
developed. The head is blackish
but the rest of the body is bright
orange with golden or silvery
iridescence. The underparts are
paler. The flanks are noticeably
marked with six or seven dark
transverse bars, which may
become less prominent in older
individuals. The adipose fin is
whitish with a dark edge, and the
other fins are blood-red. In young
individuals the dorsal fin often
features dark dots.
　In the wild this peaceful fish lives
in shoals that swim in the lower
water layers of rivers. It can grow
quite large and is, of course,
suitable for a home aquarium only
when relatively young and small.
The tank can have rocks and
roots both to decorate and to
provide hiding-places, but it
should contain no plants because
this species likes to eat the
young shoots. The plant
requirements of the diet can be
supplied by soaked oat flakes, and
boiled lettuce and spinach leaves.
The water must be soft and
slightly acid. This species has not
yet been bred in captivity.
　The genus *Distichodus* contains
several species, varying in length
from 3.2 to 24in (8 to 60cm), and
some of them are caught for
food in certain parts of Africa.

Below: **Distichodus sexfasciatus**
*Only young specimens of this fish
are suitable for the aquarium.
Breeding behaviour is not known.*

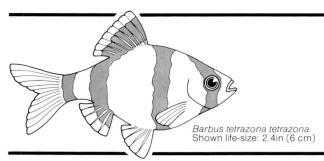

Barbus tetrazona tetrazona
Shown life-size: 2.4in (6 cm)

Family CITHARINIDAE

Nannaethiops unitaeniatus

One-striped African Characin

- **Distribution:** Tropical West Africa to the White Nile
- **Length:** Up to 2.6in (6.5cm)
- **Tank length:** 24in (60cm)
- **Diet:** Worms, crustaceans, insects, dried food
- **Water temperature:** 73 to 79°F (23 to 26°C)
- **Community tank**

The One-striped African Characin is elongated with moderate lateral compression, a small mouth, a deeply forked caudal fin, and a rather large adipose fin. The upperparts are brownish and the underparts yellowish white; they all show silvery iridescence. A narrow dark longitudinal band runs from the mouth across the eye to the root of the caudal fin. This band is bordered above by an iridescent golden line. The fins are yellowish to pale green, and the first rays of the dorsal fin are black. The larger females have duller coloration than the males. At spawning time the front part of the dorsal fin and the upper lobe of the caudal fin become blood-red in the male.

This is a peace-loving but quite active fish that lives mostly in the upper and middle water layers. It can be kept in a tank with a sandy substrate and a few areas of vegetation, leaving sufficient space for swimming. The water should be soft, slightly acid, and filtered through peat. If possible, the tank should be positioned so that it receives a certain amount of sunshine, preferably in the morning, as this stimulates spawning. This is a very productive species. The eggs are laid at random among the plants or in the open water. They will be attacked by the parent fishes, which should therefore be removed from the tank as soon as spawning has ceased. At temperatures of 77 to 79°F (25 to 26°C) the eggs hatch in 26 to 32 hours. The fry live on the contents of the yolk-sac for about five days and are then free-swimming and ready for rotifers and small nauplii.

Right: **Nannaethiops unitaeniatus** ♀
The only species of its genus, this fish is ideal for a community tank.

90

A practical reminder
Gravel size should not be too fine or too coarse; 0.125in (3mm) is about right. A gravel depth of at least 2 to 3in (5 to 7.5cm) is needed for good plant growth. Fragments of smashed rock can be used to 'color match' the gravel.

Phago maculatus
Pike Characin
● **Distribution:** Tropical West Africa
● **Length:** Up to 6in (15cm)
● **Tank length:** 24in (60cm)
● **Diet:** Large insects, fish
● **Water temperature:** 79 to 83°F (26 to 28°C)
● **Species tank**

This elongated, pikelike fish has a flat forehead and little lateral compression. The mouth is deeply cleft with beaklike jaws. Each jaw has two rows of teeth; the upper jaw moves upwards. The fins are relatively small. The caudal fin is deeply forked and the adipose fin is very small. The upperparts are chestnut-brown to dark brown, and the belly is very

Left: **Phago maculatus**
Although not suitable for a beginner, this fish provides a rewarding challenge for the serious aquarist.

pale yellow. The flanks are yellow-brown or reddish brown with several thin brown transverse bars. The fins are yellowish. The dorsal and caudal fins have black longitudinal bands, usually two on the dorsal and three or four on the caudal.

This predatory fish must be kept away from smaller fishes, it is said to swim with lightning speed out of its hiding-place to bite off the fins of larger fishes. It should be kept in a tank with subdued lighting and plenty of vegetation to provide cover as it lies in wait for prey. The composition of the water is not critical. The species has not yet been bred in captivity.

The closely related species *Phago loricatus* is an even more slender fish that comes mainly from the Niger Basin. It has a dark brown back and yellowish white underparts. The flanks are reddish brown with two or three dark longitudinal bands, of which the central one is the broadest. These bands are separated by narrow golden-yellow lines. The fins are similar to those of *P. maculatus* but the central rays of the caudal fin have a black wedge-shaped marking. And like *P. maculatus*, *P. loricatus* has not yet been bred in captivity.

Neolebias ansorgei
African Redfin
● **Distribution:** Central Africa
● **Length:** Up to 1.4in (3.5cm)
● **Tank length:** 24in (60cm)
● **Diet:** Worms, crustaceans, insects, dried food
● **Water temperature:** 73 to 83°F (23 to 28°C)
● **Species tank**

The African Redfin, a relatively short fish with little lateral compression, has no adipose fin. The caudal fin is slightly forked, and the dorsal and anal fins are relatively short. The back is brownish green and the underparts are yellowish with iridescent grayish green or blue-brassy iridescence. The flanks are green and are marked with a broad grass-green to moss-green longitudinal band. There is a narrow black longitudinal bar on the caudal peduncle. The dorsal, caudal, and ventral fins are reddish. At spawning time the fins of the male, except the pectoral fins, become blood-red. The females have a more rounded belly, and just before spawning the eggs can be seen in the body cavity when the fish is viewed in transmitted light.

This is a peaceful fish that swims in the lower water layers and can be kept in a small shoal.

The tank should have some large rocks, areas of dense vegetation around the edges, and a sandy substrate. If kept in a community tank, this species will retreat into the vegetation and its colors will become much paler. The water should be soft. Spawning is preceded by a period of driving, during which the male tries to coax the female into the vegetation. The male and female come together side by side very briefly and the sperm and eggs are shed. The female may lay 50 to 60 eggs per day, in batches of five to 10. This may go on for two to four days, giving a total of about 200 eggs. The eggs hatch in about 40 hours and the fry usually lie on the bottom for four or five days. They can then be fed on infusorians and very small sieved nauplii. After eight days they can be given brine shrimp nauplii. However, they are not easy to rear.

Right: **Neolebias ansorgei**
After spawning, the male has been seen to use his tail to flick the fertilized eggs in among the plants.

THE CARPS AND BARBS

Above: *Barbus nigrofasciatus,* a prolific fish
from the fresh waters of Sri Lanka.
Right: A quiet backwater in Sri Lanka, the type
of habitat in which many barbs live.

This very large family of fishes includes about 1,250 species distributed throughout Europe, Africa, Asia, North America, and northern Central America, almost exclusively in fresh waters. The body is typically elongated and torpedo-shaped with the dorsal and ventral profiles equally convex. The jaws have no teeth, but there are rows of teeth in the pharynx, which are used to grind up the food. The number, shape, and position of these teeth are used by ichthyologists to distinguish species that are otherwise very similar. In many cyprinids, often known colloquially as carps and barbs, there are one or two pairs of barbels at the corners of the mouth; but there is never an adipose fin. There are usually scales on the body but not on the head.

Most cyprinid species live in standing or slow-flowing warm waters, although a few have become adapted to living in colder, fast-flowing waters. Almost all species live in shoals, particularly when young. Many feed on small invertebrates or solely on plants, but the majority are omnivorous, a fact that helps the aquarist in his task of supplying a suitable diet.

Most cyprinids spawn at random above or among plants, and the small eggs sink and adhere to the leaves. They usually hatch in a few days and the fry then hang vertically from plants or other objects, while consuming the contents of the yolk-sac. Other species lay their eggs on the bottom. Only a few species practice any kind of brood protection. Spawnings of several thousand eggs are not uncommon.

Many of the small, attractive barbs from tropical and subtropical waters are kept in the aquarium, where they are undemanding and not at all difficult to breed. In temperate regions some members of the family, such as the Common Carp (Cyprinus carpio), are used as human food, and are also kept and bred in outside ponds or, more rarely, in cold-water aquarium tanks.

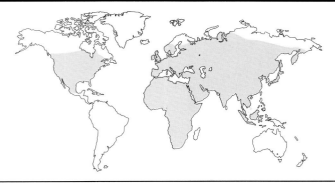

Left: Like the catfishes, the members of the family Cyprinidae are found in all continents except Australia. They do not occur in South America, which is the home of so many characins and catfishes. Unlike many of the characins, which require special types of water, the carps and barbs are most undemanding in this respect. Perhaps this accounts for their wide geographical distribution. Many are ideal for beginners.

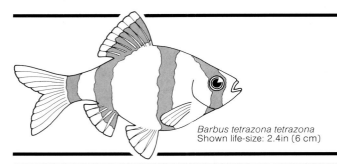

Barbus tetrazona tetrazona
Shown life-size: 2.4in (6 cm)

Family CYPRINIDAE
Barbus arulius
Arulius Barb
- **Distribution:** Southern and southeastern India
- **Length:** Up to 4.7in (12cm)
- **Tank length:** 36in (90cm)
- **Diet:** Worms, crustaceans, insects, plant matter, dried food
- **Water temperature:** 73 to 79°F (23 to 26°C)
- **Community tank:** May be too active for smaller varieties, such as characins.

Arulius is a hardy barb that swims mostly in the middle and lower water layers. Its body is elongated and moderately compressed laterally, and a pair of fairly long barbels appears on the upper jaw. The general coloration is greenish to reddish with silvery or violet iridescence, the scales being marked with several very small shiny dots. The gill cover has an iridescent green spot. The main pattern on the flanks consists of dark blue vertical markings, the most distinct being below the front of the dorsal fin, just above the anal fin, and on the caudal peduncle. The iris of the eye is dark and marked with iridescent green dots. In mature males the rays of the dorsal fin are elongated, but in females they are quite short. The anal and caudal fins are yellowish or reddish yellow with a red border.

The tank for this species should have clumps of plants with tough leaves—this may prevent the fishes from nibbling them. The substrate should be soft to allow them to dig. Adult fishes will usually tolerate medium-hard water, but for breeding the water should be soft.

For spawning, a tank containing 8 gallons (30 liters) of water should be quite sufficient. The females are usually put in the breeding tank a day or two before the males are introduced, in the evening. After intense driving, spawning takes place. The eggs must then be

Above: **Barbus arulius**
This barb is not very prolific in the aquarium; a brood of 100 young would be a good result.

protected from the voracious parent fishes. The eggs hatch in about 25 hours; the fry are free-swimming about two days later and ready to feed on tiny live food.

A practical reminder
Coarse gravel may trap uneaten food where it will rot and cause pollution; and the water flow through the biological filter will be too fast. But very fine gravel will impede filter water flow and plant root growth.

Family CYPRINIDAE
Barbus chola
Swamp barb
- **Distribution:** Eastern India and Burma
- **Length:** Up to 6in (15cm)
- **Tank length:** 36in (90cm)
- **Diet:** Worms, crustaceans, insects, plant matter, dried food
- **Water temperature:** 72 to 77°F (22 to 25°C)
- **Community tank:** May be too large for smaller tankmates

Another hardy shoaling barb, Swamp barb has a rather stocky body and a single pair of relatively short barbels on the upper jaw. Its back is olive-green, its flanks are yellowish with silvery iridescence, and the belly is whitish. On the gill cover there is an ill-defined golden-yellow marking; and the caudal peduncle has a black spot, which may be surrounded by a golden area. The eye is a brilliant orange or red. The dorsal fin is yellowish or orange, sometimes with brown dots in older specimens. The other fins are pale yellowish, possibly slightly reddish in the smaller males.

This is a peaceful fish that mostly swims in the middle and lower water layers. The tank should have a soft substrate, some vegetation around the edges, and a few separate clumps of plants with tough leaves to curb the barb's nibbling tendency. Adults are not fussy about the water and will do well in medium-hard water. For breeding, however, the water should be soft. Spawning takes place after a period of courtship, the female laying eggs at random, usually among the plants. The Swamp Barb is a remarkably hardy fish and has been known to spend the winter in water as low as 62 to 68°F (17 to 20°C).

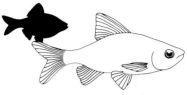

Below: **Barbus chola**
In the wild this barb is quite common in rice fields. In an aquarium it is hardy and prolific.

Family CYPRINIDAE
Barbus bariloides
Orange Barb
- **Distribution:** Southern Africa: Angola, Zimbabwe
- **Length:** Up to 2in (5cm)
- **Tank length:** 18in (45cm)
- **Diet:** Worms, crustaceans, insects, plant matter, dried food
- **Water temperature:** 73 to 79°F (23 to 26°C)
- **Community tank**

An attractive shoaling barb, Orange Barb lives mainly in the middle and lower water layers. Its body is elongated, with a distinctly arched back and a relatively long caudal peduncle. There is a pair of quite long barbels at the front of the upper jaw. The general coloration is orange to reddish, becoming more brownish on the back and silvery on the belly. The flanks are conspicuously marked with 12 to 16 transverse dark bars. The iris is bright red. In general, the fins are reddish or yellowish; the front part of the dorsal fin has a large carmine-red marking, which is sometimes not very clearly defined.

A peaceful barb, this fish is not difficult to keep in a tank with clumps of robust vegetation placed around the edges to leave sufficient room for swimming. The substrate should be dark and the lighting subdued. If the lighting is too bright, the fishes become timid and scared. Although the composition of the water is not critical, it is always better to use 'old' or 'mature' water. This means water that has stood in a tank with plants for a few weeks. A portion of the water—about 20 per cent—should be renewed about every month. The species has been bred in the aquarium, although probably not very often.

Left: **Barbus bariloides** ♂(t),♀(b)
This is a shy barb that is easily upset by bright lighting levels.

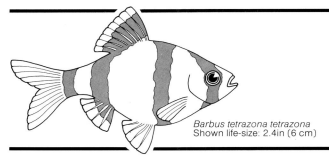

Barbus tetrazona tetrazona
Shown life-size: 2.4in (6 cm)

Family CYPRINIDAE

Barbus conchonius
Rosy Barb, Red Barb

- **Distribution:** Northeastern India, particularly Bengal and Assam
- **Length:** Up to 5.5in (14cm)
- **Tank length:** 24in (60cm)
- **Diet:** Worms, crustaceans, insects, plant matter, dried food
- **Water temperature:** 72 to 77°F (22 to 25°C)
- **Community tank:** May be too active for some small characins.

Rosy Barb has been an extremely popular aquarium fish for about 80 years. It is ideal for a beginner. The body is stocky and the female is somewhat stouter than the male. These fishes have no barbels. The back is iridescent olive-green and the belly is silvery, sometimes with a reddish tinge. The flanks are reddish with silvery iridescence, becoming brilliant red around spawning time. The female is not as brightly colored as the male. At the front end of the caudal peduncle there is a black marking usually with a yellow border. In the male the fins are pink and the tip of the dorsal fin is black. In the female the fins are almost colorless, the dorsal fin showing only a darkish tinge.

This is a most undemanding fish, and can be kept in a tank with rather subdued lighting, conveniently achieved by having a few floating plants at the surface. The substrate should be soft sand because the fishes like to burrow. Adult Rosy Barbs do well in medium-hard water, but for breeding the water should be soft, neutral, and preferably mature. After a very vigorous driving the pair spawn among the plants. The eggs must be protected by the aquarist immediately to prevent them from being eaten by the parents. Some aquarists do this by removing the parents from the tank. The eggs hatch in about 24 hours and the fry live for a few days on the contents of the yolk-sac before becoming free-swimming. They should then be fed on rotifers and small nauplii.

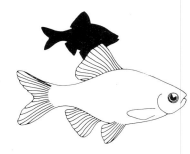

Below: **Barbus conchonius**
This is one of the best species for a beginner, but if spawning takes place you must try to prevent it from eating the eggs.

A practical reminder
Wood is a favorite aquarium decoration. Any wood used must be long dead and should be boiled and sealed before being put into the tank. A plate bolted to the wood and buried in the gravel will prevent floating.

Family CYPRINIDAE
Barbus cumingi
Cuming's Barb
● **Distribution:** Sri Lanka
● **Length:** Up to 2in (5cm)
● **Tank length:** 18in (45cm)
● **Diet:** Worms, insects, crustaceans, plant matter, dried food
● **Water temperature:** 77 to 81°F (25 to 27°C)
● **Community tank**

Cuming's Barb is a relatively tall-bodied barb with no barbels. The back is grayish brown, but the general coloration of the flanks is grayish white with some silvery or golden iridescence, each scale having a dark edge. The eye is an iridescent golden color. Just behind the gill cover there is a dark (sometimes black) vertical bar, which extends down to the rear end of the pectoral fins. There is a similar dark marking on the caudal peduncle. The dorsal and ventral fins are orange, the anal and caudal fins pale yellow, and the pectoral fins colorless. The fins of the slightly larger female are not as brightly colored.

This is an active barb from the forest streams in the mountains of Sri Lanka. In an aquarium it usually swims in the middle and lower water layers. The tank should have a soft substrate and some tough-leaved plants arranged to leave sufficient open water for swimming. The composition of the water is not critical for adults, but breeding should be attempted only in a tank with soft, neutral water. The parents perform an active courtship drive before spawning. The eggs, usually laid among vegetation, hatch in about 25 hours. The fry should be free-swimming in a few days and can be fed at first on rotifers.

Below: **Barbus cumingi**
An active fish best kept in a shoal.

Family CYPRINIDAE
Barbus everetti
Clown Barb, Everett's Barb
● **Distribution:** Singapore and Borneo
● **Length:** Up to 6in (15cm)
● **Tank length:** 36in (90cm)
● **Diet:** Worms, crustaceans, insects, plant matter, dried food
● **Water temperature:** 77 to 81°F (25 to 27°C)
● **Community tank:** Very active. May be quarrelsome with smaller species

This is a hardy Asiatic barb that has two pairs of barbels. Clown Barb's back is brownish or red-brown, sometimes with an orange tinge, and the belly is almost white. The flanks are reddish with golden or silvery iridescence and marked with somewhat irregular black or blue-gray vertical markings. Unlike certain related species, this barb has no dark stripe running through the eye. The fins are mostly a pale reddish color and may occasionally have dark tips. The slightly larger and stouter females are not as colorful as the males.

This is a lively barb living in the lower water layers and best kept in a small shoal. The tank should have marginal vegetation and a soft substrate, but the plants should have tough leaves, as this fish is another plant nibbler. The water should be soft.

The Clown Barb is not always easy to breed. Experience has shown that it is best to keep the prospective breeding fishes apart for about three weeks. During this time give them a varied and plentiful diet of white worms, insect larvae, and greens such as lettuce. They spawn in the sunshine of early morning, preferably among fine-leaved plants, such as Milfoil (*Myriophyllum*).

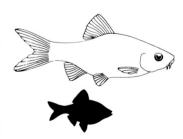

Left: **Barbus everetti**
A relatively large fish for an aquarium, this species has two pairs of barbels and thrives best when kept in a small shoal. It will nibble any soft-leaved tank plants.

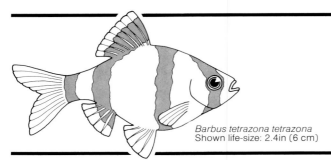

Barbus tetrazona tetrazona
Shown life-size: 2.4in (6 cm)

Family CYPRINIDAE
Barbus fasciatus
Striped Barb
- **Distribution:** Malaya, Sumatra, Borneo
- **Length:** Up to 2.4in (6cm)
- **Tank length:** 24in (60cm)
- **Diet:** Worms, crustaceans, insects, plant matter, dried food
- **Water temperature:** 72 to 79°F (22 to 26°C)
- **Community tank**

A species with the typical barb shape and a laterally compressed body, Striped Barb has two pairs of barbels. Its back is greenish with a few irregular black markings; the flanks are red, with a violet sheen that becomes paler ventrally so that the belly is almost white. The flanks are marked with four or five dark blue longitudinal stripes that extend back from the rear end of the gill cover to the base of the caudal fin. The dorsal and anal fins are red or sometimes pale yellow, but the other fins are nearly colorless. The female is slightly larger than the male, and has paler coloration and a more rounded belly profile.

This is a very active barb and is not difficult to keep in a domestic aquarium. The tank should have a soft substrate to allow for burrowing, and the plants should be mostly installed along the back and sides to leave plenty of open water for swimming. For breeding the temperature should be 81 to 83°F (27 to 28°C) and the water preferably soft. After the usual driving the female lays eggs at random among the vegetation. These hatch and can be reared in the same way as fry of the Rosy Barb.

There is a very similar species known as the Lined Barb *(Barbus lineatus)*, which comes from southern Malaya. It has almost the same pattern on the flanks, but it has no barbels.

Right: **Barbus fasciatus**
This is an active barb that thrives in an aquarium. It needs plenty of open water for swimming.

Family CYPRINIDAE
Barbus gelius
Golden Dwarf Barb
- **Distribution:** India, Bengal, and Assam
- **Length:** Up to 1.6in (4cm)
- **Tank length:** 18in (45cm)
- **Diet:** Small crustaceans and insects, dried food
- **Water temperature:** 68 to 72°F (20 to 22°C)
- **Community tank**

A somewhat transparent small barb, the female Golden Dwarf Barb is stouter than the male and has no barbels. Backs of both sexes are olive-green to brownish; the underparts are white with a silvery sheen. The flanks are iridescent gold with irregular dark blotches. In addition there is a reddish gold longitudinal stripe that extends back to the caudal peduncle, where it widens into a shiny coppery marking. The eye is pale green. The caudal fin is pale red; the pectoral fins are colorless and the other fins yellowish.

In the wild this tiny but hardy barb lives in standing and slow-flowing waters. It is one of the most undemanding aquarium fishes and can even be kept at temperatures as low as 61 to 64°F (16 to 18°C). For breeding, the water temperature should not exceed 70 to 72°F (21 to 22°C). The eggs are laid among the plants, to which they adhere, and hatch in about 24 hours. For a few days the tiny fry live on the contents of the yolk-sac and then swim free. At this point they can be fed on rotifers and nauplii, and possibly a little finely powdered dried food. The parents do not eat their own eggs, but it is probably best to remove them from the tank anyway as soon as they have finished spawning.

Below: **Barbus gelius**
This is an excellent barb for a beginner or for anyone without sufficient space for a large tank. The markings on the flanks are rather variable between individuals.

A practical reminder
Of the artificial aquarium decorations available, molded logs are the most natural looking. Sunken galleons, mermaids, and opening shells are quite out of place. Other pre-cast 'rocks' may be toxic.

Family CYPRINIDAE

Barbus lateristriga
Spanner Barb

- **Distribution:** Thailand, Malaysia, Indonesia
- **Length:** Up to 7in (18cm)
- **Tank length:** 36in (90cm)
- **Diet:** Worms, crustaceans, insects, plant matter, dried food
- **Water temperature:** 66 to 77°F (19 to 25°C)
- **Community tank:** May be too active for smaller species

This handsome barb would be too large for a home aquarium if it were to reach the maximum size of Spanner Barbs grown in the wild. In practice, however, this does not happen, and a good aquarium specimen would be 2.4 to 4in (6 to 10cm) long. The body of a young fish is slender, but with increasing age it becomes deeper and dorsally more arched; there are two pairs of barbels.

The back is greenish orange, the belly orange, and the flanks are yellowish brown with golden iridescence. On the front of the body there are two prominent blue-black markings, which straddle the back and extend down each flank to end in a tapered point. A black longitudinal bar extends from below the dorsal fin to the caudal peduncle and onto the caudal fin. The fins are red, more noticeably so in the male. In general, however, the colors and patterns of this species vary greatly, but this is not surprising in view of its wide geographical distribution.

Breeding is not difficult. After a period of vigorous driving,

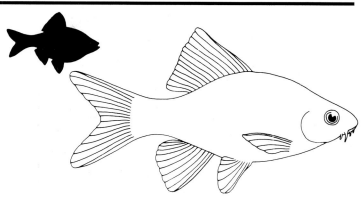

spawning takes place among the plants. As soon as this has finished, the parent fishes should be removed from the tank because they sometimes eat their own eggs. Although the composition of the water is not critical for the parents, it is probably best to use soft water for successful breeding.

Below: **Barbus lateristriga**
Half-grown specimens are more suitable; the pattern fades with age.

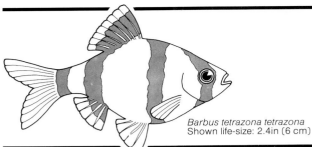

Barbus tetrazona tetrazona
Shown life-size: 2.4in (6 cm)

Family CYPRINIDAE
Barbus nigrofasciatus
Black Ruby, Purple-headed Barb
● **Distribution:** Sri Lanka
● **Length:** Up to 2.4in (6cm), possibly more
● **Tank length:** 36in (90cm)
● **Diet:** Worms, insects, crustaceans, plant matter, dried food
● **Water temperature:** 72 to 75°F (22 to 24°C)
● **Community tank:** Tank size often affects behavior; a larger tank usually results in less aggression

This is a hardy, deep-bodied fish without barbels, and it is very suitable for a beginner. In both sexes the head of Black Ruby is a beautiful crimson color. The flanks are mainly yellowish gray marked with three or four dark transverse bars. The edges of the scales are silvery, so that together they form rows of glistening dots. In males the dorsal fin is black, the anal fin is dark red, and the ventral fins are reddish. In females the colors are much paler, and the fins are yellowish without dark edges.

This is one of the most accommodating barbs for an aquarist. The tank should have a soft substrate and marginal vegetation arranged to leave sufficient open water for swimming. A few floating plants will help to subdue the light and this will benefit the fishes. For decorative purposes there can be a few isolated plants with tough leaves.

At spawning time the males assume a dramatic color change. The whole of the front part of the body becomes deep purplish red, the back velvety green, the caudal peduncle and the caudal fin almost black, and the rows of dots on the flanks green. For spawning the temperature of the water should be raised to 77 to 83°F (25 to 28°C). The female lays a large number of eggs, usually in the morning sunshine, and these hatch in about 25 hours.

Right: **Barbus nigrofasciatus**
For spawning, many aquarists recommend that the tank should have plants with feathery leaves, to which the eggs will adhere. It is important to remember, however, that the parents are spawn-eaters.

A practical reminder
Tap water is quite suitable for the majority of fishes providing the chlorine in it is neutralized by dechlorinators before use. Aeration will also help to drive out chlorine.

Family CYPRINIDAE

Barbus oligolepis
Island Barb, Checker Barb
- **Distribution:** Sumatra
- **Length:** Up to 2in (5cm)
- **Tank length:** 18in (45cm)
- **Diet:** Worms, small crustaceans, insects, plant matter, dried food
- **Water temperature:** 72 to 77°F (22 to 25°C)
- **Community tank**

The name Island Barb refers to the fact that this species was originally found only on the island of Sumatra. It was introduced into the aquarium world about 1925. The body has the typical barb shape, and there is a single pair of small barbels at the corners of the mouth. There may also be a pair of very small barbels on the snout.

The general coloration is a delicate ocher to red-brown, the back somewhat darker with bluish iridescence, the belly yellow; the flanks have a mother-of-pearl sheen. The scales on the flanks each have a broad black edge and a bluish spot at the base. In males the dorsal and anal fins are

reddish, with dark edges. In females these fins are yellowish, without dark edges. It is sometimes known as the Checker Barb because the pattern formed by the scales on the flanks resembles a checkerboard. This barb should be kept in a tank with a soft substrate and a reasonable amount of vegetation, mainly around the edges. The water composition is not critical for adults, but it should be mature and not straight from the tap. For

Above: **Barbus oligolepis** ♀
This attractive barb is best kept in a shoal. It is easy to breed.

breeding, which presents no special problems, the water should preferably be on the soft side. Spawning takes place in the same way as the Black Ruby.

Family CYPRINIDAE

Barbus phutunio
Dwarf Barb, Pygmy Barb
- **Distribution:** Eastern India and Sri Lanka
- **Length:** Up to 3.2in (8cm)
- **Tank length:** 12in (30cm)
- **Diet:** Worms, crustaceans, insects, plant matter, dried food
- **Water temperature:** 70 to 77°F (21 to 25°C)
- **Community tank**

This is another of the very small barbs. The body, which has the typical barb shape, becomes deeper with increasing age. There are no barbels. The back is brownish green or grayish green, and the belly white with a silvery

sheen. The flanks are also silvery, but with bluish or violet iridescence. The scales are relatively large and each has a dark base and a pale glistening edge. When the fish is excited, five blue transverse bars can be seen on the flanks, but these later fade leaving usually three dark blotches. The coloration is less pronounced in the stouter female. The pectoral fins are colorless but the other fins are yellowish to red. In the male an oblique dark bar often runs across the dorsal fin.

This is a peaceable, hardy barb that lives mostly in the middle water layers. It should be kept in a small shoal, in a tank with marginal vegetation and a good

Above: **Barbus phutunio** ♂
For best results a breeding pair of this species needs a separate tank.

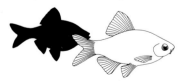

space in the center for swimming. The water should be soft. This is not a very prolific species, and a spawning of 60 to 80 eggs at a time can be regarded as successful. The fry can be reared in the usual way in a planted breeding tank, but they often turn out to be rather delicate.

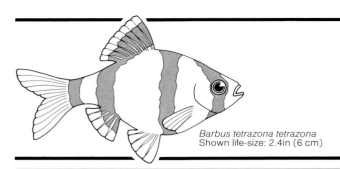

Barbus tetrazona tetrazona
Shown life-size: 2.4in (6 cm)

Family CYPRINIDAE
Barbus schwanenfeldi
Schwanenfeld's Barb, Tinfoil Barb
- **Distribution:** Thailand, Malaysia, Indonesia
- **Length:** Up to 14in (35cm), may grow larger
- **Tank length:** 36in (90cm)
- **Diet:** Worms, crustaceans, insects, plant matter, dried food
- **Water temperature:** 68 to 77°F (20 to 25°C)
- **Community tank:** Keep with larger species only

This elegant barb has a compressed body with a profile that looks like an elongated lozenge. It has two pairs of barbels on the upper jaw. The back, flanks and underside are all silvery, sometimes with yellow or bluish iridescence. This brilliant coloration has earned the fish its

other common name, Tinfoil Barb. The iris of the eye is golden. The dorsal fin is bright red with a dark marking near the tip. A thin dark stripe running along the edge of each lobe marks the red caudal fin. The other fins are paler and usually yellowish or orange. The sexes cannot be distinguished on the basis of coloration.

This is a very active barb, which should be kept in a small shoal. The fishes are only suitable for a home aquarium when they are relatively small, 2.4 to 3.2in (6 to 8cm) in length. Large specimens become somewhat aggressive and may attack and eat smaller species. The tank should be spacious enough to allow for swimming and the substrate should be soft. Like so many other barbs this species is partial to vegetation and will eat aquarium

plants. This annoying habit can be prevented, to some extent, by giving Tinfoil Barb plenty of lettuce leaves.

Tinfoil Barb has not yet been bred in captivity.

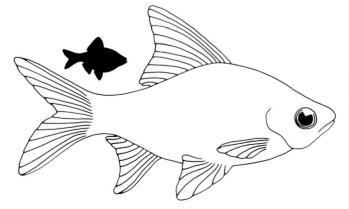

Above: **Barbus schwanenfeldi**
Small specimens of this barb are suitable for the home aquarium. It needs a good supply of plant food to prevent it from eating the tank vegetation. It grows very rapidly.

A practical reminder
Some fishes require special water conditions whose quality may be checked by the use of inexpensive test kits. Any necessary changes to the water must be introduced gradually to avoid stressing the fishes.

Family CYPRINIDAE

Barbus semifasciolatus
Green Barb, China Barb, Half-banded Barb
- **Distribution:** Southeastern China
- **Length:** Up to 4in (10cm)
- **Tank length:** 24in (60cm)
- **Diet:** Worms, crustaceans, insects, plant matter, dried food
- **Water temperature:** 72 to 77°F (22 to 25°C)
- **Community tank**

The Green Barb is a fairly elongated barb with a slightly arched back, which is more pronounced in old specimens. On the upper jaw at the corners of the mouth is a single pair of very short barbels. The back is brown to reddish brown and the belly is whitish. The flanks, which are greenish to yellow with some iridescence, are usually marked with from five to seven narrow black transverse bars. The scales all have dark edges and the upper part of the iris is blood-red. The dorsal, caudal, and anal fins are brownish red or sometimes brick-red, the pectoral fins are colorless, and the ventral fins are brownish to yellowish.

This is a hardy barb, which should be kept in a small shoal. It swims mainly in the middle and lower water layers. The tank should have a soft substrate and a reasonable amount of vegetation, and should be set up with bright lighting. Although the optimum water temperature is 72 to 77°F (22 to 25°C), an occasional drop to 64 to 68°F (18 to 20°C) will not be harmful. The water should be soft and slightly acid.

For breeding, the tank needs to be at least 24in (60cm) long to allow for the very vigorous courtship behavior. During this time the male circles around the female, pushing her with open mouth and striking her with his tail to drive her in among the plants, where they will spawn. The yellowish eggs hatch in about 25 hours and the fry should be reared in the same way as those of the Rosy Barb.

Right: **Barbus semifasciolatus**
This is a peaceful shoaling fish that will thrive in conditions of relatively low oxygen concentration.

Family CYPRINIDAE

Barbus 'Schuberti'
Golden Barb, Schubert's Barb
- **Distribution:** Unknown
- **Length:** Up to 2.8in (7cm)
- **Tank length:** 18in (45cm)
- **Diet:** Worms, crustaceans, insects, plant matter, dried food
- **Water temperature:** 68 to 77°F (20 to 25°C)
- **Community tank**

This barb first appeared in the aquarium world several years ago in North America. Apparently nobody knew where the fish came from. It was named 'Schuberti' without giving it a proper description in a recognized scientific journal. The name 'Schuberti' is therefore invalid and can only be regarded as a nickname. This fish is now thought to be a yellow form of *Barbus semifasciolatus*.

Notwithstanding such an illegitimate origin, Golden Barb is quite attractive, and perfectly hardy in the aquarium. The ground coloration is golden-yellow, the underparts being more silvery. Just below the dorsal fin there is a single black blotch, and the base of the tail also has distinct very dark markings. Old specimens sometimes have small black spots on the flanks. The fins are reddish. The females are less colorful but more robust than the males.

This barb should be kept in a small shoal, which will swim in the middle and lower water layers. The tank can be furnished in exactly the same way as for the Green Barb, described on this page. The fish spawns very freely; some aquarists, in fact, find that it spawns even more readily than the Green Barb.

Below: **Barbus 'Schuberti'**
Although of unclear origin, this fish is a perfect aquarium subject. It is hardy and breeds very easily.

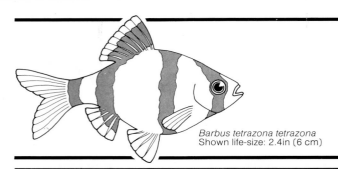

Barbus tetrazona tetrazona
Shown life-size: 2.4in (6 cm)

Barbus ticto stoliczkae
Stoliczka's Barb
● **Distribution:** Southern Burma, in the lower Irrawaddy River
● **Length:** Up to 2.4in (6cm)
● **Tank length:** 24in (60cm)
● **Diet:** Worms, crustaceans, insects, plant matter, dried food
● **Water temperature:** 68 to 77°F (20 to 25°C)
● **Community tank**

This small deep-bodied barb with no barbels is often known as *Barbus stoliczkanus,* but here it is treated as a subspecies of *B. ticto.*

The back is dark olive-green, sometimes moss-green, and the belly whitish. The flanks are silvery with yellowish to bluish iridescence, depending upon the angle of the light, and the scales have dark edges. There are two large dark markings, one just behind the gill cover, the other at the start of the caudal peduncle. In the male the dorsal fin is reddish at the base and black above, the base of the caudal fin is yellowish, the anal and ventral fins are reddish, and the pectoral fins are colorless. The female has

Above: **Barbus ticto stoliczkae**
In this popular aquarium fish the mouth faces slightly upward. It differs from Barbus ticto ticto *in the arrangement of the scales on the flanks. It is easy to breed.*

colorless fins except for the dorsal fin, which is a delicate red.

This is a popular shoaling fish, mostly swimming in the middle and lower water layers. It requires a tank with a soft bottom but the composition of the water is not critical. For breeding the temperature range should be 75 to 79°F (24 to 26°C). The eggs hatch in 25 to 30 hours.

The related and very similar Two-spot Barb *(Barbus ticto ticto)* comes from India and Sri Lanka. It can be kept in water as cool as 61°F (16°C).

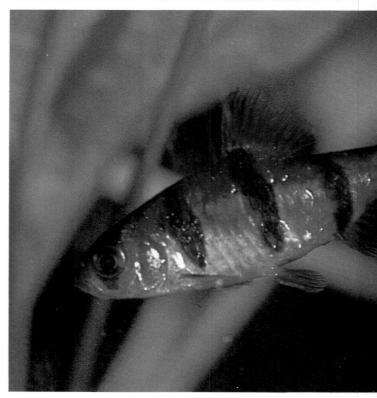

A practical reminder
Fishes from rivers in tropical rain forests
are used to soft water. Cichlids from
African Lakes like very hard water. But both
can be gradually acclimatized to live
happily in normal tap water.

Left: **Barbus tetrazona tetrazona**
*This is the most widespread of the
barbs with dark vertical bars. The
male may become pale when
spawning male may become pale.*

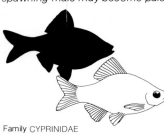

Family CYPRINIDAE
**Barbus tetrazona
tetrazona**
Sumatran Barb, Tiger Barb
● **Distribution:** Sumatra and
Borneo
● **Length:** Up to 2.4in (6cm)
● **Tank length:** 24in (60cm)
● **Diet:** Worms, small crusta-
ceans, plant matter, dried food
● **Water temperature:** 68 to 77°F
(20 to 25°C)
● **Community tank:** May be
quarrelsome with other
community species; a larger
tank often reduces aggression

One of the more colorful barbs
and one particularly suitable for a
beginner is the Sumatran or Tiger
Barb. The body is relatively high-
backed and the mouth area has
no barbels. The back is brown or
brownish red and the belly is
whitish. The flanks are silvery with
reddish or yellowish iridescence
and the scales, particularly those
on the upper part of the body,
have dark edges. The
characteristic pattern on the flanks
consists of four broad, black,
transverse bars, from which the
common name Tiger Barb is
derived. The first bar runs through
the eye and the second is just in
front of the dorsal fin. The third
bar is at the back of the dorsal fin
and extends onto the base of this
fin and the anal fin. The fourth
bar is at the base of the tail. The
outer parts of the dorsal and anal
fins are blood-red.

This species should be kept in a
small shoal, which will swim about
in the middle layers of the water.
The tank should have a soft
substrate and some vegetation
around the edges, with plenty of
space left for swimming since this
is a very active fish. Medium-hard
water can be used but it is
preferable to have soft water,
especially for the breeding tank.
Spawning habits are the same as
those of the Green Barb
described on page 103.

The Sumatran Barb has a
reputation for nibbling the fins of
Angelfishes, so it is best to keep
the two species apart.

Family CYPRINIDAE
**Barbus tetrazona
partipentazona**
Banded Barb
● **Distribution:** Thailand and
Malaysia
● **Length:** Up to 2.4in (6cm)
● **Tank length:** 18in (45cm)
● **Diet:** Worms, insects, small
crustaceans, plant matter, dried
food
● **Water temperature:** 68 to 79°F
(20 to 26°C)
● **Community tank:** May harass
smaller species

The body of this subspecies is
slightly more slender than that of
the Sumatran Barb. The Banded
Barb's back is brownish red and
the underparts are white. The

Left:
Barbus tetrazona partipentazona
This is a very prolific breeder.

flanks are silvery with a brilliant
yellowish or red sheen, and the
scales on the upperparts have
dark edges. However, the
distinguishing feature of the
Banded Barb is the short bar that
runs down from the dorsal fin to
the middle of the body, giving the
flanks a rather incomplete
appearance. The fins are more or
less the same as those of the
Sumatran Barb. Tank conditions
should also be similar, but
Angelfishes should be excluded to
prevent their fins from being
nipped.

For breeding it is best to use
fishes that are one to two years
old. The tank should have soft
water and a soft susbtrate. After a
short period of driving, during
which the female becomes paler,
the male coils the rear part of his
body (from above) around the
rear part of the female. The eggs
are then shed with the pair in this
position. A female in good
condition may produce 600 to
1000 eggs at each spawning and
these hatch in 26 to 30 hours. The
fry become free-swimming a few
days later and can be fed at first
on rotifers and brine shrimp nauplii.

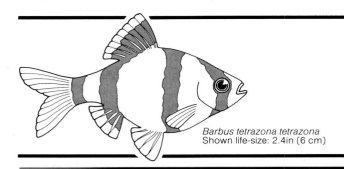

Barbus tetrazona tetrazona
Shown life-size: 2.4in (6 cm)

Family CYPRINIDAE

Brachydanio albolineatus

Pearl Danio

- **Distribution:** Southeast Asia
- **Length:** Up to 2.4in (6cm)
- **Tank length:** 18in (45cm)
- **Diet:** Worms, small crustaceans, dried food
- **Water temperature:** 70 to 77°F (21 to 25°C)
- **Community tank:** Very active

Slender and rather elongated, the Pearl Danio is slightly compressed laterally and has two pairs of barbels. The caudal fin is somewhat forked and the anal fin is relatively long. When seen in reflected light the body is iridescent violet or blue, but in

transmitted light it appears green. The belly is pale bluish and the back is darker blue or blue-gray. There is a longitudinal red streak, edged in blue-green, starting in the center of the body and ending on the caudal peduncle. The basal part of the anal fin is red or orange-red, its outer part transparent greenish. The other fins are also translucent green, with a tinge of red. The female is slightly larger, stouter, and less brightly colored than the male.

This peaceable fish was introduced to the aquarium in about 1911. It swims mostly in the upper and middle water layers. Unlike some of the other members of the family Cyprinidae, such as the rather shy Cherry Barb, this species loves sunshine; in fact, it develops the full delicate colors only when kept in sunlight.

The tank should have some vegetation, and a good lid to prevent jumping. The water can be soft or medium-hard, even for breeding. Spawning typically takes place in the morning sunshine and may last some hours. A fully mature female may lay up to 600 eggs and these must be protected from the parents; they hatch in about 24 hours. The fry take several days, usually six or seven, before they are free-swimming and ready to be fed on tiny live food such as rotifers.

Left: **Brachydanio albolineatus**
In the wild this is a very active fish and the same liveliness is seen in good aquarium specimens. The flanks are beautifully iridescent.

A practical reminder
Do not worry unduly about the water quality. The chances are that if the fishes survive in your local store's water then they will be at home in yours.

Barbus titteya
Cherry Barb
- **Distribution:** Sri Lanka
- **Length:** Up to 2in (5cm)
- **Tank length:** 18in (45cm)
- **Diet:** Worms, small crusta-ceans, plant matter, dried food
- **Water temperature:** 73 to 81°F (23 to 27°C)
- **Community tank**

An elegant small barb, the Cherry Barb has a relatively elongated body and one pair of barbels on the upper jaw at the corners of the mouth. The back is chestnut-brown with greenish iridescence. Flanks are silvery with red tones. A dark brown or blue-black stripe

Left: **Barbus titteya**
This is a beautiful but shy barb. During spawning the parent fishes can be fed on white worms.

extends from the mouth to the center of the tail base, being broadest in the middle of the body. Above this dark stripe there is a broad iridescent yellow band, which becomes greenish towards the rear. When the fish is excited a double row of dark dots may be discerned below the dark stripe. The iris of the eye is golden-red, and the gill cover is red. The whole body of the male, especially the underparts, becomes an intense red as spawning approaches. The fins are red in the male, yellowish in the female. In general, the coloration of the female is considerably paler than that of the male.

In the wild, Cherry Barbs live in shady streams, so in captivity the tank should be given subdued lighting and marginal vegetation. A few isolated plants with tough leaves will provide shelter. The water should be soft, and for spawning the water temperature should be 79 to 81°F (26 to 27°C). This is not a very prolific fish, the female usually laying 150 to 250 eggs at each spawning. These hatch in about 24 hours, and the fry should be free-swimming a few days later, and ready to feed on rotifers and nauplii. They are timid at first.

Brachydanio rerio
Zebra Danio
- **Distribution:** Eastern India and Bangladesh
- **Length:** Up to 2in (5cm)
- **Tank length:** 12in (30cm)
- **Diet:** Worms, small crusta-ceans, dried food
- **Water temperature:** 64 to 77°F (18 to 25°C)
- **Community tank**

Zebra Danio is a slender fish with a slightly compressed body and two pairs of barbels. The female, with a more rounded belly profile, is a little larger than the male. The back is brownish olive, the belly whitish. The coloration and pattern of the flanks are quite characteristic.

In males the background color is golden, strikingly marked by four deep blue longitudinal streaks, which extend the whole length of the body from the gill cover to the end of the tail. This pattern is repeated on the anal fin. The dorsal fin is olive with a bluish white border, and the pectoral and ventral fins are colorless. The gill cover has rather indistinct blue markings.

This is a remarkably hardy tropical fish, highly suitable for a

beginner because it has no special requirements. The tank can have a reasonable amount of vegetation, leaving plenty of space in the upper water layers for swimming, and it must have a good lid to prevent the fishes from leaping out. For breeding the tank should have soft or medium-hard water and a few clumps of plants with feathery leaves, such as Milfoil *(Myriophyllum)*. After vigorous driving the male chases the female in among the plants, where spawning takes place. The eggs must be protected from the parents, which are notorious spawn-eaters.

Below: **Brachydanio rerio**
This is an old favorite, introduced into the aquarium in 1905. For breeding, many aquarists recom-mend using dark males with shiny gold stripes and white-tipped fins.

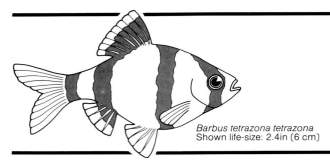

Barbus tetrazona tetrazona
Shown life-size: 2.4in (6 cm)

Family CYPRINIDAE
Danio malabaricus
Giant Danio
- **Distribution:** Sri Lanka and west coast of India
- **Length:** Up to 4.7in (12cm), but mature at 2.8in (7cm)
- **Tank length:** 36in (90cm)
- **Diet:** Worms, crustaceans, insects, dried food
- **Water temperature:** 68 to 75°F (20 to 24°C)
- **Community tank:** Very active. May disturb other species

A giant only in relation to the other danios, *Danio malabaricus* is a more slender fish than *Danio devario,* and it has one pair of barbels. The body is markedly compressed laterally. The back is gray-green to bluish and the underparts are pale pink. Flanks have three or four pale blue or indigo bands separated by thin golden-yellow longitudinal stripes. In the male the central blue band runs straight, but in the female it turns upwards at the base of the caudal fin. The gill cover has a bright yellowish green or golden marking and the iris is iridescent golden. Apart from the pectoral fins, which are colorless, all the other fins are pink or a delicate blue, sometimes with a reddish tinge at their bases. The stouter female is not as brightly colored as the male.

Giant Danio is a very handsome fish and should be kept in a shoal swimming in the upper water layers. The tank should have plants around the edges, leaving sufficient space in the center for swimming. For breeding the substrate can be fine gravel, which will provide some shelter for the eggs after spawning. This is a prolific species and it is not unusual for the female to lay over 1000 eggs.

The related *Danio regina* from southern Thailand is similar in coloration, but has a blue-back marking behind the gill cover.

Right: **Danio malabaricus**
This striking and undemanding fish is suitable for a community tank with other robust fishes.

Family CYPRINIDAE
Danio devario
Bengal Danio
- **Distribution:** Pakistan, northern India, Assam, Bangladesh
- **Length:** Up to 4in (10cm)
- **Tank length:** 24in (60cm)
- **Diet:** Worms, small crustaceans, insects, dried food
- **Water temperature:** 68 to 75°F (20 to 24°C)
- **Community tank:** Very active. May distrub smaller species.

This is a stockier fish than the Zebra Danio with a markedly convex belly profile and no barbels. The basic coloration of Bengal Danio varies somewhat, but is usually a pale silvery-green, the back a little darker and the belly silvery-white. Behind the iridescent green gill cover, the flanks show vertical blue and yellow streaks. The rear part of the body has three longitudinal blue stripes, bordered by thin yellow lines. The dorsal fin is grayish brown with a whitish border, and the ventral and anal fins are brownish or red. The upper lobe of the caudal fin is a delicate pink, the lower lobe usually more or less colorless. The iris of the eye is an attractive golden-green.

This active fish, introduced to the aquarium world in about 1939, is best kept in a small shoal, which will swim mainly in the upper water layers. The composition of the water is not critical and even during breeding it can be kept medium-hard. The tank should have clumps of fine-leaved plants, such as Milfoil *(Myriophyllum)*. If the tips of the shoots are held together by a rubber band, the fish will drive through the middle part of the plant when spawning. The plants will also help to give the sinking eggs some degree of protection from the greedy parents.

Above: **Danio devario** ♀(t), ♂(b)
Like the Giant Danio, this is an active fish that may jump out of the tank unless a lid is fitted.

Family CYPRINIDAE
Epalzeorhynchus kallopterus
Flying Fox
- **Distribution:** Sumatra and Borneo
- **Length:** Up to 5.5in (14cm)
- **Tank length:** 24in (60cm)
- **Diet:** Worms, crustaceans, insects, plant matter, dried food
- **Water temperature:** 72 to 81°F (22 to 27°C)
- **Community tank**

This barb has an elongated but only slightly compressed body, a mouth facing downward, and two pairs of barbels. The back is brown to olive-green and the underparts are white. Below the back there is a broad golden-

A practical reminder
The level of unwanted substances in the aquarium water can be kept to a safe minimum by efficient filtration (mechanical, chemical, and biological) and by regular partial water changes (20 to 25% per month).

yellow longitudinal band, which reaches from the tip of the snout to the caudal peduncle. Immediately below this band there is a blackish band running from the snout to the central rays of the caudal fin. The fins are mainly pink or reddish brown; the dorsal, anal, and ventral fins have a black bar and a white border. The iris of the eye is bright red.

This is a hardy fish that should be kept in a tank with dense vegetation and scattered rocks and roots. The substrate should be soft. The species is perfectly peaceful in a community tank. However, the Flying Fox will fight with other members of its own kind because each individual likes to have its own territory near the bottom, usually among dead branches and tree roots. When at rest they like to balance on their pectoral fins in the same way as marine bottom-living gurnards.

The ventral position of the mouth is adapted for rasping algae from rocks and roots, and also from the aquarium glass. It is unlikely that this species has been bred in captivity.

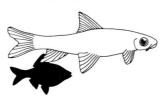

Right: **Epalzeorhynchus kallopterus**
In addition to algae, this fish also browses on flatworms.

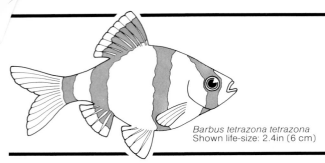

Barbus tetrazona tetrazona
Shown life-size: 2.4in (6 cm)

Family CYPRINIDAE
Rasbora borapetensis
Red-tailed Rasbora
- **Distribution:** Thailand
- **Length:** Up to 2in (5cm)
- **Tank length:** 18in (45cm)
- **Diet:** Worms, insects, crustaceans, dried food
- **Water temperature:** 68 to 79°F (20 to 26°C)
- **Community tank**

Red-tailed Rasbora is an elegant, elongated fish, with a typically forked tail and a mouth turned slightly upward. The back is olive-green. The front of the dorsal fin is just behind the insertion of the ventral fins. The flanks are greenish yellow with silvery iridescence. A wide black longitudinal stripe extends from the rear of the gill cover to the rear of the caudal peduncle, and is bordered by a thin golden line that has a tinge of green. There is also a thin black line running along the midline of the back, and a similar line along the base of the anal fin. The dorsal and caudal fins are delicate red, but the other fins are more or less colorless. The sexes are similar in coloration, but the female is slightly more robust.

This is an active small fish, which should be kept in a shoal. The tank should have a certain amount of vegetation, but there should be plenty of open water so that the fishes can swim freely. The water must be soft and slightly acid with some added peat, or it can be filtered through peat. For breeding, the same type of water should be used. The tank should have no substrate, but should be provided with scattered groups of anchored feathery plants such as *Cabomba*. During spawning the male curls his body around the female, who lays eggs at random. Those eggs that fall among the plants have some protection from the parent fishes.

Below: **Rasbora borapetensis**
Shallow water and subdued light will help this species to breed.

Family CYPRINIDAE
Labeo bicolor
Red-tailed Labeo
- **Distribution:** Thailand
- **Length:** Up to 4.7in (12cm)
- **Tank length:** 24in (60cm)
- **Diet:** Worms, crustaceans, insects, plant matter, dried food
- **Water temperature:** 72 to 79°F (22 to 26°C)
- **Community tank**

This elongated fish has slight lateral compression and a dorsal profile more convex than the ventral. The mouth faces slightly downward and has swollen lips and two pairs of barbels. The fins, particularly the dorsal fin, are well developed and usually held spread out. The females grow larger than the males. When in good condition the whole body—including the dorsal, anal, and ventral fins—is velvety-black, while the caudal fin is orange or red. The pectoral fins are also orange, but are sometimes very dark. There are local races that lack the velvety-black coloration; in this case, the body is pale gray or very dark brown and the caudal fin is yellowish red. Specimens kept in unsuitable conditions are also paler.

Right: **Labeo bicolor**
Many aquarists use coconut shells or flowerpots to provide hiding-places for this species.

This is a hardy fish that has been known to live for several years in the home aquarium. It can be kept in a tank furnished with rocks and roots; these provide hiding-places and enable the fishes to establish territories. Although aggressive towards other members of its own species, the Red-tailed Labeo normally does not molest other species. The tank can also have patches of dense vegetation. The water must be soft, slightly acid, and filtered through peat. It is also advisable to have subdued lighting. The species has been bred on only very few occasions. The eggs hatch in 30 to 50 hours and at first the fry are gray.

This species is sometimes known as the Red-tailed 'Shark', but this is very misleading as it is in no way related to true sharks.

A practical reminder
Before setting up your tank, plan everything ahead and have all the necessary tools at hand. Gravel can be washed beforehand and rocks can be contoured and glued together to make cliffs and caves.

Family CYPRINIDAE

Rasbora einthoveni
Brilliant Rasbora
- **Distribution:** Southeast Asia: Thailand to Indonesia
- **Length:** Up to 3.5in (9cm)
- **Tank length:** 36in (90cm)
- **Diet:** Worms, crustaceans, insects, dried food
- **Water temperature:** 75 to 79°F (24 to 26°C)
- **Community tank**

Sometimes known as Einthoven's Rasbora, this is an elegant elongated shoaling species that swims mainly in the upper water layers. The back is yellow-brown to greenish brown and the belly is yellowish or silvery. The flanks are grayish blue with silvery iridescence and they are marked with a longitudinal black band, showing greenish iridescence, which extends from the tip of the snout to the caudal peduncle. Just above this band there is a reddish golden iridescent stripe. In some individuals the front rays of the dorsal fin are dark, but otherwise the fins are colorless. The female has a more convex ventral profile than the male.

This is a hardy species that can be kept in a tank with some

Above: **Rasbora einthoveni**
For breeding, this species needs a spacious, infusorian-free tank.

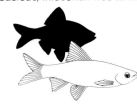

vegetation around the edges, leaving the shoal a good length of water for swimming. Although this species will live in medium-hard water it is much better—and essential for breeding—to use soft water that has been filtered through peat. For breeding, some aquarists use a tank without substrate, but with a few plants anchored at the bottom by glass rods. Spawning takes place at random in the water and when it has finished the parents must be removed, as they are spawn-eaters. The eggs will normally hatch in 26 to 30 hours and the fry will be free-swimming in three or four days. They can then be fed initially on rotifers and later on brine shrimp nauplii. About 25% of the water should be changed every month.

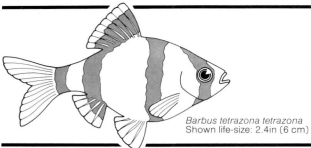

Barbus tetrazona tetrazona
Shown life-size: 2.4in (6 cm)

Family CYPRINIDAE
Rasbora dorsiocellata
Eye-spot Rasbora
● **Distribution:** Malayan Peninsula
and Sumatra
● **Length:** Up to 2.4in (6cm)
● **Tank length:** 18in (45cm)
● **Diet:** Worms, crustaceans,
insects, dried food
● **Water temperature:** 75 to 79°F
(24 to 26°C)
● **Community tank**

This is a relatively slender species
of *Rasbora*. However, the females
are slightly larger than the males,
with more rounded bellies. The
back of the Eye-spot Rasbora is
brown or brownish olive, and the
underparts are silvery-white. The
flanks are also silvery but with
bluish or violet iridescence,
depending upon the angle of the
light. There are two narrow black
longitudinal lines that may be
somewhat indistinct, running from
the back of the head to the base of
the tail. However, the
distinguishing feature of this fish is
the very prominent eye-spot in the
middle of the dorsal fin. The
caudal fin is yellow or pale red and
the iris of the eye is yellowish.

This is one of the smaller
Rasbora species and it should be
kept in a tank with marginal
vegetation and a sufficient length
of open water for swimming. The
water should be soft, slightly acid,
and filtered through peat. For
breeding, the tank can have a few
isolated clumps of plants. The
female will lay eggs among the
plants and both parents should
then be removed from the tank.
The eggs hatch in about 30 hours
and the fry at first hang more or
less motionless from the plants.
After three to five days they should
be free-swimming and can then
be fed on rotifers and small
nauplii.

The subspecies *R. dorsiocellata
macrophthalma*, which grows to
1.4in (3.5cm) long, has relatively
larger eyes, with the lower half of
the body iridescent blue-green.

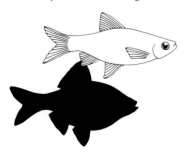

Right: **Rasbora dorsiocellata**
*This is an elegant and normally
very prolific member of the genus.
The eggs may be observed adhering to the uppersides of leaves.*

A practical reminder
Decide on the type of filtration system first.
If you have already put the gravel into the
tank, you will have to take it out again when
you come to fit a biological filter! Keep
thinking ahead at all times.

Rasbora maculata
Spotted Rasbora
- **Distribution:** Malay Archipelago, Sumatra
- **Length:** Up to 1in (2.5cm)
- **Tank length:** 12in (30cm)
- **Diet:** Worms, small crustaceans, dried food
- **Water temperature:** 70 to 77°F (21 to 25°C)
- **Community tank**

This is the pygmy of the *Rasbora* genus, and indeed one of the smallest aquarium fishes. The body is fairly squat, the female having distinctly rounded underparts. The general coloration of the Spotted Rasbora is brick-red with a tinge of greenish brown on the back. The belly is usually yellowish. There are blue-black markings of varying sizes above the pectoral fins, at the base of the anal fin, and on the caudal peduncle. The front rays of the dorsal and anal fins are dark, the other parts being yellowish or red. The caudal and ventral fins are reddish at the base.

This diminutive fish should be kept in a small shoal, in a tank with a dark substrate and areas of dense vegetation. The water should be soft, slightly acid, and filtered through peat. As in some of the other *Rasbora* species, breeding is not always easy. The breeding tank should not contain other species. It is best to keep the breeding pair in separate tanks for a week or two, and to supply them with a rich and varied diet. After they have been put together there is often a delay of some days before spawning takes place. After spawning has finished, the parents must be removed from the tank to prevent them from eating their own brood. The eggs hatch in 24 to 30 hours and the fry are free-swimming three or four days later, and ready to feed on the smallest live food.

Right: **Rasbora maculata** ♀
*The colors of this fish appear
vivid against a dark substrate.*

Rasbora heteromorpha
Harlequin Fish
- **Distribution:** Thailand, Malay Archipelago, Indonesia
- **Length:** Up to 1.8in (4.5cm)
- **Tank length:** 12in (30cm)
- **Diet:** Worms, crustaceans, insects, dried food
- **Water temperature:** 72 to 77°F (22 to 25°C)
- **Community tank**

This is an old favorite, introduced into the aquarium as long ago as 1906. The body is stockier than the other species of *Rasbora,* but the male is more slender than the female. The general coloration of the Harlequin Fish is silvery. The back is bright pink to violet and the flanks are a more delicate pink. The underparts are pale silvery-white. The characteristic feature is the wedge-shaped blue-black marking on the rear half of the body. In the male this marking is sharply defined and its lower, front edge reaches down to the center point of the belly. In the female, this marking has a much hazier outline and does not extend as far down the belly. The dorsal fin is red, becoming yellowish towards the tip. The outer rays of the caudal fin are red, the inner rays pale yellow.

Harlequin fishes should be kept in a small shoal, in a tank with areas of dense vegetation arranged to leave sufficient space for swimming. This will mostly take place in the upper water layers. In this species it is important that the water be soft, slightly acid, and filtered through peat. After vigorous driving, the breeding pair arrive beneath a leaf. The male curls his tail around the female and spawning takes place. The eggs hatch in 26 to 30 hours and the fry are free-swimming three to five days later. Feed them on rotifers and small nauplii. The fry grow quickly.

Left: **Rasbora heteromorpha** ♂♂
*Many aquarists breed this species
successfully, but sometimes only
with difficulty. Spawning is often
delayed for a few days after the
breeding pair is put together.*

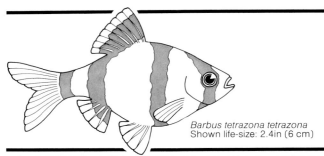

Barbus tetrazona tetrazona
Shown life-size: 2.4in (6 cm)

Family CYPRINIDAE
Rasbora trilineata
Scissors-tail
● **Distribution:** Malay Archipelago, Sumatra, Borneo
● **Length:** Up to 6in (15cm)
● **Tank length:** 24in (60cm)
● **Diet:** Worms, crustaceans, insects, dried food
● **Water temperature:** 66 to 77°F (19 to 25°C)
● **Community tank**

This is an elongated, laterally compressed *Rasbora* species with a deeply forked and well-developed tail. Females can be distinguished by their more rounded underparts. In general, the body of the Scissors-tail is

very translucent, particularly in young fish. The back is green to olive-yellow, and the belly is silvery-white. The flanks are grayish yellow, becoming more silvery when seen in reflected light. A narrow dark longitudinal line starts above the ventral fins and extends back along the middle of the flanks to the tail. A thinner dark line runs from the base of the anal fin along the underside of the caudal peduncle to the tail. The pattern of the caudal fin lobes is particularly striking. Each lobe has a broad black transverse marking, but the main characteristic of this species is the continuous scissoring action of the two lobes, hence the popular name.

This is an active shoaling fish, unlikely to exceed a length of 2.8in (7cm) in an aquarium. The tank should have a dark substrate and marginal vegetation to leave a good length of open water for swimming. After an active courtship with driving, spawning takes place in the open water. The eggs sink to the bottom, and hatch in 26 to 30 hours. The

Above: **Rasbora trilineata**
This is an active fish that needs soft water for breeding. Water should be low on infusorians.

parents must be removed as soon as spawning has finished. The fry should be free-swimming in three to five days and can then be fed on rotifers and the smallest brine shrimp nauplii.

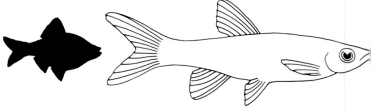

A practical reminder
Large rocks should be stood on the tank floor (or filter plate) before any gravel is added. This gives them extra stability. Otherwise, digging fishes may easily cause them to topple and crack the tank glass.

Left: **Tanichthys albonubes**
This is one of the most undemanding of all fishes, partly because of its temperature range.

Family CYPRINIDAE
Tanichthys albonubes
White Cloud Mountain Minnow
- **Distribution:** China, near Canton
- **Length:** Up to 1.6in (4cm)
- **Tank length:** 12in (30cm)
- **Diet:** Worms, small crustaceans, dried food
- **Water temperature:** 68 to 72°F (20 to 22°C) in summer; 61 to 64°F (16 to 18°C) in winter
- **Community tank**

A Chinese boy named Tan is said to have discovered this fish on the White Cloud Mountain near Canton around 1930. The genus name, *Tanichthys,* comes from the boy's name; the species name, *albonubes,* means 'white cloud'.

The body is elongated and moderately compressed. The small mouth faces slightly upward and there are no barbels. The back is dark brown or olive-brown with greenish iridescence, and the belly is white. The flanks are paler than the back and strikingly marked with a narrow iridescent golden band, bordered below by a thin dark blue line. Under this line is a broader red to chestnut-brown longitudinal band. The base of the dorsal fin is red, and the edge is silvery-blue.

This is a particularly hardy species and ideal for a beginner. In the wild it is found in mountain streams, so a regular replacement of a portion of the water is beneficial. The tank can have short plants around the edges and isolated clumps of Milfoil (*Myriophyllum*). The composition of the water is not important.

For breeding, the water temperature should be allowed to rise to 68 to 72°F (20 to 22°C). Spawning takes place among the plant clumps. The male curls the rear part of his body around the female, and the eggs adhere to the plants. Provided they are well fed, the parents do not usually attack their eggs, which hatch in about 48 hours. The fry feed at the surface on pulverized dried food or tiny live food such as rotifers.

Family CYPRINIDAE
Rasbora vaterifloris
Pearly Rasbora
- **Distribution:** Sri Lanka
- **Length:** Up to 1.6in (4cm)
- **Tank length:** 18in (45cm)
- **Diet:** Worms, small crustaceans, dried food
- **Water temperature:** 75 to 77°F (24 to 25°C)
- **Community tank**

This is a relatively short, tall-bodied, and laterally compressed *Rasbora* species, with a deeply forked tail and pointed fins. The back is green and the belly pale orange to almost white. Flanks are grayish green with a delicate pearly iridescence that varies

according to the angle of the light. The iris of the eye is golden-red. The dorsal and anal fins are orange or red and the base of the caudal fin is similarly colored. The fins of the female are more yellowish, but the pectoral fins of both sexes are colorless.

For this very beautiful species of *Rasbora,* the tank should have a certain amount of vegetation and subdued lighting. For breeding, it is strongly recommended that there be no substrate, but the tank should have groups of plants with feathery leaves, such as Milfoil (*Myriophyllum*). These plants can be anchored to the bottom with glass rods. The water must be soft, slightly acid, and filtered

Above: **Rasbora vaterifloris**
Opinions differ, but this fish is not usually difficult to breed.

through peat. After a period of driving, spawning takes place among the plants and the parents should then be removed. The eggs hatch in about 30 hours, and once the fry are free-swimming they should be fed at first on rotifers. After about a week they can be offered very small brine shrimp nauplii.

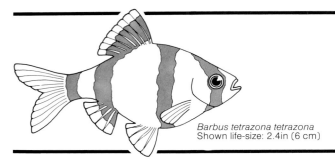
Barbus tetrazona tetrazona
Shown life-size: 2.4in (6 cm)

Family COBITIDAE

Small to medium-sized, these are mainly bottom-living fishes with species in North Africa, Europe, and particularly Southeast Asia. They have a characteristic spine in front of the eye. Air swallowed at the surface passes along the alimentary tract to the hind-gut where its oxygen is absorbed by blood capillaries.

Family COBITIDAE

Botia hymenophysa
Banded Loach
- **Distribution:** Thailand, Malaya, Borneo, Sumatra, Java
- **Length:** Up to 8.3in (21cm), possibly more
- **Tank length:** 24in (60cm)
- **Diet:** Worms, crustaceans, insects, dried food
- **Water temperature:** 77 to 86°F (25 to 30°C)
- **Species tank**

This is an elongated and slender loach with a conical pointed head. Its mouth faces downward and it has three pairs of barbels. Below the eye there is a forked, erectile spine; its length is the same as the diameter of the eye. The upperparts are brownish or yellowish brown and the underparts are pale yellow. The flanks are grayish yellow or gray-green; 11 or more dark transverse

Below: **Botia hymenophysa**
The pattern is variable; there may be up to 15 dark transverse bars.

bars, which are positioned slightly obliquely, mark the flanks. These bars are separated by narrow pale areas, but they do not reach the belly. The fins are yellowish or greenish; the dorsal and caudal fins have thin dark bands.

This rather shy loach can be aggressive. It lives on the bottom, remaining hidden by day but coming out at night to burrow for insect larvae and worms. It can be kept in a tank with a soft substrate and sufficient rocks and roots to provide plenty of hiding-places. The water should be soft, and at least a quarter of it should be renewed every month. As with Hora's Loach, there are no external sex differences and the species has not yet been bred in captivity.

The related *Botia berdmorei*, up to 10in (25cm) long, comes from Thailand and Burma. It is an elongated loach, similar in shape to *B. hymenophysa,* and it also has three pairs of barbels. The general coloration is cream or pale yellow. The flanks have 10 or 11 rather indistinct transverse bars—much fainter than in *B. hymenophysa*—and numerous dark dots and streaks arranged in longitudinal rows. The fins are yellowish. This species, too, has not yet been bred in captivity.

Family COBITIDAE

Botia macracantha
Clown Loach
- **Distribution:** Sumatra, Borneo
- **Length:** Up to 12in (30cm)
- **Tank length:** 24in (60cm)
- **Diet:** Worms, crustaceans, plant matter, dried food
- **Water temperature:** 75 to 86°F (24 to 30°C)
- **Community tank**

The most colorful and most popular of the loaches, the Clown Loach is moderately elongated and laterally compressed. It has an arched back, an almost straight belly profile, and four pairs of barbels. The barbels located on the lower jaw are very small. The head is large and the mouth faces downward, with thick fleshy lips, The spine in front of the eye is quite short. The general coloration is bright orange and the flanks are crossed by three wide, wedge-shaped black bands. The first band runs from the top of the skull across the eye and then obliquely down to the region of the mouth; the second starts in front of the dorsal fin and extends down to the

belly; and the third covers a large part of the caudal peduncle and runs down onto the anal fin. The pectoral, ventral, and caudal fins are red; the dorsal and anal fins are yellowish with black markings.

This is a very attractive loach that is not as shy as the other species. Often active by day, it can be kept quite successfully in a community tank with other fishes. In fact, Clown Loaches have even been seen to form a small shoal with armored catfishes. The tank should have a soft substrate that will allow the fishes to burrow for live food. Rocks and roots suitably placed will provide shelter. The water should be soft.

Once they are established, Clown Loaches live for several years in an aquarium, where they grow slowly but never reach the size recorded for wild specimens. They have not been bred in captivity—perhaps because they do not reach full sexual maturity.

Right: **Botia macracantha**
Also known as the Tiger Botia, this is the most colorful loach. There are no external sex differences.

A practical reminder
Most aquarists contour the gravel to add the interest of varying levels in the tank. If it slopes down from the back to front, accumulated detritus is easily seen and siphoned off before it becomes a menace.

Left: **Botia horae**
This very active loach can be kept successfully with larger tankmates.

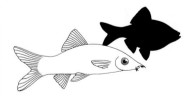

Family COBITIDAE
Botia horae
Hora's Loach
- **Distribution:** Thailand
- **Length:** Up to 4in (10cm)
- **Tank length:** 12in (30cm)
- **Diet:** Worms, crustaceans, insects, plant matter, dried food
- **Water temperature:** 79 to 86°F (26 to 30°C)
- **Species tank:** Possible for community tank, but should be carefully watched

This is a squat, laterally compressed loach with a straight belly profile and prominently arched back. The dorsal fin lies directly above the ventral fins and therefore well forward of the anal fin. There are only eight soft rays in the dorsal fin. The head is pointed and relatively long, and the mouth faces downward and has three pairs of quite short barbels. Below the eye there is a two-pointed spine that can be

erected and locked into position. The general coloration is yellowish green with a paler belly and grayish upperparts. The flanks have four quite short narrow transverse bars but these are sometimes not very distinct. A black stripe starts at the tip of the snout and runs along the ridge of the back. It ends just in front of the caudal fin where it joins an intense black transverse bar on the caudal peduncle. The caudal fin is

yellowish, and sometimes has dark spots. The other fins are either almost colorless or gray-green.

This is a hardy and quite peaceful loach that lives near the bottom. It remains hidden by day but comes out at night (unless the aquarium is brightly lit) to search for food. It can be kept in a tank with a soft substrate and a number of rocks and roots arranged to give plenty of hiding-places. The water should be soft, and about a quarter of it should be changed once a month or so. There are no external sex differences and the species has not yet been bred in captivity.

117

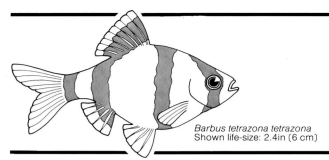

Barbus tetrazona tetrazona
Shown life-size: 2.4in (6 cm)

Family COBITIDAE
Botia modesta
Orange-finned Loach
- **Distribution:** Thailand, Vietnam, Malaysia
- **Length:** Up to 4in (10cm)
- **Tank length:** 12in (30cm)
- **Diet:** Worms, crustaceans, insects, dried food
- **Water temperature:** 77 to 86°F (25 to 30°C)
- **Species tank**

Though rather stocky and lacking the typical snakelike body of most loaches, the Orange-finned Loach has a laterally compressed shape and other features that easily identify it as a cobitid. It has three pairs of barbels. The back is moderately arched and the belly profile very slightly convex. The front rays of the dorsal fin lie directly above the ventral fins and well in front of the anal fin—again, this is a characteristic of most tropical loaches. The caudal peduncle is short but quite high. The general coloration is gray-green to grayish blue and slightly darker on the head. There is a dark marking at the root of the tail but it is usually indistinct. Otherwise, there are no transverse bars or other markings that are usually found in so many of the related species. The caudal fin is bright yellow, and the other fins are grayish yellow.

This is a hardy but rather shy loach that usually hides away during the day and comes out at night when it burrows for small

crustaceans and insect larvae. It can be kept in a tank with a soft substrate and scattered rocks and roots. Since this fish is a vigorous digger, rooted plants are not suitable for this aquarium. However, a few floating plants would provide decoration in the upper parts of the tank. This species has not yet been bred in captivity.

Loaches utilize their intestines

as an accessory respiratory organ. This enables them to live in oxygen-depleted waters. They rise to the surface and gulp a mouthful of air, which passes along the alimentary canal to the hind gut. There the oxygen is extracted by the dense accumulation of capillaries that line this part of the gut; the residue of air is passed out at the anus. However, clean water and aeration are important.

Above: **Botia modesta**
Active at night, this species, like other loaches, uses its barbels to detect food in the substrate.

A practical reminder
Terraces can be formed by using pieces of rock embedded in the gravel to hold back higher areas. Try to achieve an illusion of space and avoid perfectly flat 'aquascapes' and symmetrically grouped plants.

Family COBITIDAE
Botia sidthimunki
Dwarf Loach
- **Distribution:** Thailand
- **Length:** Up to 1.4in (3.5cm)
- **Tank length:** 12in (30cm)
- **Diet:** Worms, crustaceans, insects, plant matter, dried food
- **Water temperature:** 77 to 86°F (25 to 30°C)
- **Species tank**

The dorsal and ventral profiles of this elongated small loach are only slightly convex. The scales are very small but are not present on the head. The mouth has three pairs of barbels. The back is brownish and the belly is silvery-white. The flanks are golden-brown with a very variable pattern of dark brown markings arranged in four longitudinal bands. Two of these bands are close to the ridge of the back; the others appear at about the level of the vertebral column. These longitudinal bands are connected to one another by similarly colored transverse bars giving an almost netlike appearance. In young individuals the dark markings are black. The fins are almost colorless.

In the wild this loach lives in shoals that, unlike most other species of *Botia,* swim above the bottom—mostly in the middle water layers. It is active by day and night. In an aquarium, Dwarf Loaches can be kept in a small shoal in a tank with a soft substrate and a number of rocks and roots arranged to form suitable hiding-places. The water should be soft and approximately one quarter of it should be replaced every month.

The spines in front of the eyes, which occur in all loaches, are raised when the fish is excited or threatened. The spines may get caught in the meshes of a net when the fish is being moved from one tank to another. It is important to disentangle the fish very gently. Also, great care should be taken to avoid the sharp spines, which can cause painful wounds to the hands.

Below: **Botia sidthimunki**
An active loach best kept in a shoal.

Family GYMNOTIDAE
This is a small family with species in Central and South America. These fishes have no dorsal, caudal, or ventral fins. The very long anal fin is the main organ of propulsion. Air swallowed at the surface is used for respiration. The scales are small and very numerous.

Family GYMNOTIDAE
Gymnotus carapo
Banded Knifefish
- **Distribution:** Central and South America, Guatemala to Rio de la Plata
- **Length:** Up to 24in (60cm)
- **Tank length:** 48in (120cm)
- **Diet:** Worms, insects, meat, fish, plant matter, dried food
- **Water temperature:** 73 to 83°F (23 to 28°C)
- **Species tank**

The front part of the body of this eellike fish is almost cylindrical; the rear part is compressed and ends in a point. There are no dorsal, caudal, or ventral fins. However, the anal fin has a very long base that starts below the head. This fin

Left: **Gymnotus carapo**
Active mainly at night, this fish uses its long anal fin to move.

is the main organ of propulsion—its undulations enable the fish to move backward or forward. The numerous scales are very small. The mouth is very broad and armed with conical teeth. Coloration varies. Young individuals are flesh-colored to pale yellow and marked with several broad transverse bars. Old specimens, on the other hand, have dark background coloration marked with oblique pale bars.

The Banded Knifefish has a weak electric organ which emits pulses that help the fish orientate in murky waters. It also has accessory respiration, so that it can rise to the surface and swallow air from which the oxygen is absorbed. This enables the fish to live in waters that are poor in oxygen. It is aggressive towards other members of its own species, so that the tank must be spacious and furnished with numerous roots to provide hiding-places. It is mainly active at night when it comes out to hunt for food. If the tank is kept fairly dark it may come out by day to feed.

The Banded Knifefish has not yet been bred in captivity.

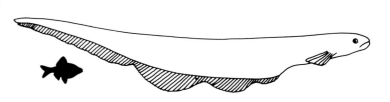

THE CATFISHES

Above: *Corydoras aeneus,* one of the best-known
of the South American armored catfishes.
Right: A swampy area in Trinidad. Such places
are home to many types of catfishes.

The order Siluriformes contains some 30 families with about 2,000 species, which have an almost worldwide distribution in fresh waters, particularly in Africa and South America. A few marine species occur in tropical and subtropical coastal waters.

The skin of catfishes is naked or covered with bony plates, but it never has true scales. Most species live on or near the bottom. They are solitary fishes, mainly active at dusk or during the night. Only a few form shoals. Their nocturnal habits are related to their poorly developed eyes, and the possession of highly sensitive barbels around the mouth. These structures help the fish to orientate in darkness and to find food.

Several of the families contain species that make excellent aquarium fishes. These include:

The Siluridae of Europe, Africa, and Asia, which lack scales or bony plates and an adipose fin, but have a long anal fin, a very small dorsal fin, and one to six pairs of long barbels.

The Schilbeidae of Africa and southern Asia, with two to four pairs of barbels and a small adipose fin. Some are active by day.

The Clariidae of Africa and southern Asia, usually with a long dorsal and anal fin, no adipose fin, and four pairs of long barbels. Most species in this family are too large for domestic aquariums.

The Mochocidae (or Mochokidae) of Africa south of the Sahara, which have three pairs of barbels and a very large adipose fin.

The Pimelodidae of tropical America with three pairs of long barbels and an adipose fin.

The Callichthyidae of South America and Trinidad, with a well-developed armor of overlapping bony plates, an adipose fin, and a varying number of barbels.

Finally, the Loricariidae, restricted to northern and central South America, with a few rows of bony plates along each flank, and an adipose fin in some species, not in others.

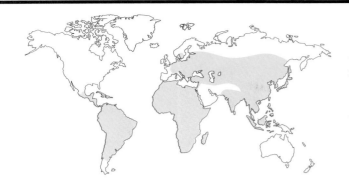

Left: The many catfish families have an extremely wide distribution, occurring in all continents except Australia. Most catfishes live in tropical fresh waters but a few occur in marine habitats, particularly off the coasts of southern Asia. Within the group there are vegetarians that suck algae from rocks, carnivores that pursue other fishes, and also true scavengers that burrow in the substrate for scraps of food.

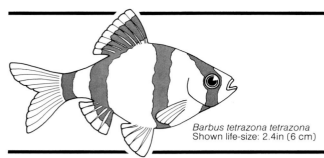

Barbus tetrazona tetrazona
Shown life-size: 2.4in (6 cm)

Family SILURIDAE
Kryptopterus bicirrhis
Glass Catfish
- **Distribution:** Thailand, Java, Sumatra, Borneo
- **Length:** Up to 4in (10cm)
- **Tank length:** 18in (45cm)
- **Diet:** Worms, crustaceans, insects, dried food
- **Water temperature:** 70 to 79°F (21 to 26°C)
- **Community tank**

The body of the Glass Catfish is scaleless and very strongly compressed. The backbone and other internal organs are clearly visible; in fact, this is one of the most transparent of all tropical fishes. There is one pair of long

Below: **Kryptopterus bicirrhis**
Many aquarists have tried to breed this attractive and unusual fish, but so far without success.

barbels on the upper jaw and these can be extended forwards. The dorsal fin consists of only a single ray and there is no adipose fin. The caudal fin is deeply forked and its lower lobe may be slightly longer than the upper lobe. The anal fin is very long, but its rear end does not connect with the caudal fin. In general, the body is highly iridescent and the actual colors seen depend upon the angle of the light.

Kryptopterus bicirrhis is a delicate species. It swims mostly in the upper and middle water layers with the body positioned obliquely and head turned upward. The tail constantly moves from side to side. These diurnal catfishes can be kept in a tank with patches of vegetation where they can hide. They do swim about in the open water, but not as actively as the African Glass Catfish, *Eutropiellus debauwi.* They should be kept in a small shoal, possibly with other species of about the same size. Under no circumstances should a single specimen be kept on its own because it will soon languish.

This species is not known to have been bred in captivity.

Family SCHILBEIDAE
Eutropiellus debauwi
African Glass Catfish
- **Distribution:** Central Africa: Congo Basin
- **Length:** Up to 3.2in (8cm)
- **Tank length:** 24in (60cm)
- **Diet:** Worms, crustaceans, insects, dried food
- **Water temperature:** 73 to 79°F (23 to 26°C)
- **Community tank**

African Glass Catfish is elongated and small with the caudal peduncle much laterally compressed. Its short dorsal fin—positioned above the pectoral fins—has a spiny first ray. There is a relatively well-developed adipose fin. The anal fin is very long and the caudal fin deeply forked. There are three pairs of short barbels on the upper jaw. The body is translucent with silvery underparts. The flanks are marked with three prominent longitudinal bands, which become more pronounced with increasing age. The head is quite short with a small terminal mouth. The eyes are large.

This is a very peaceful but active

Right: **Eutropiellus debauwi**
This species is not as delicate as the Glass Catfish, but it has the same characteristic tail-wagging. A shoal of six is ideal.

catfish. It does well in a tank with other species of a similar size. Because single specimens do not thrive, it should always be kept in a shoal. The tank should have a few areas of vegetation. However, there must be plenty of open space for swimming—this species seems to be always on the move. The water should be soft and slightly acid. When swimming, the body is positioned rather obliquely in the water with the tail downward. The caudal fin appears to beat from side to side constantly—an activity that is not completely understood.

This species has not yet been bred in captivity.

A practical reminder
Heaters should be mounted clear of the
gravel to ensure adequate water circulation
around them. Nonmetallic heater/thermostat
clips are preferable as they are nontoxic to
fishes and rust-proof.

Family MOCHOCIDAE
Synodontis nigriventris
Upside-down Catfish

- **Distribution:** Central Africa: Congo Basin
- **Length:** Up to 3.2in (8cm)
- **Tank length:** 24in (60cm)
- **Diet:** Insects, crustaceans, plant matter, dried food
- **Water temperature:** 73 to 81°F (23 to 27°C)
- **Community tank**

Upside-down Catfish is squat, scaleless, and only slightly compressed laterally. It has three pairs of barbels—one smooth pair on the upper jaw, and two feathered pairs on the lower jaw. The adipose fin is particularly long, and the caudal fin is deeply forked with pointed lobes. The general coloration is cream to pale gray with dark brown or black markings. These patterns sometimes fuse to form transverse bars. Though the fins are colorless, they have dark markings. The belly is black. The light-colored back and black belly, in accordance with its usual upside-down position, give the fish its popular name.

This is a peaceful catfish that is generally active at night and swims in shoals. By swimming upside-down the fish is able to browse algae from the under-surfaces of leaves. It can be kept in a tank furnished with rocks and roots and a number of plants with large leaves. The composition of the water is not critical.

This unusual fish has been bred on only a few occasions. Shortly before spawning, the brownish coloration changes to yellowish white and this makes the markings of the fish even more conspicuous. The pale yellowish eggs, with a diameter of about 0.1in (2.5mm), hatch in seven or eight days, and the fry live for four days on the contents of the yolk-sac. They can then be fed on tiny brine shrimp nauplii. At first they swim belly downward, but after about eight weeks they start to swim upside-down.

Left: **Synodontis nigriventris**
*The mottled pattern of the upturned
belly probably helps this catfish
to remain undetected by
predatory birds. Difficult to breed.*

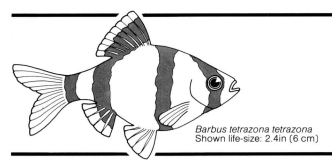
Barbus tetrazona tetrazona
Shown life-size: 2.4in (6 cm)

Family PIMELODIDAE
Pimelodella gracilis
Graceful Pimelodella
- **Distribution:** South America: in Orinoco, Amazon, La Plata
- **Length:** Up to 6.7in (17cm), possibly more
- **Tank length:** 24in (60cm)
- **Diet:** Worms, insects
- **Water temperature:** 66 to 75°F (19 to 24°C)
- **Community tank:** Keep with larger species only

Young specimens of *Pimelodella gracilis* have dark gray upperparts and silvery-white or silvery-green flanks. A black longitudinal band extends from the gill cover to the base of the caudal fin. Adult females are similarly colored, but adult males are a uniform blue-black with strong iridescence. The fins in both sexes are colorless. There is a pair of very long barbels on the upper jaw, and two pairs of shorter barbels on the lower jaw.

The Graceful Pimelodella is a fish suitable for a tank with other fishes of its own size, but it should not be kept with smaller species.

The tank should have rocks and roots to provide hiding-places and some plants around the edges. However, sufficient space should be allowed for swimming. The water should be soft. This species is mainly active at dusk, when it swims about in the middle and lower water layers. It is not known to have been bred in captivity.

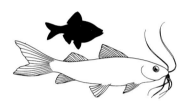

Below: Pimelodella gracilis
This is a useful fish to have in a community tank as it spends much of its time scavenging for waste food. Keep in subdued light.

Family CALLICHTHYIDAE
Corydoras aeneus
Bronze Corydoras
- **Distribution:** South America: Trinidad, Venezuela, southwards to La Plata
- **Length:** Up to 2.8in (7cm)
- **Tank length:** 18in (45cm)
- **Diet:** Worms, crustaceans, insects, plant matter, dried food
- **Water temperature:** 66 to 79°F (19 to 26°C)
- **Community tank**

This is perhaps the most commonly kept species of *Corydoras.* The body is stocky and deep, with a very arched back. The female is more robust than the male, and is usually a little longer. Each side of the body has two rows of bony plates, the upper row having 21 to 23 plates, the lower 19 to 21. The upper jaw has two pairs of barbels, which, if folded back, would reach almost as far as the gill opening. The background coloration is yellow-brown or a delicate reddish brown. The head and flanks have strong iridescence that appears greenish, coppery, or golden,

depending upon the angle of the light. The middle part of the flanks is usually darker. The fins are grayish and without markings.

The tank should have a sandy substrate. Decorative plants, such as *Cryptocoryne,* can be used sparingly. The composition of the water is not critical although it should not be too acid.

Spawning is preceded by very vigorous driving, and it has been observed that the female often takes the more active part. The actual spawning may go on for one to three hours, with the female laying from five to 12 eggs at a time, with a final total of up to 200 eggs. The eggs are usually laid on the plants and they hatch in five or six days. The fry fall to the bottom, where they feed at first on infusorians and rotifers.

Right: Corydoras aeneus
This is another fish that scavenges for waste food in the aquarium.

Family CALLICHTHYIDAE
Callichthys callichthys
Armored Catfish
- **Distribution:** South America: eastern Brazil to La Plata
- **Length:** Up to 4in (10cm), possibly more
- **Tank length:** 24in (60cm)
- **Diet:** Fish, insects, plant matter, dried food
- **Water temperature:** 68 to 79°F (20 to 26°C)
- **Community tank**

This elongated catfish has an arched back and an almost straight belly profile. The caudal peduncle is tall and laterally

compressed. The head of the Armored Catfish is broad and flattened, and it has relatively small eyes. The upper jaws carry two pairs of barbels. The body is enclosed in two series of bony plates—a characteristic of the whole family. The upper row has 26 to 29 plates, the lower row 25 to 28. In addition, between the dorsal and adipose fins there are some small bony plates separated by naked skin from the upper row of lateral plates. The adipose fin has a powerful spine in front and the caudal fin is rounded. In the males the first pectoral finray is thickened. The coloration is not particularly attractive. The upper-parts are dark olive-green or dark

green with a slight bluish or violet sheen; the underparts are grayish blue. Both areas have a variable number of dark spots. The fins are translucent and grayish with dark spots, the edges red or yellowish orange. In general, the colors are more intense in the males than in the females.

This catfish remains more or less hidden by day and comes out at night to hunt for fish and insects. For this reason the aquarium should have rocks and roots to provide hiding-places, and some areas of dense vegetation. For breeding, a nest of air bubbles coated with saliva is built on the underside of a large leaf. The eggs are attached to the

nest and guarded by the male. They hatch in four to six days. The parents should then be removed. The fry live for about two days on the contents of the large yolk-sac and will then eat small live food.

Right: Callichthys callichthys
It is quite normal for this species to swallow air at the surface for intestinal respiration The male grunts while guarding the eggs.

A practical reminder
Make all electrical connections *outside* the aquarium. Do not switch on heaters unless they are covered by water. Always switch off the power before putting your hands into the aquarium for any reason.

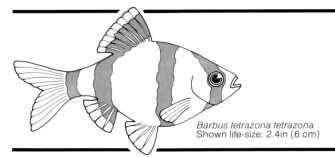

Barbus tetrazona tetrazona
Shown life-size: 2.4in (6 cm)

Right: **Corydoras julii**
This is one of the most striking species in the genus Corydoras. *The barbels are relatively short.*

Family CALLICHTHYIDAE
Corydoras julii
Leopard Corydoras
● **Distribution:** South America: Brazil, in lower Amazon tributaries
● **Length:** Up to 2.4in (6cm)
● **Tank length:** 18in (45cm)
● **Diet:** Worms, crustaceans, insects, plant matter, dried food
● **Water temperature:** 66 to 79°F (19 to 26°C)
● **Community tank**

Leopard Corydoras is a fairly squat armored catfish with an arched forehead and two pairs of relatively short barbels on the upper jaws. The armor on the flanks consists of 21 or 22 bony plates in the upper row and 20 or 21 in the lower row. There is a spine towards the front of the adipose fin. The general coloration is silvery-gray with delicate green iridescence. A characteristic pattern of black spots covers the back and flanks but not the underparts. On the gill cover and the upper side of the head, the spots are replaced by a pattern of wormlike squiggles. Near the midline of the body, between the two rows of bony plates, there is a wavy or almost jagged dark longitudinal band that extends from the end of the gill cover to the end of the caudal peduncle. A silvery-gray line borders each side of this prominent band. The outer part of the dorsal fin has a large black marking, and the caudal and anal fins have a few rows of dark spots.

Corydoras julii is an active fish best kept in a small shoal. The tank should have a soft sandy substrate because—like other species of *Corydoras*—Leopard Corydoras lives on or near the bottom, where it likes to burrow. It has been bred though not easily or often. Spawning may take place over a period of several days.

This catfish has also been known as *Corydoras leopardus*.

Family CALLICHTHYIDAE
Corydoras melanistius
Black-spotted Corydoras
● **Distribution:** South America: Guyana, in the Essequibo River
● **Length:** Up to 2.4in (6cm)
● **Tank length:** 18in (45cm)
● **Diet:** Worms, crustaceans, insects, plant matter, dried food
● **Water temperature:** 66 to 79°F (19 to 26°C)
● **Community tank**

A small squat catfish with an arched back, the Black-spotted Corydoras has two pairs of barbels on the upper jaw. The armor on the flanks consists of 21 to 23 bony plates in the upper row and 19 or 20 in the lower row. The rear edge of the dorsal fin is concave. A scattered, irregular pattern of brown dots marks the flanks, which can be grayish white or yellowish white with a slight reddish tinge. Starting at the top of the head, an almost triangular marking runs down across the eye to the lower part of the head. Also a wedge-shaped black bar extends from the front of the dorsal fin to a position just above the insertion of the pectoral fins. Small dark dots, which may be arranged in rows, mark the caudal and anal fins. The other fins are usually colorless and without markings.

Corydoras melanistius is a hardy, active catfish best kept in a shoal. The fishes swim near the bottom, where they scavenge for scraps of food. In fact, all the species of *Corydoras* are marvelous scavengers that help to keep the tank clean. The tank should have a soft, sandy substrate, in which the fishes will burrow with their snouts. However, this activity will usually discourage plant growth. After a period of driving, spawning may take place at intervals over several days. The eggs hatch in five or six days. The fry fall to the bottom, where they feed at first on various kinds of very tiny live food.

Right: **Corydoras melanistius**
This rather soberly colored armored catfish with short barbels is an efficient scavenger.

A practical reminder
The air pump should be situated above the water level if possible. Failing this, an anti-siphon loop in the air tubing will prevent water siphoning into the pump if it stops due to an electrical failure.

Left: **Corydoras myersi**
This particularly attractive species has been bred in the aquarium, but probably not very frequently. It is a hardy, inquisitive fish that is well worth keeping.

Family CALLICHTHYIDAE
Corydoras myersi
Myers' Corydoras
- **Distribution:** South America: upper Amazon River in small tributaries
- **Length:** Up to 2.4in (6cm)
- **Tank length:** 18in (45cm)
- **Diet:** Worms, crustaceans, insects, plant matter, dried food
- **Water temperature:** 66 to 79°F (19 to 26°C)
- **Community tank**

A fairly deep-bodied armored catfish with a slightly arched back and three pairs of barbels, *Corydoras myersi* was first given a scientific description in 1942. The lateral armor has 22 or 23 bony plates in the upper row and 20 or 21 plates in the lower row. This is one of the more brightly colored of the *Corydoras* species. The general coloration is orange, but the top of the head and the throat are yellowish. Starting behind the head there is a broad, almost black band that extends back to the upper part of the tail base. The area around the gill cover may be iridescent green, and the eye and its immediate surroundings are very dark. The fins, which have no markings, are pale gray.

The many species of *Corydoras,* and also *Callichthys callichthys,* supplement the oxygen-gathering activity of their gills with an accessory respiratory organ. When living in waters that are low in oxygen or polluted, they rise to the surface and take in air through the mouth. The air is then passed through the alimentary tract to the hind-gut, where blood vessels extract the oxygen. Residual air passes out through the anus. If the atmosphere is sufficiently humid, it is not unusual for this and other species of *Corydoras* to come out on land and move about, using the spines of the pectorals as stilts to raise the body above the ground.

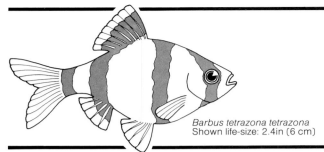

Barbus tetrazona tetrazona
Shown life-size: 2.4in (6 cm)

Family CALLICHTHYIDAE

Corydoras paleatus
Peppered Corydoras
● **Distribution:** South America, in southeastern Brazil and La Plata Basin
● **Length:** Up to 2.8in (7cm)
● **Tank length:** 18in (45cm)
● **Diet:** Worms, crustaceans, insects, plant matter, dried food
● **Water temperature:** 66 to 79°F (19 to 26°C)
● **Community tank**

Peppered Corydoras is a tall-bodied catfish with two pairs of rather short barbels. The lateral armor has 22 to 24 bony plates in the upper row and 20 to 22 in the lower row. In the caudal fin the upper lobe is somewhat larger than the lower lobe. The dorsal fin is tall and pointed, and in the male the outer edge is ragged. The upperparts are dark olive-green or olive-brown and the underparts are pale yellow. The flanks are greenish with some iridescence, marked with large black spots that sometimes fuse to form transverse bands. This happens to some extent in the upperparts, and the body is more or less covered with small black dots. The dorsal and anal fins are gray, with a few dark dots. Dark spots also mark the caudal fin. These spots increase in number towards the tip of the fin.

Corydoras paleatus is probably the best-known and most widely kept species of *Corydoras*. This is not surprising, since the fish is very undemanding. The tank should have a soft bottom—preferably of sand—so that the fish can burrow. The composition of the water is not critical.

This is undoubtedly the beginner's catfish. It came into the aquarium world in the early 1890s, but it had already been bred in Paris in 1878 by M. Charbonnier. The breeding behavior is the same as in other species of *Corydoras*. This species may sometimes continue to spawn over several days.

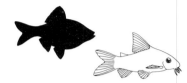

Below: **Corydoras paleatus** ♂
This is the easiest to breed of all the Corydoras *catfishes. It is ideal for a beginner, being hardy and long-lived in the aquarium.*

Family CALLICHTHYIDAE

Corydoras reticulatus
Reticulated Corydoras
● **Distribution:** South America, in the Amazon River near Monte Alegre
● **Length:** Up to 2.8in (7cm)
● **Tank length:** 18in (45cm)
● **Diet:** Worms, crustaceans, insects, plant matter, dried food
● **Water temperature:** 66 to 79°F (19 to 26°C)
● **Community tank**

First described in 1938, Reticulated Corydoras is one of the most attractive of the armored catfishes. The body is high-backed and rather short and it has two pairs of barbels. The head, flanks, and back are iridescent greenish or dark brown, marked with a bold netted pattern in black. The much paler belly shows little trace of this pattern. The young are gray to reddish with rather inconspicuous markings, and the full netted pattern is attained only when the fishes are sexually mature. There is a thin yellowish stripe running along the back from the base of the dorsal fin to the caudal fin. The dorsal fin itself is dark at the base with black dots in its outer part. The anal and caudal fins also have dark markings, but those on the caudal fin are arranged in rows. In general, the female is not as brightly colored as the male.

Spawning behavior follows the customary pattern for species of *Corydoras*. As usual the parents must be removed from the tank as soon as the female stops laying eggs. Some aquarists prefer to rear the brood in a carefully cleaned tank without substrate. This cuts down the risk of infection, and also enables any food remains to be removed.

Left: **Corydoras reticulatus**
Often rests on smooth rocks.

A practical reminder
Plant the aquarium when it is three-quarters full. Use plants of the same species for best effect. Remember, not all plants tolerate the same water conditions and some will not grow happily together.

Family LORICARIIDAE

Loricaria filamentosa
Whiptail

● **Distribution:** South America, in Rio Magdalena
● **Length:** Up to 10in (25cm)
● **Tank length:** 24in (60cm)
● **Diet:** Worms, insects, plant matter, dried food
● **Water temperature:** 72 to 79°F (22 to 26°C)
● **Community tank**

This elongated catfish has a dorso-ventrally flattened body that is covered by several rows of bony plates. Whiptail's mouth is ventral with lobed lips. The caudal peduncle is very long, and the upper lobe of the caudal fin ends in a whiplike prolongation. There is no adipose fin. The upperparts are gray-brown to yellowish brown and are marked with numerous irregular dark brown streaks and dots. On the caudal peduncle the markings coalesce to form transverse bars. The fins have dark tips and, with the exception of the caudal fin, they all start with a powerful spine. The sexes can be distinguished by the bristly outgrowths, which occur only in the adult male.

Whiptail is not difficult to keep in a tank with patches of dense

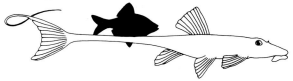

vegetation and an arrangement of rocks and roots. This is all kept clean by the suction feeding of the fish. The water should be soft to medium-hard.

Before spawning the fishes clean a flat rock. The male and female lie over this spawning site as the eggs and sperm are shed. The eggs are guarded by the male, who fans fresh water over them with his fins. As many as 100 to 200 amber-colored eggs may be laid. They are about 0.08in (2mm) in diameter. Hatching occurs in about nine days, and the fry should be kept in shallow water and fed on fine food.

Below: **Loricaria filamentosa**♀♂
This fish will keep the aquarium clean as it scavenges for food.

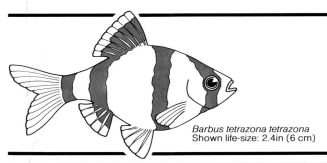

Barbus tetrazona tetrazona
Shown life-size: 2.4in (6 cm)

Family LORICARIIDAE

Otocinclus affinis
Golden Otocinclus

- **Distribution:** South America, in Brazil around Rio de Janeiro
- **Length:** Up to 1.6in (4cm)
- **Tank length:** 12in (30cm)
- **Diet:** Worms, plant matter, dried food
- **Water temperature:** 66 to 77°F (19 to 25°C)
- **Community tank**

This is a small catfish with a moderately elongated body covered with bony plates. The mouth is ventral and acts as a sucker, and there is no adipose fin. The flanks of the Golden Otocinclus are silvery-white with a broad black longitudinal band that extends from the gill cover to the base of the tail. The belly is whitish and the fins are colorless, without any pattern.

Otocinclus affinis is a bottom-living fish that does well in a tank with areas of vegetation and some rocks and roots, preferably covered with algae. This fish is mainly active at night. During this time it browses algae, which helps to keep the tank clean.

After a period of courtship the eggs are laid—more or less at random—on rocks, leaves, or the glass panes of the tank. They hatch in about two days and the fry can be reared on tiny nauplii, micro-worms, and sieved hard-boiled egg yolk.

The very similar *Otocinclus flexilis* can be distinguished by its pattern of spots on the dorsal, anal, and ventral fins.

Right: **Otocinclus affinis**
This small, mainly nocturnal catfish is not very easy to breed.

A practical reminder
Avoid disturbing the contoured gravel
when filling your tank. Direct the water into
a jug or shallow dish standing on the
gravel. Bring the water up to the
appropriate temperature by adding hot water.

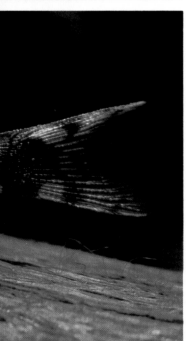

Family LORICARIIDAE

Plecostomus punctatus
Suckermouth Catfish
● **Distribution:** South America, in southern Brazil
● **Length:** Up to 12in (30cm)
● **Tank length:** 24in (60cm)
● **Diet:** Worms, plant matter, dried food
● **Water temperature:** 66 to 79°F (19 to 26°C)
● **Community tank**

This catfish can grow to a length of 6 to 8in (15 to 20cm) in a public aquarium but is unlikely to reach this size in a home aquarium. The body is elongated and only slightly compressed laterally.

Suckermouth Catfish is covered in bony plates everywhere except on the belly. The head is very broad and flattened with a ventral sucking mouth and two barbels. The back and flanks are brown or brownish gray with dark dots and five oblique transverse bars. The belly is whitish to pale brown and the fins are brownish with fairly large rounded spots arranged in rows. The dorsal fin is particularly tall and flaglike, and the first ray is spiny. An adipose fin is present.

The Suckermouth is a very hardy and peaceful catfish. It is best kept in a tank with rocks and roots to provide hiding-places and with a few floating plants at the surface. It is mainly nocturnal and can scarcely be described as colorful. This is an excellent consumer of algae, browsing

Above and above left:
Plecostomus punctatus
This is an excellent fish when small. It cleans the tank as it browses algae with its large sucking mouth.

from rocks and aquarium glass. The tank should have medium-hard water. Approximately one teaspoonful of sea salt should be added to every 2.5 gallons (10 liters) of fresh water.

Plecostomus punctatus and the related *P. commersoni* are not known to have bred in captivity.

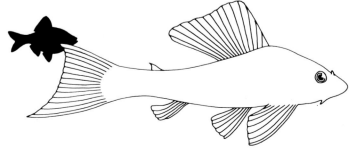

THE EGG-LAYING TOOTHCARPS

Above: *Aphyosemion australe*, a toothcarp from
the acid waters of western Africa.
Right: A lake in Senegal, West Africa, the
typical home of many egg-laying toothcarps.

*These egg-laying toothcarps form a family of mostly small
fishes with representatives in Africa, America, Asia, and
Europe. The majority live only in fresh waters, a few in
brackish waters, and very few in the sea. The body is always
elongated and the top of the head is flattened. The mouth is
usually protrusible and faces upward; thus it is well adapted for
feeding at the surface. Many species vary in color and pattern
and there are numerous subspecies or local forms. Sex differences
are almost always quite distinct, the males being larger with
longer fins and having more intense coloration.*

*There are two main breeding patterns. Some species lay their
eggs among the vegetation, and the eggs adhere to the leaves; others
spawn within the substrate. Almost all the substrate spawners
are annual fishes. This means that they live in relatively small
bodies of water that dry up at certain times of the year.
Spawning takes place before this occurs and the parents leave the
eggs in the substrate. Then the parent fishes die when the water
recedes. The eggs, which have remarkably hard shells, remain in
the damp substrate for a resting period of several weeks or
months, and hatch only when the rains return. The fry grow
rapidly and become sexually mature during a single season in
much the same way as annual plants. This unusual method of
reproduction means that, during the dry season, each species
survives only as a varying number of fertilized eggs—without any
adult individuals.*

*Skilled home aquarists have contributed much to our knowledge
of the biology of fish reproduction from observing fishes of the
Cyprinodontidae.*

Left: The family Cyprinodontidae contains about 450 species, classified into eight subfamilies. The majority live in tropical America, Asia, or Africa. There are very few species in Europe or North America. Some live only in acid waters; others prefer alkaline waters, sometimes with a certain amount of salt. A few egg-laying toothcarps in South America and Africa live in temporary ponds.

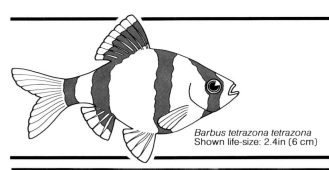

Barbus tetrazona tetrazona
Shown life-size: 2.4in (6 cm)

Family CYRINODONTIDAE

Aphyosemion australe
Lyretail

- **Distribution:** West Africa: Gabon, Cameroon, Congo
- **Length:** Up to 2.2in (5.5cm)
- **Tank length:** 12in (30cm)
- **Diet:** Worms, crustaceans, insects, dried food
- **Water temperature:** 73 to 83°F (23 to 28°C)
- **Species tank**

Lyretail is an elongated species. The dorsal and anal fins are set far back on the body and their tips are more prolonged in the male. The upper and lower rays of the caudal fin are also elongated and pointed in the male. The whole body is markedly lyre-shaped. The fins of the female are more rounded.

The coloration of the sexes differs considerably. The background coloration of the male is yellowish brown to brownish orange. Bright red dots appear on the flanks and on the dorsal and caudal fins. The area of the gill cover is bluish or pale green. The caudal fin has a blue center, surrounded by a red

Above: **Aphyosemion australe** ♂
Sometimes known as the Cape Lopez Lyretail, this toothcarp is fairly hardy when kept in soft water.

border. The elongated tips of the lobes are white. A white border encloses the dorsal fin. Comparatively plain, the female is pale brown with scattered red dots.

This species is best kept as a pair in a tank without other fishes. The substrate should be dark and the vegetation fairly dense. The water must be soft, slightly acid, and filtered through peat. The eggs are laid on leaves and they adhere to them. It is best to remove the eggs to a separate small tank with shallow water. The eggs hatch in 12 to 20 days and the young can be fed immediately on rotifers and tiny nauplii.

A very attractive orange variety — Hjerresen's Aphyosemion has been bred in the aquarium.

Family CYPRINODONTIDAE

Aplocheilus blocki
Green Panchax, Dwarf Panchax

- **Distribution:** Southern India and Sri Lanka
- **Length:** Up to 2in (5cm)
- **Tank length:** 12in (30cm)
- **Diet:** Worms, crustaceans, insects, dried food
- **Water temperature:** 72 to 83°F (22 to 28°C)
- **Species tank**

Aplocheilus blocki is a moderately elongated toothcarp. The front part of its body is roundish in the cross section and the rear part is laterally compressed. When viewed from the side its head appears flat and rounded. The dorsal fin is positioned far back over the rear end of the anal fin. The general coloration of the male is yellow-green or olive-green with longitudinal rows of bright yellow or reddish dots. The underparts are more blue-green. The dorsal, anal, and caudal fins are slightly yellowish with brown or red dots. Though far less colorful — usually yellowish gray — the female has a characteristic black marking at the base of the dorsal fin.

This is the smallest of the *Aplocheilus* species from

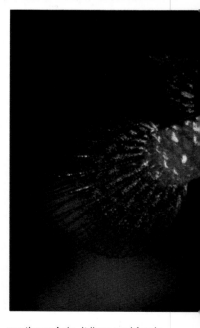

southern Asia. It lives and feeds mainly just below the surface of the water. The tank should have some vegetation, but, more important, the water should be soft and preferably filtered through peat. The male swims around the female in a kind of aquatic

A practical reminder
Specimen plants may be grown in shallow pots buried in the gravel. This will enable you to give them special feeding if necessary and the plant will not be unduly disturbed if it is transplanted to another tank.

Family CYPRINODONTIDAE

Aphyosemion filamentosum
Plumed Lyretail

● **Distribution:** West Africa, in Nigeria.
● **Length:** Up to 2.2in (5.5cm)
● **Tank length:** 12in (30cm)
● **Diet:** Worms, crustaceans, insects, dried food
● **Water temperature:** 68 to 75°F (20 to 24°C)
● **Species tank**

The dorsal and anal fins of this relatively short-bodied toothcarp lie opposite one another and are positioned far back on the body. In the male these fins are well developed and have toothed edges, but in the female they are somewhat smaller and the edges are not toothed. The upper and lower rays of the male's caudal fin are elongated, but not as much as in the Lyretail *(Aphyosemion australe)*.

The general coloration of the male is sky-blue to greenish marked with bright red dots. The belly is violet. The red markings on the flanks may appear to be arranged in diagonal rows. This is particularly so on the gill cover.

Above: **Aphyosemion filamentosum** ♂(t),♀(b)
Some aquarists carefully transfer the newly laid eggs of this species to a separate unlit tank.

The dorsal and caudal fins have smaller red dots. The anal fin is blue and marked with a red horizontal band. The female is similarly colored but not nearly as brightly.

This species swims mainly in the middle water layers. It should be kept as a pair in a tank with some vegetation and a dark substrate. However, some aquarists dispense with the substrate and place a sheet of black paper below the bottom glass of the tank. The water must be soft, slightly acid, and filtered through peat. The eggs are laid on plants or sometimes on the bottom of the tank. They hatch in 20 to 40 days and the fry can be fed immediately on rotifers and very small brine shrimp nauplii.

courtship dance. Spawning takes place among the plants. The eggs are laid on the leaves and hatch in 12 to 15 days. It is best to remove the parent fishes before this happens. The fry should be fed on very tiny live food, such as rotifers and small nauplii.

Above: **Aplocheilus blocki**
A tiny fish best kept as a pair.

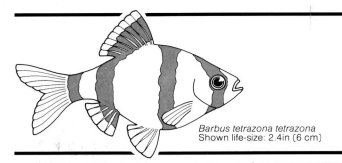

Barbus tetrazona tetrazona
Shown life-size: 2.4in (6 cm)

Family CYPRINODONTIDAE

Aplocheilus dayi
Ceylon Killifish

- **Distribution:** Sri Lanka
- **Length:** Up to 2.8in (7cm)
- **Tank length:** 12in (30cm)
- **Diet:** Worms, crustaceans, insects, fish, dried food
- **Water temperature:** 70 to 77°F (21 to 25°C)
- **Community tank:** Keep with larger species only

This elongated, laterally compressed toothcarp has a flat head and a pointed snout. The short dorsal fin of the Ceylon Killifish is positioned over the last few rays of the much longer anal fin, which is pointed in the male and rounded in the female. The back of the male is golden-brown and the belly is pale bluish. The flanks are an iridescent yellow-green and each scale is marked with a shiny yellow dot. The fins are mainly yellow-green with small red markings. The iris of the eye is greenish or pale yellow. Although the female has the same type of coloration, she is much duller. Also a few dark transverse bars appear on the rear part of the body. These markings are evident

Above: **Aplocheilus dayi** ♀(t),♂(b)
The growing fry should be sorted into sizes to prevent cannibalism.

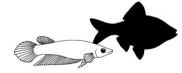

in young males, but are lost in adult males.

Aplocheilus dayi is a hardy toothcarp that should be kept only with larger fishes. The tank must have a good lid to prevent jumping. Some areas of dense vegetation, a few floating plants, and some well-washed roots should be included. Soft water, filtered through peat if possible, is best. During courtship the male swims in circles around the female. They spawn together near the bottom, often on the plants or roots. Spawning may go on for one or two weeks. The female lays eight to 10 eggs a day. Plants with attached eggs can be transferred to a separate tank. Hatching should take place in 12 to 14 days, and the fry can be reared on very tiny live food.

Family CYPRINODONTIDAE

Aplocheilus panchax
Blue Panchax

- **Distribution:** India to Malaysia
- **Length:** Up to 3.2in (8cm)
- **Tank length:** 12in (30cm)
- **Diet:** Worms, crustaceans, insects, fish, dried food
- **Water temperature:** 70 to 77°F (21 to 25°C)
- **Community tank:** Keep with larger species only

This old favorite, introduced into the aquarium around 1899, is usually considered to be the most suitable toothcarp for a beginner. The body of the Blue Panchax is similar in shape to the other two species of *Aplocheilus* described in this book, but the coloration is quite different. In general, the male is a grayish yellow that becomes darker on the back and paler with blue iridescence on the underparts. The popular name refers to the scales on the flanks, which are iridescent blue in the middle with a thin dark edge. The dorsal fin is pale blue in the center and blackish at the base and edge. The anal fin is orange at the base and becomes reddish towards the edge. The caudal fin

is also orange at the base but white towards the rear edge. The female shows paler colors and more rounded fins.

Like many other toothcarps, *Aplocheilus panchax* is somewhat predatory so it can only be kept in a community tank with larger fishes. In addition to a good lid, the tank should have roots on the bottom, dense vegetation, and a few floating plants. If possible, the water should be soft. After vigorous driving by the male, the pair spawn among the plants. This goes on for some days. During this period plants with eggs should be moved to a separate tank with exactly the same type of water. The eggs hatch in 12 to 14 days and the fry are then fed on rotifers and small nauplii.

Right: **Aplocheilus panchax** ♂
With a rich and varied diet the young usually grow very rapidly.

A practical reminder
Sandwich activated carbon between filter wool when placing it in the filter body. Fill box filters with water by siphon tubes before switching on the air supply to start a water flow through the filter.

Aplocheilichthys macrophthalmus
Lamp-eye Panchax

- **Distribution:** Tropical West Africa
- **Length:** Up to 1.6in (4cm)
- **Tank length:** 24in (60cm)
- **Diet:** Worms, crustaceans, insects, dried food
- **Water temperature:** 72 to 79°F (22 to 26°C)
- **Species tank**

Lamp-eye Panchax is a handsome toothcarp with a slender, elongated body and strikingly large eyes that reflect golden-green iridescence. The dorsal fin is positioned far back on the body. It is pointed in the male and rounded in the female. The rear edge of the caudal fin is truncated or slightly convex. The body, as a whole, is more or less translucent. The upperparts are pale olive or yellowish gray and the underparts are yellowish with a bright sheen. There is a reddish stripe along the midline of the back. The pale yellow flanks have two iridescent blue-green stripes running back from behind the gill cover. The upper stripe is bordered by a thin black streak. The dorsal and anal fins are translucent with pale gray or blue edges. The caudal fin is blue with orange dots.

This very small toothcarp lives in

the upper water layers, often right below the surface. It should be kept in a small shoal and in a tank with some vegetation planted to leave sufficient space for swimming. The water flowing out of a filter can be allowed to produce a surface current. For juveniles and adults the water should be hard or neutral because this reduces the risk of tuberculosis. On the other hand, breeding is more successful in soft or medium-hard water. Spawning goes on over a period of about two weeks. The female lays 15 to 20 eggs a day. These hatch in 11 to 14 days, and the fry can be reared on *Paramecium*, rotifers, and pulverized dried food.

Above:
Aplocheilichthys macrophthalmus
Well-aerated water is recommended.

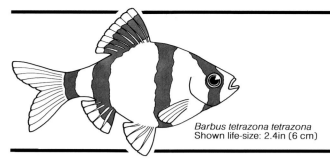

Barbus tetrazona tetrazona
Shown life-size: 2.4in (6 cm)

Family CYPRINODONTIDAE
Cynolebias bellotti
Argentine Pearlfish
- **Distribution:** South America, in Rio de la Plata
- **Length:** Male up to 2.8in (7cm), female slightly less
- **Tank length:** 18in (45cm)
- **Diet:** Worm, crustaceans, insects, dried food
- **Water temperature:** 66 to 86°F (19 to 30°C)
- **Species tank**

The body of the Argentine Pearlfish is tall and laterally compressed. It has rounded fins. The dorsal fin is directly above the anal fin. These fins have about four more rays in the male than they do in the female. The dark blue male is covered with whitish or pale blue iridescent dots, which extend onto the head and the bases of the dorsal, caudal, and anal fins. During spawning the background coloration becomes almost black. A dark diagonal band runs from the nape across the eye. The pale yellow female has irregular dark markings and a large round dark spot in the middle of the flanks.

Cynolebias bellotti is an annual or seasonal toothcarp. In the wild it lives in waters that dry up during the dry season. The adult fishes then die, but they have spawned, leaving fertilized eggs in the mud.

These habits are so deeply ingrained that the fishes live only a short period in an aquarium, and their eggs require a resting period in a semi-dry state. A mature pair placed in an all-glass tank with peat and soft water will start to spawn almost immediately— usually after some courtship display. The eggs may be pushed into the soft substrate by the anal fin of the female, or both fishes may burrow into the substrate to spawn. This procedure sometimes goes on for two or three weeks. The eggs should be kept for six weeks or longer in damp peat at 64 to 68° (18 to 20°C). They hatch when the tank is flooded, and the fry should be fed immediately on pulverized dried food.

Below: **Cynolebias bellotti** ♂♀♀
The males quarrel, so this species is best kept as a single pair.

Family CYPRINODONTIDAE
Cynolebias nigripinnis
Dwarf Argentine Pearlfish
- **Distribution:** South America, in Rio de la Plata and Rio Paraná
- **Length:** Male up to 2in (5cm), female slightly less
- **Tank length:** 12in (30cm)
- **Diet:** Worms, crustaceans, insects, dried food
- **Water temperature:** 64 to 77°F (18 to 25°C)
- **Species tank**

Cynolebias nigripinnis is a smaller, but somewhat more slender, version of *Cynolebias bellotti*. The rear edges of the dorsal and anal fins of the male are more pointed than those of the female. In mature males, body and fins are a brilliant blue-black with numerous iridescent blue or green dots. Just below the edge of the dorsal fin, the dots fuse to form an iridescent longitudinal band. On the caudal fin and the edge of the anal fin, the dots are arranged in rows. The female is yellow with irregular dark markings, but lacks the flank spot seen in *Cynolebias bellotti*.

Although the Dwarf Argentine Pearlfish is a rather delicate fish, it often behaves quite aggressively. So at no time should the tank contain two males. A mature pair should be placed in a small tank with a soft peat substrate, some marginal vegetation, and open water for swimming. The water should be soft and slightly acid. The pair should have been well fed in separate tanks for at least a week before being put together. After a period of driving they spawn on the bottom and the eggs are laid in the peat substrate. This usually continues for eight to 10 days. Afterwards the pair should be removed from the tank, and the water should be drained. The eggs must be left in the damp peat—in the dark—for 90 days at 68 to 72°F (20 to 22°C). The eggs start to hatch as water is added to the tank. The fry should be fed immediately on pulverized dried food.

Right: **Cynolebias nigripinnis** ♂(t)♀
More strikingly patterned than C. bellotti, this species is not always easy to keep and is certainly not suitable for a beginner.

A practical reminder
Reduce pressure of water returning from power filters by the use of a spray bar, which distributes the water across the whole aquarium. Ensure that all the hose connections and fixtures are secure.

Family CYPRINODONTIDAE
Epiplatys sexfasciatus
Six-barred Epiplatys
- **Distribution:** West Africa: Ghana to Gabon
- **Length:** Up to 4in (10cm)
- **Tank length:** 18in (45cm)
- **Diet:** Worms, crustaceans, insects, fish, dried food
- **Water temperature:** 72 to 83°F (22 to 28°C)
- **Species tank**

Six-barred Epiplatys is an elongated, predatory toothcarp that was introduced to the aquarium around 1910. Both the dorsal and anal fins are positioned far back on the body, giving the fish a pikelike appearance. The dorsal fin, however, is considerably shorter than the anal fin. The back of the male is pale brown to olive-brown and the belly is whitish. The flanks are iridescent bronze, green, or blue, and the scales have red dots that are sometimes edged with black. There are six transverse bars on the lower part of the body. The dorsal, caudal, and anal fins are blue, orange, red, or green. The dorsal and anal ones have pointed tips. The eye is dark green enclosed within a narrow golden circle. The lips are black. The female is much paler and has rounded anal and dorsal fins. The great variation in coloration of this species is related to the very extensive geographical range.

This is a surface-living fish that can be kept in a tank with some areas of dense vegetation around the edges and a few floating plants. The water should be soft, slightly acid, and filtered through peat. The substrate should consist of fine sand. Spawning takes place among the plants and the

Above: **Epiplatys sexfasciatus** ♂
The eggs of this rather timid fish hatch over a long period and the fry must be sorted according to size to prevent cannibalism.

female usually lays one egg at a time. This may continue for 12 to 15 days with a final yield of 120 to 300 eggs. These usually hatch in 10 to 12 days, but the period varies. Soon after hatching, the fry start to swim at the surface and to feed on nauplii.

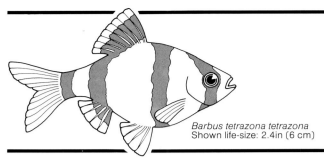

Barbus tetrazona tetrazona
Shown life-size: 2.4in (6 cm)

Family CYPRINODONTIDAE

Jordanella floridae
American Flagfish

- **Distribution:** North America. Florida and Mexico
- **Length:** Up to 2.4in (6cm)
- **Tank length:** 24in (60cm)
- **Diet:** Worms, crustaceans, insects, plant matter, dried food
- **Water temperature:** 66 to 72°F (19 to 22°C)
- **Community tank**

Jordanella floridae is a short, rather squat species with a tall caudal peduncle and a dorsal fin that starts in the middle of the back and forwards of the anal fin. The caudal fin has a rounded rear edge. The back is brownish olive and the belly is yellowish to silvery-white. The flanks are olive-green and each scale has an iridescent blue or yellow-green spot. This combination of colors produces rows of glistening dots, which are particularly striking when seen in reflected light. The anal and dorsal fins are greenish or yellowish with rows of red-brown dots or bands. The general coloration of the female is yellow with a checkerboard pattern of dark markings on the sides of the body and a dark spot at the rear of the dorsal fin.

This species can be kept at a relatively low temperature in a tank with a dark substrate, dense

Right: **Jordanella floridae** ♂
This hardy fish has interesting breeding habits that resemble those of the brood-protecting cichlids.

marginal vegetation, and a few isolated plants with tough leaves. If the aquarium glass has a growth of algae, it will not matter because the American Flagfish is largely a vegetarian and will soon clear up any soft plant matter. The males establish territories, and when placed in an aquarium they become quite aggressive towards one another. For breeding, it is best to have only a single male in the tank. The composition of the water is not important. After vigorous driving, the pair spawn in a small pit that was previously prepared by the male. About 100 eggs are laid. The male will carefully guard them until they hatch in six to nine days. The fry will feed at first on tiny live food and can later be moved to a tank with a good growth of algae, which are their favorite food.

Family CYPRINODONTIDAE

Oryzias melastigma

- **Distribution:** India and Sri Lanka
- **Length:** Up to 2in (5cm)
- **Tank length:** 18in (45cm)
- **Diet:** Worms, crustaceans, insects, dried food
- **Water temperature:** 73 to 79°F (23 to 26°C)
- **Community tank**

Oryzias melastigma is a moderately elongated, laterally compressed toothcarp with a very convex belly profile. The head and nape region are noticeably flat. The dorsal fin is small and positioned close to the rear of the body. The anal fin has a long base and is rounded in the

male, but truncated or slightly concave in the female. The caudal fin is fanlike. When viewed in reflected light the body appears rather translucent with pale blue iridescence. There are several dark markings on the flanks and a narrow longitudinal streak. The dorsal, caudal and anal fins are colorless or pale orange. In the slightly larger female the dorsal and anal fins are smaller than in the male.

This is an active small fish that should be kept in a shoal in a tank with a substrate of fine sand and a few floating plants. For adults the water should be hard, but for spawning it should be soft and slightly acid. This is the same paradoxical situation seen in the Lamp-eye Panchax. At spawning time the male and female nudge each other with the rear part of the body, and the male wraps his anal fin around the female. The eggs are laid, then fertilized by the male. For a few hours the female swims around with the eggs still attached to her, but eventually she rubs them onto the plants. They hatch in 12 to 16 days and the fry are then fed on infusorians, rotifers, and tiny nauplii.

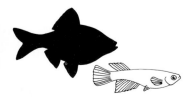

Left: **Oryzias melastigma** ♂♀
This photograph shows the female (below the male) just after spawning, with the eggs still attached.

A practical reminder
Learn to recognize a fish's likely living and feeding habits by its appearance. Torpedo shape—fast swimmer. Upturned mouth—surface feeder. Underslung mouth and flat belly—bottom-dweller.

Family CYPRINODONTIDAE
Pachypanchax playfairi
Playfair's Panchax
● **Distribution:** Seychelles, Zanzibar, probably also East Africa
● **Length:** Up to 4in (10cm)
● **Tank length:** 18in (45cm)
● **Diet:** Worms, crustaceans, insects, fish, dried food
● **Water temperature:** 72 to 77°F (22 to 25°C)
● **Community tank**

Playfair's Panchax is an elongated toothcarp with a flattened forehead and nape region. The body is round in front and laterally compressed at the back. The dorsal fin is positioned above the rear half of the anal fin. The back of the male is brown, and the underparts are yellowish. The flanks are bright emerald-green with longitudinal rows of red dots. The dorsal, caudal, and anal fins are yellow-green with rows of tiny red dots; the caudal and anal ones have a narrow black border. The female is more uniformly colored, with colorless fins, except that the dorsal fin has a prominent black spot at the base.

This is an active—often aggressive—toothcarp that can be kept in a tank with clumps of dense vegetation. Any other occupants of the tank should be equal in size or larger. The substrate should be fine sand; the water should be soft or medium-hard. A few floating plants would also be suitable. For breeding, it is usually best to put one male and two females together. After a short period of courtship, with the male and one female pressing against each other, spawning takes place among the plants. The female may lay 100 to 150 eggs over a period of 12 to 14 days, and these hatch in 10 to 12 days. The fry start to feed shortly after hatching. By that time most of them will already be swimming at the surface. Some aquarists remove the eggs from the breeding tank and put them into a separate tank for hatching and rearing.

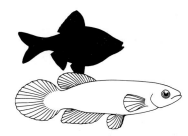

Below: **Pachypanchax playfairi** ♂
At certain times, and particularly during spawning, the scales of the male stick out. This is wrongly interpreted as a sign of disease.

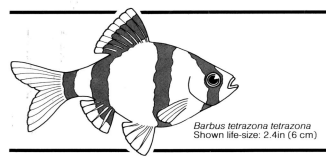

Barbus tetrazona tetrazona
Shown life-size: 2.4in (6 cm)

Family CYPRINODONTIDAE

Pterolebias longipinnis

Featherfin Panchax

- **Distribution:** South America, in Brazil.
- **Length:** Up to 4in (10cm)
- **Tank length:** 18in (45cm)
- **Diet:** Worms, crustaceans, insects, dried food
- **Water temperature:** 72 to 79°F (22 to 26°C)
- **Species tank**

An elongated, short-lived toothcarp, Featherfin Panchax has some lateral compression in the region of the caudal peduncle. In the male the dorsal and anal fins are particularly well developed and their pointed tips extend back far beyond the base of the caudal fin. In the slightly smaller female the fins are rounded and not as large. The male is mainly dark brown with paler brown on the underparts. The flanks show grayish blue iridescence and oblique rows of green or yellow dots. The smaller female is paler brown and lacks the rows of dots. Just above the base of the pectoral fins the male has an irregular cinnabar-red shoulder marking. The fins are brown with dark spots and streaks.

Pterolebias longipinnis is one of the annual species and it is best kept in a separate tank with a substrate of peat, marginal vegetation, and sufficient space for swimming. The water should be soft and slightly acid. For breeding, the tank can have a pair or, if the male drives too vigorously, one male and two females. Before this the fishes should be kept apart and fed for at least a week on a rich diet, such as white worms and insect larvae. They usually spawn very soon after being put into the breeding tank. The eggs are laid in the substrate. Spawning may continue for eight to 10 days. When spawning is over, the parents must be moved to another tank. The breeding tank water should then be drained off carefully, leaving the eggs in the damp peat. They should remain there for 55 to 70 days. They will hatch when water is subsequently added to the tank.

Left: **Pterolebias longipinnis** ♂
Some eggs of this species may remain dormant for several months.

Family CYPRINODONTIDAE

Roloffia occidentalis

Red Aphyosemion

- **Distribution:** Africa, in Sierra Leone
- **Length:** Up to 3.5in (9cm)
- **Tank length:** 12in (30cm)
- **Diet:** Worms, crustaceans, insects, dried food
- **Water temperature:** 70 to 75°F (21 to 24°C)
- **Species tank**

Red Aphyosemion is a moderately elongated, short-lived toothcarp. The dorsal fin sits roughly above the anal fin in the rear part of the body. The caudal fin is fan-shaped in the male, but ovate in the female. The coloration of the male—though always brilliant—varies. The back is orange-yellow with a yellow border. The usually bright blue throat becomes even darker at spawning time. The flanks are orange-red to golden with irregular dark red dots and streaks. The dorsal fin has areas of blue and red. The anal fin is similarly colored, but may have a white tip. There are two red bands on the caudal peduncle, one above and one below, and these extend back to the rear edge of the caudal fin. The female is red-

brown with indistinct brown markings.

This rather aggressive fish swims mostly in the middle and lower water layers. The tank should have a few areas of dense vegetation and a substrate of peat. The water must be soft and slightly acid. After a period of courtship the pair spawn in the substrate. In the wild the waters dry up, and the parents die. The eggs, which were left in the mud, hatch only when the waters return at the start of the next rainy season. In an aquarium the water should be drained off and the eggs should remain in the damp peat for at least six weeks. They hatch when the tank is refilled with water. The fry start to feed almost immediately on rotifers and small nauplii. The eggs should be checked for mold during storage.

Above: **Roloffia occidentalis** ♂
The eggs of this African toothcarp may hatch after several weeks rather than a rest of several months.

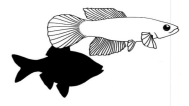

A practical reminder
Disk-shaped fishes inhabit slow-moving or still waters. Fishes with large eyes live in deep or muddy waters. Fishes with no eyes navigate with lateral line systems, sensing obstructions by reflected vibrations.

Family ANABLEPIDAE
This is a very small family (only two species) distributed from southern Mexico to northern South America. The horizontal partitioning of each eye allows the fish to see above and below water at the same time.

Family ANABLEPIDAE
Anableps anableps
Four-eyes
- **Distribution:** Southern Mexico to northern South America
- **Length:** Up to 8in (20cm), possibly more
- **Tank length:** 36in (90cm)
- **Diet:** Insects
- **Water temperature:** 73 to 77°F (23 to 25°C)
- **Community tank:** May eat smaller fishes

Four-eyes has a flat head and very protruding eyes. The dorsal fin of this elongated fish is very small and set far back on the body; the caudal fin is oval. The male is easily distinguishable by the prominent gonopodium. The back is bluish gray, and the flanks and underparts are yellowish with no distinct markings. The fins are blue-gray.

The cornea, pupil, and retina of the eyes are separated into two parts by a horizontal bridge of tissue. The fish swims at the surface of the water with the upper half of the eye above the surface. Distant objects out of the water are perceived by the upper eye and registered on the lower half of the retina, while closer objects under water are seen by the lower half-eye and registered in the upper half of the retina. The upper eye, therefore, allows the fish to see enemies approaching.

This unusual-looking fish requires a shallow tank with a well-fitting lid, as it is a good jumper. The water must have added sea salt (about 5 teaspoonsful to every 2.5 gallons/ 10 liters of fresh water).

The genital opening of about half of all female Four-eyes faces to the left, and in the other half it

Above: **Anableps anableps**
Bifocal eyes enable this fish to see both above and below the water.

faces right. Some of the males have the gonopodium turning to the right, others to the left. Males with a gonopodium turning to the right mate with females that have the genital opening facing left, and vice versa. The females produce a small number of live young (about six) twice a year, but these are already 1.2 to 2in (3 to 5cm) long.

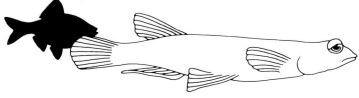

THE LIVE-BEARING TOOTHCARPS

Above: *Xiphophorus variatus,* a live-bearer
from Mexico that breeds very freely.
Right: A river in Mexico, the natural habitat
of many of the popular live-bearers.

These live-bearing toothcarps are mostly small fishes distributed from the southern United States, throughout Central America including the West Indies, and south to northern Argentina. However, some species have now been taken by man to many other tropical areas, where they are bred in large numbers for the aquarium trade. A few species have been introduced into malarial areas to control mosquito larvae.

Female live-bearers are usually larger than the males, but the latter have more striking colors and patterns, and often longer fins. The males also have a special organ, known as the gonopodium, which develops from the anal fin and is used to transfer packets of sperm to the female. The gonopodium consists of the third, fourth, and fifth rays of the anal fin; the other rays of this fin are much smaller. During mating the gonopodium is turned forward and its fin rays form a trough that is closed by the ventral fin to form a tube. The packets of sperm pass down this tube into the oviduct of the female. There the packets break up to release the sperm, some of which fertilize the ripe eggs, while the remainder are stored in the folds of the oviduct wall. A single mating is sufficient for several pregnancies. The yolky eggs develop within the oviduct and the young are born alive. In most species the female's tissues do not nourish the embryo, but in a few species the female may pass nutrients to the embryos.

The live-bearing toothcarps are among the most popular aquarium fishes. This is due to their small size and handsome coloration, and the ease with which they can be bred. Over a period of several years, aquarists have bred and selected a large number of new color variants and also new fin shapes.

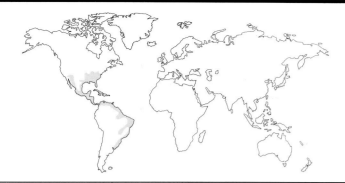

Left: The map shows the natural range of the family Poeciliidae, of which about 130 species are known, in addition to the numerous varieties produced in the aquarium. Most of the species occur in areas north of the equator. The Amazon River evidently forms a barrier, and few species occur further south. Most live-bearing toothcarps live in lakes or close to river banks, and some extend into brackish waters.

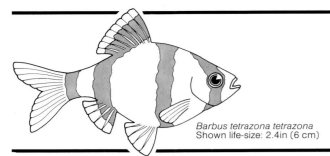
Barbus tetrazona tetrazona
Shown life-size: 2.4in (6 cm)

Family POECILIIDAE
Gambusia affinis
Mosquito Fish

- **Distribution:** Southeastern United States, Texas and northern Mexico
- **Length:** Male up to 1.6in (4cm), female to 2.6in (6.5cm)
- **Tank length:** 24in (60cm)
- **Diet:** Worms, crustaceans, insects, plant matter, dried food
- **Water temperature:** 64 to 68°F (18 to 20°C)
- **Species tank**

There are two subspecies of *Gambusia affinis.* The typical one is *Gambusia affinis affinis* from Texas, and the very similar *G. affinis holbrooki* comes from the southeastern United States and northern Mexico. The following description is based on the typical subspecies. *Gambusia affinis affinis* is a spindle-shaped fish with a dorsal fin that starts behind the middle of the body, and with a fan-shaped caudal fin. As in other members of the Poeciliidae, part of the anal fin is modified to form a gonopodium. The back of the male is brown or olive-brown, and the underparts are silvery. In general, the flanks are gray with a delicate bluish iridescence and are sometimes marked with a few black dots. These markings also occur on the dorsal and caudal fins. The fins are otherwise colorless or very pale yellow. The female usually has the same coloration as the male but a larger anal fin. The Mexican subspecies differs only in that it has irregular black markings on the flanks.

Although quite small in size, Mosquito Fish is an aggressive live-bearer that nips the fins of other fishes. Therefore, it is best kept in a species tank. The composition of the water is not at all critical. In an aquarium the fishes breed at all times of the year. The females produce up to 60 live young after a gestation period of six to eight weeks. The parents are apt to eat their young.

G. affinis has been introduced in many areas for the control of mosquito larvae. It is very hardy and can be kept in winter at temperatures as low as 50 to 54°F (10 to 12°C).

Below:
Gambusia affinis holbrooki ♂
The gonopodium is clearly seen on this male of the Mexican subspecies.

Family POECILIIDAE
Heterandria formosa
Least Killifish

- **Distribution:** North America, from North Carolina to Florida
- **Length:** Male up to 0.8 (2cm), female to 1.4in (3.5cm)
- **Tank length:** 12in (30cm)
- **Diet:** Worms, crustaceans, plant matter, dried food
- **Water temperature:** 68 to 75°F (20 to 24°C)
- **Community tank:** Keep with small, peaceful species

Least Killifish is an elongated live-bearer with moderate lateral compression and rather poorly developed fins. The male is much more slender than the female. The background coloration is yellowish brown or red-brown with striking pearly iridescence when seen in reflected light. An irregular dark brown band extends from the tip of the snout to the base of the caudal fin and it is crossed by six to 12 similarly colored short transverse bars. These bars become paler with increasing age. The fins are yellowish to brownish. The base of the anal fin has a black spot; the base of the dorsal fin has a similar spot with an orange border.

This very active fish swims mainly in the middle and lower water layers. The tank can have some vegetation but filamentous algae should be removed. Any other occupants of the tank should be small and peaceful. The water should be hard and slightly alkaline.

The males are often aggressive towards one another. After a period of courtship, the male—using his copulatory organ (gonopodium)—introduces sperm into the female's genital opening. In this particular species, but not in the other live-bearers described in this book, the eggs derive some nourishment from the female. Over a period of six to 10 days a single female may produce two or three young per day. These fry should be fed on very fine live food and pulverized dried food, and protected from their parents.

Right: **Heterandria formosa** ♀
This fish is one of the smallest of all known vertebrates.

A practical reminder
Some bottom-dwelling species, such as Gobies, have their ventral fins joined together to form a suction disk. This anchors them to rocks and keeps them from being swept away by water currents.

Family POECILIIDAE
Poecilia hybrid
Black Molly
- **Distribution:** Venezuela, Colombia, Mexico
- **Length:** Up to 4in (10cm)
- **Tank length:** 18in (45cm)
- **Diet:** Worms, crustaceans, insects, plant matter, dried food
- **Water temperature:** 77 to 83°F (25 to 28°C)
- **Community tank**

The common name Molly comes from the genus *Mollienisia,* which is no longer used. The various species are now included in the genus *Poecilia*. The exact origin of some of the black hybrid Mollies is somewhat vague, but it is probable that the original male parent was *Poecilia sphenops.*

The dorsal fin of the male Black Molly is enormous—up to 0.6in (1.5cm) or even 0.8in (2 cm) tall—with a rather angular, only slightly rounded shape. The male is an intense black color, but females vary in coloration. Some are entirely black, but others have only black spots and black edges to the scales.

Another hybrid, known as the Crescenty Black Molly, was produced by crossing the original Black Molly with the Sailfin Molly *(Poecilia latipinna)*. In the male of this hybrid the dorsal fin is 1.6 to 2in (4 to 5cm) tall and sail-shaped like *P. latipinna*. There is yet another black hybrid that has a lyre-shaped tail.

Black Mollies do well in a tank with plenty of vegetation, and water that is medium-hard and slightly alkaline. The addition of approximately one teaspoonful of sea salt to every 2.5 gallons (10 liters) of the tank water is the concentration recommended. The period of gestation is 40 to 70 days, and the female produces a brood of 20 to 60 live young—sometimes more. They can be fed at first on brine shrimp nauplii and sieved nauplii.

Above: **Poecilia hybrid** ♂
This is one of many hybrid forms developed by aquarists. The large dorsal fin will develop only if the fish has plenty of space.

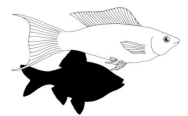

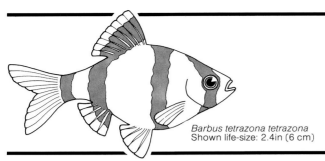
Barbus tetrazona tetrazona
Shown life-size: 2.4in (6 cm)

Family POECILIIDAE
Poecilia latipinna
Sailfin Molly

- **Distribution:** Mexico, Texas, Florida, the Carolinas to Virginia
- **Length:** Male up to 4in (10cm), female to 4.7in (12cm)
- **Tank length:** 24in (60cm)
- **Diet:** Worms, crustaceans, insects, plant matter, dried food
- **Water temperature:** 68 to 75°F (20 to 24°C)
- **Community tank**

Formerly known as *Mollienisia latipinna,* Sailfin Molly is an elongated, laterally compressed fish with a very large dorsal fin. The dark olive-green coloration is sometimes tinged with yellow, becoming slightly darker on the back and paler on the underparts. The scales on the back and flanks are pearly and iridescent and each is marked with a dark spot. These prominent markings unite to form a number of longitudinal stripes. There are six or seven dark, almost black transverse bars at the rear end of the body. The dorsal fin of the male is bluish with very dark vertical stripes and an orange-red border. The center of the caudal fin is orange surrounded by metallic green. This fin is edged in black.

This very handsome species requires a spacious tank without too much vegetation. The water should be medium-hard and slightly alkaline with an addition of approximately one teaspoonful of sea salt to every 2.5 gallons (10 liters) of fresh water. It is best to keep only a single pair in a tank because the males may fight one another. The female gives birth to 20 to 80 young after a gestation period of eight to 10 weeks; she should then be removed from the tank. The young can be reared on

Above: **Poecilia latipinna** ♂(t)♀(b)
The large dorsal fin of the male does not develop fully until the fish is two years old.

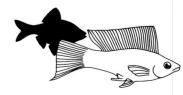

nauplii and finely sieved matter, but the water temperature should not exceed 75°F (24°C).

A practical reminder
Color is produced in the fish either by reflective guanin deposited beneath the scales or by pigmentation. Some fish genera, such as the pencilfishes *(Nannostomus)*, change their color pattern at night.

Poecilia melanogaster
Black-bellied Limia
- **Distribution:** Jamaica and Haiti
- **Length:** Male up to 1.6in (4cm), female to 2.4in (6cm)
- **Tank length:** 24in (60cm)
- **Diet:** Worms, crustaceans, insects, plant matter, dried food
- **Water temperature:** 72 to 83°F (22 to 28°C)
- **Community tank**

Black-bellied Limia, a rather squat fish, is more brightly colored than the Cuban Limia. It has a deep caudal peduncle and a relatively short dorsal fin that starts in the middle of its back. In the male, the back is olive-green and the underparts are dark orange. The iridescent steel-blue flanks have a number of ill-defined, almost black transverse bars on the caudal peduncle. The eye is a pale golden color. The fins are usually yellowish. The dorsal fin has a very dark edge and a black bar running parallel to the outer border. Sometimes the caudal fin has a black border. The female lacks the black edge to the dorsal fin but the transverse bars on her caudal peduncle are much more clearly defined than they are in the male, and their rear edges are silvery. However, the striking characteristic of this species is the very large black mark of

pregnancy on the female's belly, hence the popular name. The species name, *melanogaster,* means 'black belly'.

This fairly active live-bearer needs a higher water temperature than the Cuban Limia, and, more important, a definite amount of sunshine. The tank should have clumps of plants. The water should be medium-hard and slightly alkaline with a supplement of approximately one teaspoonful of sea salt to every 2.5 gallons (10 liters) of fresh water. The female produces a brood of 20 to 40 live young (on occasion they have been known to produce up to 80) every six or seven weeks. The offspring must be protected from the female.

Right: **Poecilia melanogaster** ♀(b)
This active, highly prolific live-bearer needs a spacious tank with plenty of open water for swimming.

Poecilia reticulata
Guppy
- **Distribution:** Northern Brazil, Venezuela, Guyana, Barbados, Trinidad
- **Length:** Males up to 1.2in (3cm); females to 2.4in (6cm)
- **Tank length:** 12in (30cm)
- **Diet:** Worms, crustaceans, insects, plant matter, dried food
- **Water temperature:** 72 to 83°F (22 to 28°C)
- **Community tank:** Fancy varieties may be harassed

The Guppy is probably the best-known of all tropical aquarium fishes. In the 1860s a few living pairs were sent to the British

Left: **Poecilia reticulata** ♂♂
This is a prolific and immensely popular fish. The females may produce young every four weeks.

Museum in London by Robert John Lechmere Guppy, hence the popular name that is now used in all parts of the world. Until 1963 this fish was mostly known as *Lebistes reticulatus.*

Even specimens caught in the wild—particularly the males—show considerable variation in color and pattern. The females have duller coloration. Since its introduction into the aquarium world, this small live-bearer has been admired for its wide range of forms. This applies not only to the numerous color variants, but also to a whole series of caudal fin variants, such as round tail, spadetail, speartail, pintail, fantail, and many others. These various possibilities are now the preoccupation of enthusiasts who have established Guppy societies in many parts of the world.

Guppies are not difficult to keep, with a certain amount of vegetation. The water should be medium-hard and slightly alkaline, but added salt is not necessary and is not always tolerated. After a gestation period of four to six weeks the female produces 20 to 100 live young. The fry should be kept in a separate tank and fed like young Mollies.

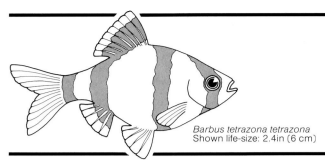

Barbus tetrazona tetrazona
Shown life-size: 2.4in (6 cm)

Family POECILIIDAE

Poecilia sphenops
Pointed-mouth Molly

- **Distribution:** Venezuela, Colombia, Mexico, Texas, Leeward Islands
- **Length:** Males up to 2.8in (7cm); females to 4in (10cm)
- **Tank length:** 18in (45cm)
- **Diet:** Worms, crustaceans, insects, plant matter, dried food
- **Water temperature:** 73 to 83°F (23 to 28°C)
- **Community tank**

Poecilia sphenops (formerly known as *Mollienisia sphenops*) varies greatly in color. In general, the coloration is bluish with four to six longitudinal rows of orange-red dots. Between these rows there are numerous iridescent bluish or greenish spots. The dorsal fin is rather angular with black dots at the base. The dots are arranged between the fin's eight to 11 rays, and the border is red or orange with an outer edging of black. The pectoral and ventral fins are colorless and the gonopodium is

orange. The much paler female has colorless fins.

Pointed-mouth Molly, an active live-bearer, lives mainly in the upper water layers. It should be kept in a tank furnished with rocks and roots, and some robust plants arranged to leave sufficient space for swimming. The water should be medium-hard and slightly alkaline with added sea salt (as recommended for *Poecilia vittata*). After a gestation period of about two months ,the female gives birth to a brood of 100 to 120 live

young, each about 0.4in (1cm) long. The female should then be removed from the tank. The young are best kept in shallow water and fed on small nauplii and finely sieved plant food.

Below: **Poecilia sphenops** ♂
This species probably provided the male parent for the Black Molly.

Family POECILIIDAE

Poecilia vittata
Cuban Limia

- **Distribution:** Cuba
- **Length:** Male to 2.4in (6cm), female to 4in (10cm)
- **Tank length:** 24in (60cm)
- **Diet:** Worms, crustaceans, insects, plant matter, dried food
- **Water temperature:** 72 to 79°F (22 to 26°C)
- **Community tank**

This species, formerly known as *Limia vittata,* is a stocky live-bearer with a fanlike caudal fin and a dorsal fin that starts in the middle of the back (behind the level of the gonopodium). The pectoral fins are positioned relatively high up on the sides of the body and are set just behind the gill cover. The back is yellow and the underparts are pink or pale yellow. The background coloration of the flanks is a darker yellow, showing some blue iridescence when seen in reflected light. The pattern of markings on the flanks varies, but there is usually a poorly defined dark longitudinal streak and a number of narrow dark cross bars that become more distinct on the caudal peduncle. These bars

are fairly short and are normally apparent only in the middle of the body. The dorsal and caudal fins are yellow to orange-red and usually have dark edges and irregular dark markings.

Cuban Limia is a very hardy and peaceful live-bearer, which can be kept in a tank with areas of dense vegetation. The water should be medium-hard and slightly alkaline; the addition of approximately one teaspoonful of sea salt to every 2.5 gallons (10 liters) of fresh water is also to be recommended. After a gestation period of three to five weeks, the female produces a brood of between 20 and 60 live young. However, larger broods of young sometimes occur.

Right: **Poecilia vittata** ♂(t)
This is an undemanding live-bearer that is ideal for a community tank.

A practical reminder
Fishes with exaggerated finnage developed by selective breeding are slow swimmers. Their aquarium conditions must be kept scrupulously clean to avoid possible bacterial damage to the fishes' delicate fins.

Poecilia velifera
Mexican Sailfin Molly
- **Distribution:** Southeastern Mexico
- **Length:** Male up to 6in (15cm), female to 7in (18cm)
- **Tank length:** 24in (60cm)
- **Diet:** Worms, crustaceans, insects, plant matter, dried food
- **Water temperature:** 77 to 83°F (25 to 28°C)
- **Community tank**

This is one of the larger Mollies, formerly known as *Mollienisia velifera*. It is very similar in appearance to *P. latipinna* but

differs in several details. The dorsal fin of the Mexican Sailfin Molly starts further forward and has 18 or 19 rays, compared with Sailfin Molly's 14 rays. In *P. velifera* the pale spots at the base of the dorsal fin are roundish, rather than elongated as in *P. latipinna*. In males of *P. velifera* the flanks have large numbers of shining blue-green spots. The females are not as brightly colored but they still have varying numbers of dots. Some individuals of this species are almost completely black.

This species should be kept in a well-lit tank with growths of algae

on at least some of the glass panes. An overcrowded tank will lead to stunted growth. The water must be medium-hard and slightly alkaline with added salt — a concentration of approximately one teaspoonful of sea salt to every 2.5 gallons (10 liters) of fresh water — and good filtration is essential. A virgin female should be mated with a well-developed male that is about 18 months old. The period of gestation is about two months, and the female should be removed as soon as she has produced her young. The broods usually contain 30 to 50 young, but births of up to 200

Above: **Poecilia velifera** ♀(t),♂(b)
The large dorsal fin will develop only in a scrupulously clean tank.

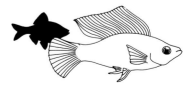

have been recorded. The young should at first be kept in shallow water (about 3.5in/9cm deep) and fed on brine shrimp nauplii with some fine plant food.

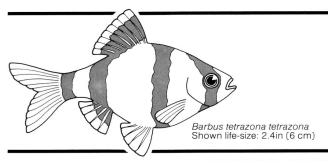

Barbus tetrazona tetrazona
Shown life-size: 2.4in (6 cm)

Family POECILIIDAE

Xiphophorus helleri
Swordtail

- **Distribution:** Southern Mexico, Guatemala
- **Length:** Males up to 4in (10cm) excluding sword; females to 4.7in (12cm)
- **Tank length:** 24in (60cm)
- **Diet:** Worms, crustaceans, insects, plant matter, dried food
- **Water temperature:** 70 to 79°F (21 to 26°C)
- **Community tank:** May be aggressive to smaller species, particularly in a small tank

Xiphophorus helleri, a slender, laterally compressed live-bearer, has a long 'sword' formed by the lowermost rays of the lower lobe of the caudal fin. The female is more squat and has no sword. The back of the original wild form is olive-green. The flanks are yellowish green and the edges of the scales are brown. A dark violet or red band extends from the snout, across the eye, and to the base of the tail. In the male it continues on towards the sword. This dark band is bordered on each side by a pale green zone. The sword may be green, orange red, or yellow. All are edged with black along the top. The dorsal fin is yellowish with one or more

Above: **Xiphophorus helleri** ♀(t),♂(b)
This is a fine pair of the very popular red variety of Swordtail.

rows of red dots. The female is similarly colored but somewhat duller.

This peaceful, lively species is very suitable for a beginner. The Swordtail can be kept in a tank with dense vegetation and areas of open water for swimming. The water should be medium-hard and slightly alkaline, and salt should not be added. For breeding, a pregnant female should be moved to a separate tank with dense vegetation. The gestation period is from four to six weeks and the female gives birth to 20 to 100 or more living young. The number of fry depends upon the size of the mother.

The Swordtail has been crossed with other members of the genus *Xiphophorus,* particularly *X. maculatus.* Some forms have lyre-shaped tails or even tails with an upper and lower sword.

Family POECILIIDAE

Xiphophorus maculatus
Platy

- **Distribution:** Southern Mexico, Guatemala, Honduras
- **Length:** Males up to 1.6in (4cm), females to 2.4in (6cm)
- **Tank length:** 12in (30cm)
- **Diet:** Worms, crustaceans, insects, plant matter, dried food
- **Water temperature:** 68 to 77°F (20 to 25°C)
- **Community tank**

Xiphophorus maculatus was known as *Platypoecilus maculatus,* hence its popular name. It is a relatively elongated live-bearer, but squat, high-backed forms also occur. The dorsal fin has nine or 10 rays and is usually quite small. In the original Platy the upper-parts are dark olive and the underparts are white. The flanks are an iridescent bluish color marked in the males with from two to five dark, though sometimes indistinct, transverse bars. The caudal peduncle has a pattern of black markings. The coloration is, however, extremely variable both in the wild and as a result of hybridization and selection in the aquarium. Hybrids include: the Red Platy with red

body and fins; the Tuxedo Platy with the underparts black and the rest of the body red or greenish; and the Gold Platy with yellow upperparts, a red dorsal fin, and a pale belly.

The tank can have some areas of dense vegetation. The water must be medium-hard and slightly alkaline, but with no added salt. A pregnant female, transferred to a separate tank, will give birth to 10 to 80 or more live young after a gestation period of four to six weeks. The young, which are 0.28 to 0.32in (7 to 8mm) long at birth, grow rapidly.

Right:
Xiphophorus maculatus ♂♂
This is a very variable fish; one authority lists over 40 different hybrids and selected forms.

A practical reminder
Male fishes are generally brighter in color and slimmer, and have longer pointed fins than the females of the same species. Male live-bearers have their anal fins adapted into a reproductive organ (gonopodium).

Family POECILIIDAE

Xiphophorus variatus
Variatus Platy
- **Distribution:** Mexico
- **Length:** Males up to 2.2in (5.5cm), females to 2.8in (7cm)
- **Tank length:** 12in (30cm)
- **Diet:** Worms, crustaceans, insects, plant matter, dried food
- **Water temperature:** 68 to 75°F (20 to 24°C)
- **Community tank**

This member of the Poeciliidae family is a moderately squat live-bearer with the belly profile of both sexes more convex than the back. The dorsal fin is large and has 11 or 12 rays. The typical body is yellowish to orange, greenish, or bluish and marked with an irregular pattern of black dots. The caudal fin is usually orange or reddish. All the other fins are yellowish green. Underparts may be silvery or golden. The females show similar coloration but are much paler—some simply yellowish or grayish brown with colorless fins.

There are several aquarium hybrids and color varieties. One such variety is the Red Variatus, showing orange or yellow flanks with a greenish golden iridescence when seen in reflected

Above left and above:
Xiphophorus variatus
This is an excellent live-bearer for a beginner, even though it may be difficult for an aquarist to discover which of the many different varieties he is keeping.

light. The dorsal fin is orange and sometimes exhibits red dots.

Variatus Platies can be kept in a well-lit tank with a few areas of dense vegetation. The water should be medium-hard and slightly alkaline, but salt should not be added. For breeding, a pregnant female can be transferred to a separate tank with the water at 73 to 81°F (23 to 27°C). Depending upon her age and size, she will produce, over a period of some days, from 20 to 150 (or even more) live young. They may reach sexual maturity in six or eight months and be fully grown in a year.

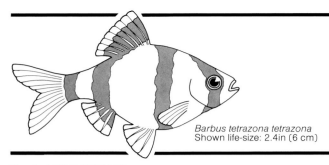

Barbus tetrazona tetrazona
Shown life-size: 2.4in (6 cm)

Family EXOCOETIDAE

This is a family of fishes from tropical seas as well as fresh and brackish waters. It includes flying fishes that are not suitable for the aquarium, but the freshwater halfbeaks are kept and bred successfully. These fishes are live-bearers that feed near the water surface.

Family EXOCOETIDAE

Dermogenys pusillus
Halfbeak, Wrestling Halfbeak

- **Distribution:** Thailand, Malaya, Sumatra, Java
- **Length:** Up to 2.8in (7cm)
- **Tank length:** 12in (30cm)
- **Diet:** Worms, crustaceans, insects, dried food
- **Water temperature:** 68 to 79°F (20 to 26°C)
- **Community tank:** Should be kept singly; two or more males may fight

This live-bearer is elongated with only moderate lateral compression. The dorsal fin is set very far back, close to the caudal fin. This gives the fish a pikelike appearance. However, the characteristic feature is the long thin lower jaw, which is not movable. The upper jaw, on the other hand, is much shorter and can move up and down with the skull. The caudal fin is ovate. In the male the front part of the anal fin is modified to form a gonopodium. Coloration varies considerably according to the locality, which is not surprising in view of the very extensive geographical distribution. The upperparts may be brownish or green, and the belly may be pale yellow or silvery-white. The flanks are silvery and, when seen in reflected light, may show blue iridescence. The iris is bright green. On each side of the long lower jaw is a red and a green line. A dark marking is usually quite distinct in the shoulder area, and there is another dark spot near the base of each pectoral fin. The fins are usually lemon-yellow. The anal fin has a black edge, and the dorsal fin of the male has a red spot.

These are lively fishes that live at the surface in both fresh and brackish waters. They can be kept in a large shallow tank with a few floating plants. The water should be medium-hard and slightly alkaline with 3 teaspoonfuls of sea salt per 2.5 gallons (10 liters) of water. During courtship the male swims up under the female and touches her belly with his snout, and at the subsequent spawning the two come alongside one another. The female has a long gestation period of up to eight weeks. Each brood consists of 12 to 20 live young, which are about 0.4in (1cm) long at birth. The female should then be removed and the young will start to feed on very tiny live food. At birth the upper and lower jaws are almost the same length, but the lower jaw starts to grow longer after about five weeks.

Below: **Dermogenys pusillus** ♂
When alarmed, this fish may dash against the tank glass and damage its lower jaw.

Family CENTRARCHIDAE

These are small to medium-sized freshwater fishes of central and eastern North Ameria. In many species the male guards the eggs in a pit on the bottom. Some species have become naturalized in Europe.

Family CENTRARCHIDAE

Elassoma evergladei
Everglades Pygmy Sunfish

- **Distribution:** North America, Carolina to Florida
- **Length:** Up to 1.4in (3.5cm)
- **Tank length:** 12in (30cm)
- **Diet:** Crustaceans, plant matter, dried food
- **Water temperature:** 50 to 77°F (10 to 25°C)
- **Species tank**

This is a moderately elongated fish with slight lateral compression. The caudal fin is fan-shaped and the anal fin lies below the rear part of the dorsal fin. The mouth is small. The body of an older female is taller than that of a comparably aged male. The general coloration is yellowish with scattered silvery and blackish dots, and it sometimes shows irregular, rather indistinct dark transverse bars. At spawning time the male becomes more intensely colored with a velvety-black body marked with numerous iridescent green dots; the fins also become black. The females are less brightly colored and at spawning time the reddish eggs can be seen through the body wall.

This is a particularly hardy fish that should definitely be kept at a temperature of 46 to 50°F (8 to 10°C) during the winter. In summer the species is usually kept at 61 to 77°F (16 to 25°C) or even higher, but at high temperatures the water must be sufficiently aerated. The tank should have dense vegetation and a number of rocks arranged so that each male can establish a territory. The water must be medium-hard or hard, and alkaline. Spawning takes place among the vegetation. The eggs are usually laid on feathery leaves. They hatch in two or three days and the fry become free-swimming about three or four days later. They can then be fed on brine shrimp nauplii. At this time they swim mostly just below the water surface.

In some areas this species will breed very successfully in an outdoor tank during summer.

Left: **Elassoma evergladei**
In this species there is no need to remove the parent fishes after spawning has finished.

Family CENTRARCHIDAE

Lepomis gibbosus
Pumpkinseed

- **Distribution:** North America: Great Lakes to Texas and Florida
- **Length:** Up to 8.7in (22cm)
- **Tank length:** 36in (90cm)
- **Diet:** Worms, crustaceans, insects, dried food
- **Water temperature:** 50 to 72°F (10 to 22°C)
- **Species tank**

This is a thick-set fish with strong lateral compression. The dorsal fin has a large number (usually 10 to 12) of spiny rays, unlike species in the genus *Elassoma*, which have only four or five such rays. This fish is at its most attractive when 1.6 to 4in (4 to 10cm) long. At this time the general coloration is brownish yellow with pearly iridescent greenish-blue transverse bars and numerous red dots. The gill cover is iridescent green and the characteristic rear flap (sometimes called the 'ear') is deep black with an orange-red marking at the back. The throat and underparts are bright orange, and the fins are greenish or yellowish. In older individuals the general coloration is more brownish and the transverse bars on the flanks are iridescent greenish blue. The head is marked with numerous dark red spots.

A practical reminder
Always buy healthy stock from a quarantined source. Fishes with spots, pimples, split fins, or wounds and those that have difficulty in swimming or maintaining a stable position should be avoided.

Family CENTROPOMIDAE
This group of mainly marine fishes is native to the tropical Atlantic, Indian and western Pacific Oceans. A few species inhabit fresh waters in Asia; these include the very translucent glassfishes that are kept in the aquarium. Some fishes in the group have two dorsal fins.

Family CENTROPOMIDAE
Chanda ranga
Indian Glassfish
- **Distribution:** India, Burma, Thailand
- **Length:** Up to 2.8in (7cm)
- **Tank length:** 18in (45cm)
- **Diet:** Worms, crustaceans, dried food
- **Water temperature:** 64 to 77°F (18 to 25°C)
- **Community tank**

Tall and diamond-shaped, this fish has strong lateral compression. In old individuals the forehead is conspicuously indented. There are two separate dorsal fins: The first has only spiny rays, the second has one spiny ray and a number of soft ones. The caudal fin is deeply cleft with pointed lobes. In transmitted light the very translucent body has a greenish yellow tinge; in reflected light it shows golden and greenish iridescence. The flanks have a violet longitudinal line at the level of the backbone and a number of thin lines composed of tiny dark dots. The fins are yellow at the base and rust-red towards the edge. The second dorsal and the anal fin have a pale blue border in the male. In reflected light the caudal fin shows iridescent gold.

This timid fish is best kept only with others that are also peaceful. The tank can have patches of vegetation and a dark substrate. The water should be hard and slightly alkaline with added sea salt (approximately 3 to 6 teaspoonfuls per 2.5 gallons/10 liters of water). For breeding, about a third of the water should be renewed and the temperature raised a few degrees. There is active driving during spawning—the female lays four to six eggs at a time, with a total of 200 or more. The eggs adhere firmly to fine-leaved plants and are not bothered by the parents. They hatch in 20 to 24 hours and the fry hang vertically from plants for three or four days

Above: **Chanda ranga**
Spawning in this timid species is stimulated by morning sunshine.

and can then be fed on very tiny nauplii. They do not chase after the food, however, but take only what is close to their mouths. They are not easy to rear.

This is a peaceful fish that in the wild lives in clear standing waters with a good growth of aquatic plants. It is best kept in a tank with patches of dense vegetation and a fine sandy substrate. The water must be clean and rich in oxygen, but the actual chemical composition is not critical. Before spawning the male digs a pit in the sand in which he and the female come together, belly to belly, as spawning takes place. The female may lay up to 1,000 eggs; the male guards the eggs, beating his fins to fan fresh water over them. He usually drives the female away as soon as spawning has finished. The eggs hatch in four to six days and the male usually fans the fry into a clump of plants. They hang onto the plants until free-swimming. At first they feed on brine shrimp nauplii and later on micro-worms.

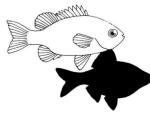

Right: **Lepomis gibbosus**
Where the climate allows, this fish can be kept in a garden pool during the summer, and it will even survive outdoors in a mild winter.

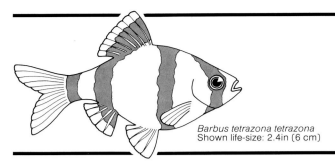

Barbus tetrazona tetrazona
Shown life-size: 2.4in (6 cm)

Family MONODACTYLIDAE

A very small family with species living in the sea and brackish coastal waters of West Africa and the Indian and western Pacific Oceans. Most species live in shoals.

Family MONODACTYLIDAE

Monodactylus argenteus

Fingerfish

- ● **Distribution:** Coastal areas, Red Sea to Australia
- ● **Length:** Up to 9in (23cm)
- ● **Tank length:** 36in (90cm)
- ● **Diet:** Worms, crustaceans, insects, plant matter, dried food
- ● **Water temperature:** 75 to 81°F (24 to 27°C)
- ● **Community tank:** A very fast-moving fish that is easily frightened. It may not be compatible with all other community varieties and will eat small specimens as it grows

The Fingerfish is a tall, disk-shaped fish with strong lateral compression. The head is relatively small, as is the mouth, which has fine teeth. The eyes are large. The dorsal and anal fins are almost opposite one another, and their front parts are much elongated. The very small scales extend onto the bases of the dorsal, caudal, and anal fins. The ventral fins are very small and positioned below the pectoral fins, and the edge of the caudal fin is almost straight. The body is very silvery, becoming yellowish green on the upperparts. The principal markings are two narrow dark transverse bars. The front bar, which starts on the nape, runs across the eye and ends on the

cheek. The second one runs from the front edge of the dorsal fin in a curve across the gill cover and on to form the dark front edge of the anal fin. The dorsal, caudal, and anal fins are mostly yellowish to orange. The sexes are almost impossible to distinguish.

In the wild this attractive shoaling fish is found in fresh, brackish, and sea water. Young individuals can be kept quite successfully in hard fresh water, but they do better if the water has a small amount of salt (about 3 teaspoonfuls to 2.5 gallons/10 liters of water). As they grow the amount of salt should be gradually increased since old Fingerfishes thrive best in pure sea water. The species has not yet been bred in the aquarium. On the other hand, the related Striped Fingerfish, *Monodactylus sebae,* from coastal areas of tropical West Africa, has been bred successfully. After a stormy courtship the female lays up to 15,000 or more eggs, which hatch in about 24 hours.

Below: **Monodactylus argenteus**
This fish should be kept in a shoal.

Family SCATOPHAGIDAE

This small family of fishes lives in coastal areas and reefs of the tropical Indo-Pacific. The juveniles are often found in fresh and brackish waters.

Family SCATOPHAGIDAE

Scatophagus argus

Argusfish

- ● **Distribution:** Tropical Indo-Pacific, in coastal areas
- ● **Length:** Up to 12in (30cm)
- ● **Tank length:** 36in (90cm)
- ● **Diet:** Worms, crustaceans, insects, plant matter, dried food
- ● **Water temperature:** 70 to 83°F (21 to 28°C)
- ● **Community tank:** Often aggressive

This is a very tall, much laterally compressed fish with a small head. The spiny front section of the dorsal fin is relatively low, except for the third and fourth rays; but the soft-rayed part of this and the anal fin are well developed and separated from the caudal fin by only a narrow gap. The mouth is small with rows of fine teeth. The body and head have

small scales and these extend onto the bases of the dorsal and anal fins. The coloration varies considerably with age. For the home aquarium only small specimens are suitable, and these are more attractively colored than old fishes. In individuals about 2 to 2.4in (5 to 6cm) long the flanks are silvery-brown or green and marked with either large round blackish blotches or irregular transverse bars. The soft-rayed parts of the dorsal and anal fins are translucent. Older individuals are greenish with black spots and the bases of the fins often have a yellowish brown or blackish pattern. Specimens with red markings on the back have often been called *S. rubrifrons* but they are really only color variants of *S. argus*.

The young are often seen in both fresh and brackish waters

A practical reminder
Choose compatible fishes. Your dealer should know what size your chosen fishes will reach. Large fishes will eat smaller ones. Slow-swimming timid fishes will not be happy with more boisterous tankmates.

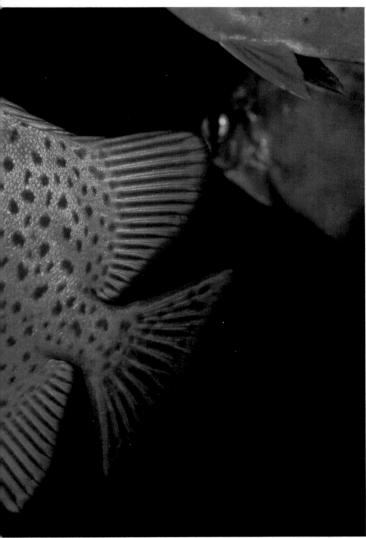

Family TOXOTIDAE
This very small family (one genus with six species) is found in the coastal waters of Southeast Asia and the western Pacific. The fishes catch some of their food by shooting down insects with drops of water.

Family TOXOTIDAE
Toxotes jaculator
Archerfish
● **Distribution:** Southeast Asia to Polynesia and northeastern Australia, mostly in brackish waters
● **Length:** Up to 10in (25cm)
● **Tank length:** 36in (90cm)
● **Diet:** Worms, insects
● **Water temperature:** 77 to 83°F (25 to 28°C)
● **Species tank**.

Also known as *T. jaculatrix,* the Archerfish is a moderately elongated, laterally compressed fish with a pointed head. The dorsal profile, between the forehead and the start of the dorsal fin, is almost straight. The eyes are strikingly large and the deeply cleft mouth faces slightly upward. The dorsal and anal fins are situated far back on the body, and the caudal fin has a slightly concave edge. The back is yellow-green or brownish; the flanks are pale gray to silvery and marked with four to six broad black transverse bars. The first bar runs across the eye and the last one is on the caudal peduncle. This last bar extends to the rear end of the dorsal fin on the top and to the border of the anal fin on the bottom. There are no reliable external sex differences.
Archerfishes are well known for their ability to shoot drops of water to dislodge insects above the water surface. The tongue and the roof of the mouth form a tube. When the mouth is filled with water, the sudden closure of the gill covers forces this water along the tube and out of the mouth. Young individuals start to learn how to shoot when only about 1in (2.5cm) long. The range of the shot varies with the size of the fish. Large, old individuals can bring a fly down at a range of 5ft (1.5m). These interesting fishes are best kept in a tank with rocks and shallow water, and with plants that grow up above the surface. The water should have added sea salt at the rate of one teaspoonful per gallon (4 liters); a quarter of the water must be renewed at regular intervals. The species has not yet been bred in captivity.

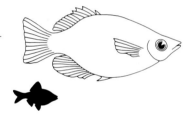

Below: **Toxotes jaculator**
In an aquarium, prey such as crickets, flies, or mealworms placed on leaves above the surface will soon be shot down.

Above: **Scatophagus argus**
This greedy fish will eat almost anything, including boiled lettuce or spinach, and soaked oat flakes.

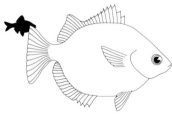

but adults mostly live in the sea, close to the coasts, where they often feed on sewage. They can be kept in a tank with rocks. The water should contain some added salt or sea water. However, because of the large amount of food these fishes consume, the tank will soon accumulate excessive amounts of detritus. This must be removed and a portion of the water replaced. There are no external sex differences. The species has probably not been bred or, if so, only very rarely.

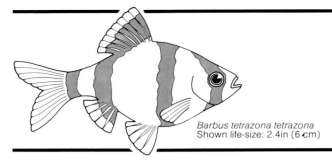

Barbus tetrazona tetrazona
Shown life-size: 2.4in (6 cm)

Family NANDIDAE

The species of this small family of voracious predators are native to South America, Africa, and southern Asia. Most species are relatively small, robust fishes with large heads and deeply cleft, usually protrusible mouths. The dorsal fin has spiny and soft rays.

Family NANDIDAE

Monocirrhus polyacanthus

South American Leaf-fish

- **Distribution:** South America: Amazon, Rio Negro, Guyana
- **Length:** Up to 3.2in (8cm)
- **Tank length:** 12in (30cm)
- **Diet:** Fish
- **Water temperature:** 75 to 83°F (24 to 28°C)
- **Species tank**

When seen from the side, this fish appears ovate with very marked lateral compression. It has a large pointed head with a slightly concave forehead. The mouth is large and protrusible, and the lower lip has a wormlike growth. The dorsal and anal fins have long bases; the front part of each is supported by numerous short spines. In general the fins are very poorly developed. The coloration, which is always inconspicuous and can change according to the surroundings, often gives the flanks the appearance of a dead leaf. When lurking among plants, the body, iris, and spiny parts of the fins are greenish yellow, but in open water they are pale yellow or brownish with irregular dark markings. There are three thin dark lines radiating from near the eye; the first runs obliquely up to the nape and on to the origin of the dorsal fin, the second obliquely down to the edge of the belly, and the third from above the gill cover to the root of the tail.

This is an extremely predatory, voracious fish, which remains mostly in an oblique position, with head down, lying in wait for prey. The prey is literally sucked into the protrusible mouth. The South American Leaf-fish should be kept in a well-established tank with dense vegetation and subdued lighting. The water must be soft, slightly acid, and filtered through peat. The pair cleans a spawning site (a rock, a leaf, or an area of the aquarium glass) and starts to spawn without a period of courtship. The male guards and fans the small eggs, which hatch after three to four days. The fry live on the yolk-sac contents until six or seven days after hatching and then feed on tiny crustaceans.

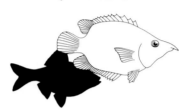

Below: **Monocirrhus polyacanthus**
The female should be removed from the tank after spawning, leaving the male to tend the brood.

Family NANDIDAE

Badis badis

Badis

- **Distribution:** India
- **Length:** Up to 3.2in (8cm)
- **Tank length:** 12in (30cm)
- **Diet:** Worms, crustaceans, insects, dried food
- **Water temperature:** 79 to 83°F (26 to 28°C)
- **Community tank**

Badis is a somewhat elongated fish with only slight lateral compression. The dorsal fin starts above the pectoral fin and it has a very long base. The caudal fin has a rounded rear edge. The females are smaller and have a more convex belly profile, while the males usually have slightly concave underparts. In the adults the general coloration of the flanks is yellowish, brownish, or greenish; healthy males exhibit a mosaiclike pattern of yellow, red, or black scales. A black streak runs from the mouth, across the eye, to the insertion of the dorsal fin. The back is olive to dark blue and the underparts are greenish or bluish. The fin colors vary and may be bluish, dark blue, or green. The dorsal fin may be marked with red or green longitudinal stripes. Females are similar, but not as brightly colored. Young individuals often have six to 10 dark transverse bars, but these usually disappear with age.

This is a very peaceful fish of the middle and lower water layers, which does not quarrel with other members of its species even in a community tank. Keep it in a tank with areas of dense vegetation and be sure to furnish the tank with rocks and roots to provide hiding-places, since this is a shy fish. The composition of the water is not critical. Spawning takes place in one of the hiding-places (a flowerpot is very suitable), and the male guards the eggs. These hatch in three days and the fry are kept together until they have consumed the contents of the yolk-sac. At this point the parent fish should be removed from the tank. The fry will only feed on live food, such as brine shrimp nauplii.

Right **Badis badis**
This is the most peaceful member of an otherwise aggressive family.

A practical reminder
Avoid wide temperature changes when introducing fishes into the tank. Float their transporting bag in the aquarium for a few minutes to equalize water temperatures before you release the new fishes.

Left: **Polycentrus schomburgki**
This interesting predatory fish is reasonably sized for an aquarium, but not suitable for beginners.

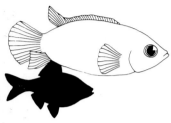

Family NANDIDAE
Polycentrus schomburgki
Schomburgk's Leaf-fish
● **Distribution:** Northern South America and Trinidad
● **Length:** Up to 4in (10cm)
● **Tank length:** 12in (30cm)
● **Diet:** Worms, insects, fish
● **Water temperature:** 73 to 79°F (23 to 26°C)
● **Species tank**

Another stocky, ovate and laterally compressed leaf-fish, the stocky *Polycentrus schomburgki* has a large pointed head and a deeply cleft, protrusible mouth. The rear edge of the gill cover is armed with a spine. The dorsal and anal fins are similar to one another. The rear parts of the fins—with soft rays—are quite small, but the front parts—with spiny rays—have relatively long bases and are quite low. The coloration changes according to the surroundings, the temperature of the water, and the mood of the fish; but it is usually gray to brownish with irregular dark and pale markings. Three dark stripes radiate from the eye—one to the nape, one to the snout, and the third to the edge of the gill cover. At spawning time the male becomes velvety-black marked with silvery and blue-green dots, while the female is very pale.

This is a highly predatory fish, which can be kept in a tank with dense vegetation and some rocks and roots where the fish can lie in wait for prey. The water must be soft, slightly acid, and filtered through peat. The lighting should be subdued. Spawning takes place in a small cave or under an overhang of rock. The eggs, which are guarded by the male, hatch in 60 to 70 hours and the fry are free-swimming about six or seven days later. They can be fed on small nauplii. However, the fry do not chase their prey but, like their parents, wait until it appears before their mouths.

THE CICHLIDS

Above: *Pseudotropheus zebra*, one of the cichlids
found only in Lake Malawi, East Africa.
Right: A Rift Valley lake in East Africa with
hard, alkaline water that suits cichlids.

*T*his is a large family of fishes, mostly heavy-bodied and
distinguished more for their interesting breeding habits than
for their intrinsic beauty. They are widely distributed in South and
Central America and tropical Africa, with a few in southern Asia,
and one species is found in southern North America. Most cichlids
live in lakes or slow-flowing waters, often in shallow areas close
to the shore where rocks and vegetation provide good hiding-places.

Breeding is in most cases based on a territory, which may not
be very large but is always vigorously defended by the male. In
most home aquariums, therefore, a single pair is usually
sufficient for the average tank. The eggs are laid on rocks, timber,
or leaves, or in a pit dug in the sand by the male. Because of this
digging behavior the tank should not contain any rooted plants,
although a few floating plants will look attractive and provide some
degree of shelter.

There are two main spawning patterns. Some species lay
their eggs out in the open; both sexes take part in clearing the
spawning site, guarding the territory, and tending the eggs and
young. In these the sexes are similar in form and coloration and
difficult to distinguish.

In other cichlids, known in general as shelter-breeders, the sexes
are clearly distinguished, the males being larger and more
brightly colored than the females. Their eggs are either laid and
guarded in small caves or laid on the substrate and then taken
immediately into the mouth, usually of the female, where they are
incubated. Such eggs hatch in six to 10 days and the fry are
then tended for a while longer by the female.

For most cichlids the composition of the tank water is not
critical. The exceptions include the rather delicate discus fishes
from South America, which require soft, acid, peat-filtered
water, and certain species from Africa. The well-known
Mozambique Mouth-brooder normally lives and breeds in fresh
water, but it has been known to spawn successfully in sea water.

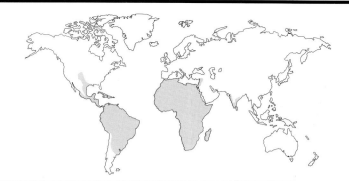

Left: The family Cichlidae has about 650 species, most of which live in the fresh waters of Africa or Central and South America. A few cichlids occur in brackish waters, but the vast majority live in rivers or standing inland waters. Most species are omnivorous, taking a wide range of foods, but some are active predators and others live mainly on a vegeterian diet, usually by scraping algae.

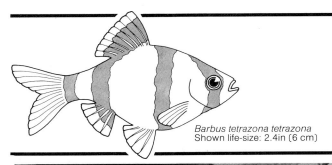

Barbus tetrazona tetrazona
Shown life-size: 2.4in (6 cm)

Family CICHLIDAE
Aequidens portalegrensis
Port Acara
- **Distribution:** Southern Brazil, Porto Alegre, Paraguay, Bolivia
- **Length:** Up to 8.7in (22cm)
- **Tank length:** 36in (90cm)
- **Diet:** Worms, crustaceans, insects, dried food
- **Water temperature:** 61 to 73°F (16 to 23°C)
- **Species tank**

Port Acara is a moderately squat cichlid with a deep, laterally compressed body and a massive head. The general coloration is greenish in the male but more brownish or red in the female. The flanks have reddish or bluish iridescence when seen in reflected light. A broad dark longitudinal band starts at the back of the eye and extends along the body. It ends in a dark greenish or brown marking on the dorsal side of the caudal peduncle. During periods of excitement, such as spawning time, the whole body in both sexes becomes almost black. The caudal and anal fins are green or brownish green, and the dorsal

Above:
Aequidens portalegrensis ♂(t),♀(b)
This is a spawning pair. Some eggs have already been laid and these can be seen on the substrate beneath the belly of the female.

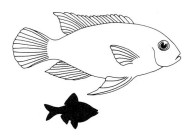

fin is bluish gray with small dark markings on its rear half.

This is a hardy cichlid that can be kept at temperatures as low as 61°F (16°C) during the winter. The tank can have rocks and roots to provide hiding-places, but should contain no rooted plants since the Port Acara is a great digger—particularly before spawning. The eggs are laid out in the open, and the newly hatched fry are assiduously guarded by both parents. Water changes are essential for healthy fishes.

Family CICHLIDAE
Aequidens maronii
Keyhole Cichlid
- **Distribution:** Guyana, Surinam
- **Length:** Up to 4in (10cm)
- **Tank length:** 36in (90cm)
- **Diet:** Worms, crustaceans, insects
- **Water temperature:** 72 to 77°F (22 to 25°C)
- **Species tank**

This fairly short, high-backed cichlid has a rounded forehead and a laterally compressed body. The dorsal and anal fins of the male are elongated and have pointed tips. In old males the dorsal fin may extend back almost to the end of the caudal fin, and the ventral fins may reach the anal fin. The upper lobe of the caudal fin is slightly longer than the lower lobe. In general, the body is beige to pale brown and the flanks have 12 or 13 longitudinal rows of darker dots. A curved black band runs from the front end of the dorsal fin, across the eye, to the lower edge of the gill cover. The most characteristic feature, however, is a very dark blotch with a pale border that lies near the back and beneath the last spiny rays of the dorsal fin.

Keyhole Cichlid is a very peaceful fish, which can be kept in a tank with a few plants and rocks to provide shelter, and plenty of open water for swimming. The composition of the water is not critical but a portion—about one third—should be changed every three or four weeks. The eggs are laid on a previously cleaned rock and are guarded by both parents. They hatch in a few days, and the fry will feed on fine live food. They will continue to be guarded by the parents.

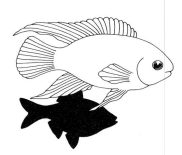

Right: **Aequidens maronii**
This is a very undemanding cichlid, which has even bred in a community tank. The young may remain with the parent fishes for a period of six months.

A practical reminder
A major contribution to keeping fishes in prime condition is a varied diet of high-quality food including living foods. Fishes will naturally become bored with any single type of food, however high the quality.

Family CICHLIDAE
Aequidens pulcher
Blue Acara
- **Distribution:** Central and northern South America
- **Length:** Up to 6.3in (16cm)
- **Tank length:** 36in (90cm)
- **Diet:** Worms, crustaceans, insects
- **Water temperature:** 72 to 79°F (22 to 26°C)
- **Species tank**

This oval-shaped cichlid has a broad forehead. The rear part of the body is laterally compressed. The dorsal and anal fins of the male are very elongated with pointed tips—the dorsal fins may even extend over the caudal fin. The fins of the female are not as well-developed as those of the male. The back is olive, and the flanks are yellow-brown or grayish brown with a bluish iridescence. The underparts are much paler. The flanks have between five and eight broad transverse bars, which are sometimes indistinct. Each scale on the flanks has a large iridescent blue-green or pale blue spot. The gill cover and cheeks are marked with shiny blue-green dots and lines. The lips are pale

Above: **Aequidens pulcher**
Beneath this spawning pair eggs can be seen on a flat rock that the fishes have cleaned.

blue. The iris of the eye is golden-yellow with a red border. Except for the caudal fin, which is reddish, the fins are greenish or bluish. The dorsal fin has a red border. At spawning time the flanks show six to eight rows of greenish dots. The female is similarly colored.

The peaceful Blue Acara can be kept in a tank with some plants as well as rocks and roots, and a sandy substrate. Both sexes clean a rock that will be the spawning site. The female lays her eggs on the rock. There they are fertilized by the male. Both sexes tend the eggs—which hatch in two to five days—and they continue to look after the fry for some weeks. Once the fry are free-swimming they will feed on rotifers and small nauplii.

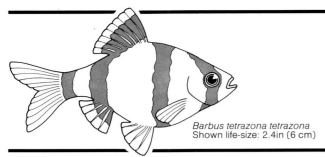

Barbus tetrazona tetrazona
Shown life-size: 2.4in (6 cm)

Family CICHLIDAE
Apistogramma agassizi
Agassiz's Dwarf Cichlid
- **Distribution:** Brazil and Bolivia
- **Length:** Up to 3.2in (8cm) in males, to 2.4in (6cm) in females
- **Tank length:** 24in (60cm)
- **Diet:** Worms, crustaceans, insects, dried food
- **Water temperature:** 73 to 77°F (23 to 25°C)
- **Community tank**

Agassiz's Dwarf Cichlid is a moderately elongated small cichlid. It has a very long dorsal fin whose rear end draws out to a point—strikingly so in the male. The caudal fin of the male has central rays that are much longer than the outer ones. In the female this fin is rounded. The back of the male is greenish blue, and the flanks are orange in front and iridescent greenish blue at the back. Both gill covers and cheeks are marked with brilliant blue dots and lines. A dark line extends from the mouth, across the eye, and back along the flanks to the root of the tail. The basal part of the dorsal fin is blackish, the front part blue-green, and the rear part smoky-gray with the edge and tip poppy-red. The inner part of the caudal fin is blue-green and the edges are gray-green. These two areas are separated by a smoky-gray section. The female is lemon-yellow with markings similar to those of the male.

This cichlid can be kept in a tank with rocks and plants. The water should be soft, slightly acid, and filtered through peat. The members of the genus *Apistogramma* spawn in small caves—not out in the open. In an aquarium provide the fishes with a small inverted flowerpot or half a coconut shell for spawning. Either one can be propped up on one side to provide an entrance. The male guards a relatively large territory; within this area a number of females occupy smaller territories. The male courts and mates with each female. The eggs are laid on the roof of the cave and tended by the females. The eggs hatch in three or four days, and the fry are tended for a time by the female. When free-swimming they can be fed on rotifers and small nauplii.

Below: **Apistogramma agassizi** ♂
One of the best dwarf cichlids, this species will not dig up the plants.

Family CICHLIDAE
Apistogramma reitzigi
Yellow Dwarf Cichlid
- **Distribution:** South America, in Rio Paraguay
- **Length:** Up to 2in (5cm)
- **Tank length:** 24in (60cm)
- **Diet:** Worms, crustaceans, insects, dried food
- **Water temperature:** 73 to 77°F (23 to 25°C)
- **Community tank**

Apistogramma reitzigi is a laterally compressed cichlid that is not as elongated as *Apistogramma agassizi*. The dorsal and anal fins of the Yellow Dwarf Cichlid are tall and pointed at the back. In the male the elongated tips of these fins reach the rear end of the caudal fin, but they are considerably shorter in the female. The caudal fin is fan-shaped. In the male the background coloration is grayish yellow, with a pale yellow belly. When in good condition, the flanks show bluish iridescence and the cheeks and gill cover are marked with numerous bright green spots. The dorsal fin is yellowish at the rear end and more greenish in front with a bluish iridescence. There are dark dots at the base. The caudal fin is yellowish. Several dark transverse or longitudinal markings may appear on the flanks. This usually occurs when the fish is excited. The female is darker, but becomes yellow at spawning time.

This cichlid requires soft, slightly acid water in a tank with rocks or other objects—artificial or otherwise—to supply shelter and caves for spawning. The male and female Yellow Dwarf Cichlids have the same territorial system as the Agassiz's Dwarf Cichlids. The female lays 30 to 60 red eggs, and she tends these and the fry. Her maternal instinct is very strong.

Left: **Apistogramma reitzigi** ♀
If her eggs fail to hatch, the female has been known to gather together a little shoal of Daphnia *and guard them as her brood.*

A practical reminder
If you catch your pets' live food, try to collect it from fish-free waters. This will avoid the risk of introducing any fish diseases into the aquarium. Check all wild-caught food for dangerous aquatic larvae.

Family CICHLIDAE
Astronotus ocellatus
Oscar
● **Distribution:** South America: Orinoco to Rio Paraguay
● **Length:** Up to 14in (35cm)
● **Tank length:** 48in (120cm)
● **Diet:** Worms, crustaceans, insects, chopped meat, dried food
● **Water temperature:** 72 to 79°F (22 to 26°C)
● **Species tank**

The Oscar is an oval cichlid with only moderate lateral

compression of the body. The ventral fins are pointed, but the dorsal, caudal, anal, and pectoral fins are rounded. The general coloration varies greatly and depends, to some extent, on age. In sexually mature specimens the flanks may be dark brown, bluish black, or olive. They are marked with very irregular pale yellowish streaks and blotches. The caudal peduncle has a black spot encircled by a bright red ring—this is one of the Oscar's few constant characteristics. The fins are dark at the outside and paler at the base. The eyes are relatively small.
　Ideally the tank should have a

substrate of sand or gravel, a number of rocks and roots, and some floating plants. Rooted plants are not advised since Oscars are great diggers. Some aquarists use potted plants well anchored in the substrate. Both sexes carefully clean a suitable spawning site—often a flat rock. The eggs adhere to this site and are guarded by both parents. They hatch in three or four days, and the parents move the fry to a shallow pit in the sand where they remain for six or seven days. Once they are free-swimming they will take rotifers and small brine shrimp nauplii.

Above: **Astronotus ocellatus**
In spite of its large size, this is quite a peaceful fish, but its digging activities make it unsuitable for a community tank.

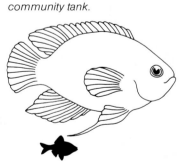

165

characins

Left: **Cichlasoma festivum**
Once established, a pair of these fishes will continue to breed. This species is peaceful enough to be kept with Angelfishes.

Above the band the upperparts are usually brown, but below it the flanks are yellow with some iridescence. The gill cover is iridescent greenish or yellow, and the caudal peduncle has a well-defined black marking surrounded by a golden-yellow area. The iris is also golden-yellow with splotches of red above.
　This shy, non-aggressive cichlid should be kept in a well-aerated tank with rocks and roots, and a few rooted plants. Spawning takes places on a rock or leaf and the parents guard the eggs and fry assiduously. The fry become free-swimming about two days after hatching, and can be fed at first on fine live food.

Also known as *Herichthys cyanoguttatus,* this species is an elongated, laterally compressed cichlid with an arched back and a bulging forehead. The dorsal fin is pointed but not elongated, and the caudal fin is slightly concave. Adults are blue-gray or chestnut-brown with an irregular pattern of blue or green streaks and dots that extend onto the dorsal, caudal, and anal fins. The pectoral fins are colorless, and the rays of the anal fin are bright blue-green. Females are similarly—but less intensely—colored. Young individuals are clay-colored with a few dark markings on the flanks.

Rio Grande Perch is an aggressive cichlid that uproots plants. The tank should contain only rocks and roots positioned to form separate compartments so that the fishes can establish territories. A few floating plants would be suitable. Good aeration is essential and a portion of the water must be replaced at regular intervals as this species is sensitive to old water. The 400 to 500 eggs are laid in the open in large spawning pits or sometimes on rocks cleaned by the fishes.
　The eggs hatch in five to seven days. The parents do not always protect their brood.

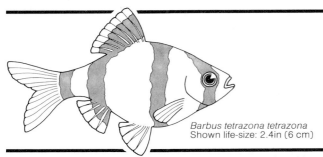

Barbus tetrazona tetrazona
Shown life-size: 2.4in (6 cm)

Right: **Cichlasoma biocellatum** ♂
This fish is such an enthusiastic digger that it will make a tank uninhabitable for more peaceful species. It takes excellent care of its brood, which may be large.

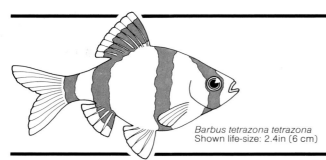

Barbus tetrazona tetrazona
Shown life-size: 2.4in (6 cm)

Family CICHLIDAE

Cichlasoma meeki
Firemouth Cichlid

● **Distribution:** Central America
● **Length:** Up to 6in (15cm)
● **Tank length:** 36in (90cm)
● **Diet:** Worms, crustaceans, insects, dried food
● **Water temperature:** 68 to 77°F (20 to 25°C)
● **Community tank**

Cichlasoma meeki is a fairly tall, laterally compressed cichlid with a large head. The forehead in front of the eyes is slightly concave. The dorsal fin starts far forward on this fish—roughly above the rear edge of the gill cover. In the male it ends behind in a pointed tip. The anal fin has a similar pointed tip. In the female the fin tips are noticeably shorter. In older inidividuals the rear edge of the caudal fin becomes slightly concave and the outer rays are elongated. The general coloration is blue-gray with violet iridescence. The belly is yellow-green to orange, but the throat and breast are characteristically bright red, hence the popular name. The flanks have from five to seven dark transverse bars, which are usually not very well defined. The scales have red edges. Apart from the pectoral fins, which are

Above: **Cichlasoma meeki** ♂
This photograph shows a male guarding a large shoal of very young fry. With its brilliant red underparts, this is one of the most striking of the cichlids.

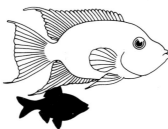

transparent, the other fins have brownish red rays, and the tissue between them is marked with blue-green dots. The edges of the caudal and anal fins are black. The edge of the dorsal fin is red.

This is a peaceful cichlid except towards smaller members of its own species. It requires a tank with a substrate of clean sand, rocks and roots, and a few robust plants. The plants will not be attacked except possibly during breeding. Spawning takes place on the bottom and then both sexes protect the eggs and, subsequently, the fry.

Firemouth Cichlids are also found in subterranean waters.

A practical reminder
Fishes needing vegetable matter may have their diet supplemented with lettuce leaves, spinach, or wheatgerm. Carnivores can be given scraps of raw, lean meat such as ox heart, and will enjoy chopped earthworms.

Family CICHLIDAE
Cichlasoma nigrofasciatum
Zebra Cichlid
- **Distribution:** Central America: Guatemala (in Lakes Atitlan and Amatitlan)
- **Length:** Up to 4in (10cm), possibly more
- **Tank length:** 36in (90cm)
- **Diet:** Worms, crustaceans, insects, fish, chopped meat, plant matter, dried food
- **Water temperature:** 68 to 79°F (20 to 26°C)
- **Species tank**

The Zebra Cichlid is moderately elongated and laterally compressed. It has a small mouth and eight or nine dark transverse bars on the flanks. In the male, the dorsal fin, which starts above the gill slit, is elongated and pointed toward the end. The tip reaches back to the middle of the caudal fin or even beyond. There is a large black spot on the caudal peduncle and on the gill cover. The caudal, dorsal, and anal fins are iridescent green, the last two having red borders. The female is not as brightly colored as the male. At spawning time the transverse bars of the male are scarcely visible, but those of the female are black.

This is a quarrelsome fish that is suitable only for a tank with large rocks, a gravel substrate, and no rooted plants. The diet should contain a high proportion of plant matter, such as boiled lettuce or spinach and soaked oat flakes. (Boiling and soaking will soften the food.) Spawning takes place on the bottom in the open, not in a cave. The eggs are laid on a previously cleaned spawning site and are guarded assiduously by both parents, who chase away any intruders. The fry are still tended by the parents, and they become free-swimming about six to eight days after hatching. They can then be fed on tiny live food, such as brine shrimp nauplii and micro-worms. Brood protection continues for three or four weeks after hatching.

Right: **Cichlasoma nigrofasciatum**
This is a boisterous fish that will quickly destroy any tank decor.

Family CICHLIDAE
Crenicichla lepidota
Pike Cichlid
- **Distribution:** Brazil to northern Argentina.
- **Length:** Up to 8in (20cm)
- **Tank length:** 36in (90cm)
- **Diet:** Worms, insects, fish
- **Water temperature:** 68 to 79°F (20 to 26°C)
- **Species tank**

Pike Cichlid is another elongated cichlid. It has moderate lateral compression, a pointed snout, and a deeply cleft mouth. The body looks somewhat like that of a pike. The upperparts are olive-green or gray-green and the underparts are whitish, pale brown, or yellowish. The flanks are green and sometimes tinged with yellow. A dark longitudinal band, sometimes broken, runs back from the mouth to a point just behind the insertion of the pectoral fins. The area behind the gill cover has a large black marking, which may be encircled with silvery or golden spots. The rear part of the caudal peduncle has a similar marking. In general, the coloration of this cichlid varies greatly, which is not surprising in view of its extensive geographical range.

This voracious cichlid should be kept in a covered tank with a sandy substrate, rocks and roots arranged to provide shelter, and a few robust rooted plants. The composition of the water is not critical. Spawning takes place in shallow pits in the substrate. The female lays a number of very small, whitish eggs. In this species the protection of the brood is carried out primarily by the male, who should be given a varied and abundant diet of large insects and small fishes during this period. Once they are free-swimming the fry can be fed on tiny live food.

Left: **Crenicichla lepidota**
This predatory cichlid needs an abundant supply of live food.

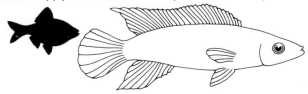

Barbus tetrazona tetrazona
Shown life-size: 2.4in (6 cm)

Right: **Etroplus maculatus**
One of the few Asiatic cichlids, this modestly sized species is highly suitable for an aquarium.

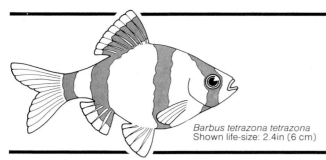

Family CICHLIDAE
Etroplus maculatus
Orange Chromide
- **Distribution:** India and Sri Lanka
- **Length:** Up to 3.2in (8cm)
- **Tank length:** 24in (60cm)
- **Diet:** Worms, crustaceans, insects, fish, plant matter, dried food
- **Water temperature:** 72 to 83°F (22 to 28°C)
- **Community tank**

The slightly elongated Orange Chromide has strong lateral compression. When viewed from the side the body is ovate and less angular than the Green Chromide. The forehead is very slightly concave, the head is pointed, and the eyes are large. The fins are not very impressive compared with those of other cichlids. The anal and dorsal fins are low and quite long. At spawning time the back is grayish blue or dark brown. The yellow or pale orange flanks are marked with three broad transverse bars that do not usually extend to the back and underparts. Each scale on the flanks has a red dot. The dorsal fin is orange with dark red dots and a red border. The anal fin is yellow at the base but dark at the edge. The caudal fin is yellow, becoming reddish towards the edge. The eyes are large with golden or iridescent red irises.

This is a better fish for the small aquarium than the Green Chromide. It can be kept in a tank with rocks and a few plants, which will not normally be attacked. The water should be hard with added sea salt (about two teaspoonsful to every 2.5 gallons/10 liters of tank water). If kept in pure fresh water this species is susceptible to fungal disease. Spawning habits are identical to those of the Green Chromide; the eggs and fry are guarded by both parents. Before they become free-swimming the fry adhere to the parents' flanks.

170

A practical reminder
Brine shrimp *(Artemia salina)* eggs hatch in salt water (4oz of natural sea salt per gallon/30gm per liter) in 24 to 26 hours. They provide nutritious, disease-free, live food just the right size for the majority of fry.

Family CICHLIDAE
Etroplus suratensis
Green Chromide
- **Distribution:** Sri Lanka
- **Length:** Up to 16in (40cm)
- **Tank length:** 36in (90cm)
- **Diet:** Worms, insects, chopped meat
- **Water temperature:** 73 to 83°F (23 to 28°C)
- **Species tank**

Etroplus suratensis is a short oval cichlid with a deep, laterally compressed body. The forehead is very slightly concave, and the caudal fin is convex with pointed corners. The dorsal and anal fins are low and very long. This is not a particularly colorful fish except at spawning time. The general coloration is grayish to gray-green and the flanks are marked with six to eight dark transverse bars, which are often very indistinct. Depending upon the angle of the light, the flanks show a certain amount of iridescence and the scales in this area have large bright blue or green spots. In general the fins are greenish or faintly blue, with the exception of the pectoral fins, which are pale yellow with a clearly defined dark marking at the base.

The Green Chromide should not be kept in fresh water for any length of time. In the wild it lives in shoals in brackish water, occasionally moving into the sea, where it suffers no harm. In fact, it has been observed that sea water enhances the colors of the fish. The tank can have some dense vegetation, and the water must be hard, with added sea salt (about two teaspoonsful to every 2.5 gallons/10 liters of fresh water). Spawning takes places on a previously cleaned rock or other object. The eggs are guarded by both parents, and they hatch in two to five days. When they are free-swimming, the fry will start to feed on brine shrimp nauplii and other very small live food.

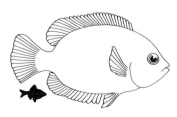

Left: **Etroplus suratensis**
This cichlid is ideal for a home aquarium when young. A shoal of mature specimens makes a splendid exhibit in a public aquarium.

Family CICHLIDAE
Geophagus jurupari
Earth-eater
- **Distribution:** Tropical South America
- **Length:** Up to 10in (25cm)
- **Tank length:** 36in (90cm)
- **Diet:** Worms crustaceans, insects
- **Water temperature:** 72 to 83°F (22 to 28°C)
- **Community tank:** Size may intimidate smaller species

Earth-eater is a moderately elongated, laterally compressed cichlid with an arched back and forehead and a strikingly massive head. The dorsal fin is very long and its rear end is pointed. The anal fin, on the other hand, is quite short but it too is pointed. The sexes are similarly colored. In general, the flanks are iridescent greenish or yellowish and the back is somewhat darker. The belly is usually pale yellow, but it may be grayish. The fins are greenish with pale dots and streaks. The head and gill cover have many shiny dots and streaks.

In spite of its somewhat predatory appearance, this is a most peaceful fish and will not bother the other occupants of the tank. It feeds on the bottom, burrowing in the substrate for its food—hence the popular and generic names *(Geophagus* means 'earth-eater'). The tank should have rocks and roots to provide hiding-places, some robust plants, and a substrate of fine sand. The continuous digging makes the water cloudy, so the filtration system must be efficient. Spawning usually takes place on a rock, where the eggs remain for about 24 hours. During this period they are fanned by the fins of both parents. They are then taken up into the female's mouth, where they are incubated. Some aquarists say that the male also takes part in mouth-brooding. So the breeding behaviour of this species falls somewhere between that of the typical open spawners such as *Cichlasoma* and that of the mouth-brooders such as *Labeotrophus.*

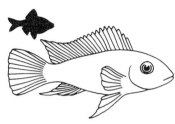

Below: **Geophagus jurupari**
Although it appears aggressive, this is a reasonably peaceful fish.

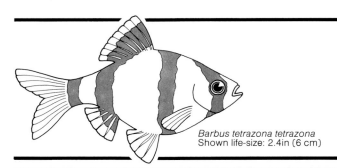

Barbus tetrazona tetrazona
Shown life-size: 2.4in (6 cm)

Family CICHLIDAE

Hemichromis bimaculatus

Jewel Cichlid

- **Distribution:** Africa (Rivers Nile, Niger, Zaire)
- **Length:** Up to 6in (15cm)
- **Tank length:** 36in (90cm)
- **Diet:** Worms, crustaceans, insects, chopped meat
- **Water temperature:** 72 to 83°F (22 to 28°C)
- **Species tank**

This elongated, laterally compressed cichlid has a roundish caudal fin, but the dorsal and anal fins are pointed. The back is gray-brown or dark olive with greenish iridescence, and the belly is yellowish. The flanks are greenish yellow with a dark longitudinal band that expands on the gill cover, mid-flanks, and tail base to form large blotches. The fins are dark ocher to greenish. At spawning time the coloration becomes much more brilliant. The back and forehead are olive with red iridescence, and the markings on the gill cover and flanks become almost black. The dorsal fin is pale red in the middle,

Above:
Hemichromis bimaculatus ♂(t), ♀(b)
Eggs can be seen just below the female of this spawning pair.

becoming deep red at the base and edge. The rays of the ventral fins are blue-green. The iris is blood-red with a thin golden inner edge.

This is a quarrelsome fish and an inveterate digger—in a short time, a small group of Jewel Cichlids will uproot all the plants, dig pits in the substrate, and undermine the rocks. This should be taken into consideration when furnishing the tank. Typical open breeders, they usually spawn on a rock. Brood protection is particularly assiduous, and the young are tended until they are 0.4in (1cm) or more in length. The digging activities make the water cloudy, so there should be a good system of filtration.

A practical reminder
Well-fed fishes can be left without food over a two-week vacation period. If you can trust a neighbor not to overfeed them, you have found a 'fish-sitter' but always remember— overfeeding kills.

Left: **Hemihaplochromis multicolor**
This excellent mouth-brooder has been a favorite since about 1905.

Family CICHLIDAE
Hemihaplochromis multicolor
Egyptian Mouth-brooder
● **Distribution:** Eastern Africa, particularly the Nile area
● **Length:** Up to 3.2in (8cm)
● **Tank length:** 18in (45cm)
● **Diet:** Worms, crustaceans, insects, chopped meat, dried food
● **Water temperature:** 68 to 79°F (20 to 26°C)
● **Community tank**

Also known as *Pseudocrenilabrus multicolor,* the Egyptian Mouth-brooder is a moderately elongated cichlid with lateral compression, particularly in the rear of the body. The caudal fin is fan-shaped and the rear parts of the dorsal and anal fins are rounded. The general coloration is yellow to pale red, with greenish or golden iridescence; the back is iridescent blue. The dorsal fin of the male is usually red with a blue-green border and a black edge; the anal fin has the same coloration, but is bright red at the rear end. The caudal fin is yellow-green with three rows of dark dots. The iris is golden-yellow and the gill cover is green with a black spot ringed in gold. The female is not as brightly colored, and the anal fin lacks the red tip.

This is altogether a truly multicolored fish, and one that is highly suitable for a beginner. It can be kept in a tank with a sandy substrate, dense marginal vegetation, a few floating plants, and rocks and roots to provide hiding-places. The composition of the water is not critical. Spawning takes place in a small pit that has been previously dug by the male. There may be 30 to 60 eggs— sometimes more—and they are immediately taken up into the mouth of the female, where they are incubated until they hatch after about 10 days. The fry start to feed immediately on very fine live food, but they continue to use the female's mouth as a refuge when threatened, and also at night, for as long as six or seven days.

Family CICHLIDAE
Julidochromis ornatus
Golden Julie
● **Distribution:** East Africa, in Lake Tanganyika
● **Length:** Up to 2.8in (7cm)
● **Tank length:** 24in (60cm)
● **Diet:** Worms, crustaceans, insects, plant matter, dried food
● **Water temperature:** 72 to 77°F (22 to 25°C)
● **Species tank**

This elongated, spindle-shaped cichlid has a small mouth, a long snout, and a fan-shaped caudal fin. The flanks are marked by

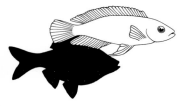

Left: **Julidochromis ornatus**
This cichlid needs plenty of swimming space in a species tank.

three well-defined, broad, dark brown or almost black longitudinal bands. The uppermost of these bands runs along the back and extends onto the base of the dorsal fin; the central band runs from the forehead above the eye to the upper edge of the caudal peduncle; and the lower band extends from the upper lip, across the lower half of the eye, to the caudal peduncle and continues onto the caudal fin as a large, round spot. All the fins are yellow and the dorsal, caudal, and anal fins have dark edges.

This is a territorial cichlid best kept as a single species to avoid male rivalry. The tank should be furnished with rocks, arranged to provide small caves. The water must be hard and slightly alkaline. A typical cave spawner, the female lays eggs in a small cave or on the underside of an overhanging rock. The male, which is larger than the female, takes the major part in brood protection. After hatching, the fry remain at the spawning site for four to six days and are then free-swimming. At this stage they can be fed on nauplii and other tiny live food.

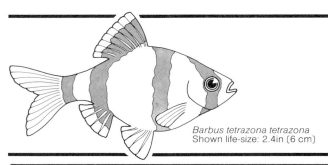

Barbus tetrazona tetrazona
Shown life-size: 2.4in (6 cm)

Above and left:
Labeotropheus fuelleborni ♂(t), ♀(l)
This active cichlid needs plenty of swimming space and rocks.

Family CICHLIDAE

Labeotropheus fuelleborni
Fuelleborn's Cichlid

- ● **Distribution:** East Africa, in Lake Malawi
- ● **Length:** Up to 4.7in (12cm)
- ● **Tank length:** 36in (90cm)
- ● **Diet:** Worms, crustaceans, insects, plant matter, dried food
- ● **Water temperature:** 72 to 77°F (22 to 25°C)
- ● **Species tank**

A moderately elongated, relatively high-backed cichlid, *Labeotropheus fuelleborni* has pointed dorsal and anal fins. The upper lip is quite large and overhangs the lower lip, so the mouth of Fuelleborn's Cichlid is ventral. The teeth are chisel-shaped and well adapted for grazing on the thick algal mats that cover the inshore rocks of their native Lake Malawi. These algal mats also contain the larvae of midges and other small insects.

The males of this species are blue with darker transverse bars. The rear edge of the caudal fin is red. Some of the females are also blue and very similar to the males, but others are orange with dark spots and blotches, giving a marbled appearance.

This active cichlid needs a tank that includes groups of plants with tough leaves and an arrangement of rocks and roots to provide hiding-places. The water should be medium-hard. These cichlids—especially the males—tend to be quarrelsome, so they are best kept as a pair in a separate species tank. Spawning takes place on the bottom. After the eggs have been laid they are taken up into the female's mouth, where they are incubated for two to four weeks. A large female may lay up to 60 eggs. Once hatched the fry will be free-swimming and ready to feed on small live food after about three weeks.

A practical reminder
Regular maintenance chores include pruning plants, removing dead leaves and detritus, and cleaning front and cover glasses. Change the filter wool when you do partial water changes. Check pump filter pads.

Labeotropheus trewavasae
Trewavas's Cichlid

● **Distribution:** East Africa Lake Malawi
● **Length:** Up to 4in (10cm)
● **Tank length:** 36in (90cm)
● **Diet:** Worms, crustaceans, insects, plant matter, dried food
● **Water temperature:** 72 to 77°F (22 to 25°C)
● **Species tank**

Another elongated, robustly built cichlid from Lake Malawi, Trewavas's Cichlid is similar in shape to Fuelleborn's Cichlid. The males are pale blue with darker transverse bars and a reddish brown dorsal fin. Some of the females are colored like the males, but many of them are yellowish brown or orange with a pattern of red and black marbling. Young males are mostly violet-blue. The upper lip is overhanging and the teeth are shaped for scraping algae off the rocks.

This is an active, rather quarrelsome cichlid, which establishes and defends a territory. The tank should be furnished with a few rooted plants with tough leaves, and some rocks and roots arranged to provide hiding-places The water should be medium-hard. Spawning takes place on the bottom, and the eggs are taken up into the mouth of the female, where they are incubated for three or four weeks. Normally a female does not lay a large number of eggs—usually about a dozen—but because of the mouth-brooding behaviour these eggs have a greater chance of survival than those spawned at random by so many other tropical fishes, such as characins and barbs.

Lake Malawi, one of the East African Rift Valley lakes, has over 200 cichlids that can be found nowhere else—these are known as endemic species.

Left and below:
Labeotropheus trewavasae ♀(l),♂(b)
As this fish scrapes algae off rocks in the wild it also takes in small crustaceans and worms.

Nannacara anomala
Golden-eyed Dwarf Cichlid

● **Distribution:** Guyana
● **Length:** Up to 3.2in (8cm)
● **Tank length:** 24in (60cm)
● **Diet:** Worms, crustaceans, insects
● **Water temperature:** 72 to 83°F (22 to 28°C)
● **Community tank**

An elongated and laterally compressed cichlid, Golden-eyed Dwarf Cichlid has an oval profile when seen from the side. The caudal peduncle is very short, but the dorsal fin is long, with a pointed tip at the rear that reaches to the middle of the caudal fin. The anal fin is similarly elongated and pointed, but the caudal fin has a rounded edge. The coloration and pattern vary considerably, but in the male the upperparts are olive to chestnut-brown and the flanks iridescent olive-green or almost golden. Each scale is marked with a dark brown spot. When the fish is excited the flanks may show two dark longitudinal bands and some transverse markings. The outer edge of the iris is brown and the center is reddish with an orange border. The gill covers and cheeks are iridescent green, characteristically marked with black spots and streaks. The female is more soberly colored, but retains some trace of the flank markings.

This peaceful cichlid swims mainly in the middle and lower water layers. It can be kept in a tank with patches of dense vegetation and a few rocks. It does not burrow in the substrate or attack the plants. The water must be soft, slightly acid, and preferably filtered through peat. The eggs are laid on a clean object and guarded only by the smaller female—she chases away the male when spawning has finished. Remove the male.

Left: **Nannacara anomala** ♂
This specimen has an exceptionally well developed dorsal fin.

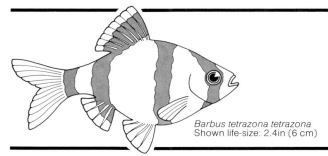

Barbus tetrazona tetrazona
Shown life-size: 2.4in (6 cm)

Family CICHLIDAE
Nanochromis parilus

- **Distribution:** Central Africa, in the Zaire River
- **Length:** Males up to 2.8in (7cm), females 2in (5cm)
- **Tank length:** 24in (60cm)
- **Diet:** Worms, crustaceans, insects, dried food
- **Water temperature:** 72 to 83°F (22 to 28°C)
- **Species tank**

Another elongated and somewhat dorso-ventrally compressed cichlid with a cylindrical body form, *Nanochromis parilus* has a fairly blunt head and a steep forehead. The dorsal fin is particularly long and low, and the caudal fin is rounded, and pale in the lower half, the upper half being attractively striped in claret and yellow with hints of blue. The caudal and dorsal fins are edged with a white inner and black outer stripe. The body is yellowish with an overlying iridescent blue sheen. There are no distinct external sex differences in this species.

This is a very attractive small cichlid. The males may quarrel among themselves, but they do not bother the females. They swim in the lower water layers and spend much time in small caves. The tank, therefore, should have dense vegetation around the edges and some rocks, which should be arranged to form caves. The water must be soft, slightly acid and filtered through peat; or some peat can be incorporated in the substrate. For breeding, it is advisable to keep only a single male with two or three females. The eggs are laid in groups on the roof of a small cave, and are guarded by the female; there may be 80 to 100 eggs in a brood. They hatch in about three days and are free-swimming three days later. The fry can be fed initially on very small live food.

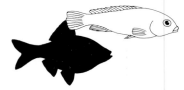

Below: **Nanochromis parilus**
A coconut or flowerpot will serve as a spawning site for this species.

Family CICHLIDAE
Pseudotropheus auratus
Malawi Golden Cichlid

- **Distribution:** East Africa, in Lake Malawi
- **Length:** Males up to 4.3in (11cm), females to 3.5in (9cm), larger specimens not unusual
- **Tank length:** 36in (90cm)
- **Diet:** Worms, crustaceans, insects, plant matter, dried food
- **Water temperature:** 72 to 77°F (22 to 25°C)
- **Species tank**

This cichlid is elongated and only slightly laterally compressed. The rear end of the caudal fin is slightly concave and the dorsal and anal fins are rounded, not elongated, at the rear. Coloration of the sexes is very different. The male is dark brown with a paler band running along the flanks from the forehead to the caudal peduncle. The back is yellow. The bases of the caudal and anal fins are dark; the outer parts are pale yellow. The dorsal fin is turquoise-blue. The female is golden-yellow with three blackish brown bands, one along the middle of the flanks, the second near to the midline of the back, and the third on the dorsal fin. The fins are yellowish. The upper part of the caudal fin shows dark markings and the tips of the dorsal fin rays are reddish to orange.

The Malawi Golden Cichlid is rather aggressive. It should be kept in a tank with gravel sub-strate, a few tough plants, and rocks and roots arranged to divide up the area. This fish will graze algae from the rocks and aquarium glass. The water should be medium-hard. For breeding the temperature should be raised to 79°F (26°C). The eggs are laid in the open and immediately taken up into the female's mouth. They remain there for about three weeks before hatching. Only about 30 eggs are laid, but they are quite large. The newly hatched fry start to feed immediately on tiny crustaceans and other small live food.

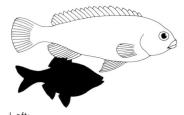

Left:
Pseudotropheus auratus ♂(t),♀(b)
In the wild this very active cichlid lives in the rocky areas of Lake Malawi. The juveniles' coloration is similar to that of the adult female. This species is suitable only for the experienced aquarist.

A practical reminder
Prevent disease by quarantining all new fishes and by disinfecting new plants. Watch each fish for the first sign of any spots, folded fins, or abnormal behavior. Isolate any doubtful fishes at once.

Family CICHLIDAE

Pelvicachromis pulcher
Kribensis

- **Distribution:** West Africa, in southern Nigeria
- **Length:** Up to 4in (10cm)
- **Tank length:** 24in (60cm)
- **Diet:** Worms, crustaceans, insects, dried food
- **Water temperature:** 75 to 83°F (24 to 28°C)
- **Community tank**

The Kribensis is an elongated, moderately compressed cichlid with a short but tall caudal peduncle and a rounded forehead. The long dorsal fin starts very far forward and the caudal fin has a convex rear edge. The tips of the dorsal and anal fins are elongated and pointed in the male, but rounded in the female. The coloration varies greatly. In general, however, the upperparts are brownish with bluish or violet iridescence, and the underparts are white with a bluish tinge. On either side of the belly there is a brilliant red blotch with poorly defined edges. The rear end of the gill cover has a dark brown marking, bordered above by a red area and below by a steel-blue area. The upper part of the male's caudal fin usually has from one to five dark spots, each with a pale yellow border. In the adult female the dorsal fin has a dark marking. On the whole the females are more brightly colored than the males, which is a rare occurence for fishes.

This cichlid was formerly called *Pelmatochromis kribensis,* hence the popular name. There is still a certain amount of confusion about the naming of this and related fishes.

The tank should have rocks and roots for shelter together with some areas of dense vegetation. The water should have added sea salt (about 5 teaspoonfuls per 2.5 gallons/10 liters of water) because this species comes from brackish waters. Spawning takes place in small caves and the red-brown

Above:
Pelvicachromis pulcher ♀(t), ♂(b)
The photograph shows a breeding pair; the free-swimming fry are clearly visible.

eggs are guarded by both parents, though some aquarists say only by the female. They hatch in two or three days, and the fry are free-swimming about four days later. They can then be fed on tiny live food.

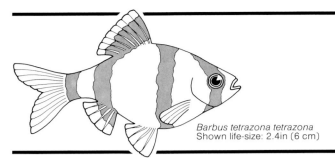

Barbus tetrazona tetrazona
Shown life-size: 2.4in (6 cm)

Right: **Pseudotropheus zebra** ♂
The pale spots on the anal fin are egg dummies; the female may bite at these marks to stimulate the male to release the fertilizing milt.

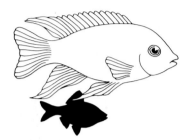

Family CICHLIDAE

Pseudotropheus zebra
Malawi Blue Cichlid
- **Distribution:** East Africa, in Lake Malawi
- **Length:** Up to 6in (15cm)
- **Tank length:** 36in (90cm)
- **Diet:** Worms, crustaceans, insects, plant matter, dried food
- **Water temperature:** 72 to 77°F (22 to 25°C)
- **Species tank**

Another fish from Lake Malawi, this squat, high-backed cichlid has thick lips, a bulging forehead, and a caudal peduncle that is short but relatively tall. The rear parts of the dorsal and anal fins are elongated and pointed. In this species there are several different color phases. The commonest has a pale blue background coloration and seven or eight blue-black transverse bars. The dorsal, caudal, and ventral fins are blue. In another color phase the body is blue, but without dark transverse bars. An alternative phase is almost white; and in another—which occurs only in females—the body is bluish white with irregular orange, brown, and black markings. There may well be other color phases.

Like *P. auratus*, the Malawi Blue Cichlid is an aggressive species, which can be kept in a shoal in a tank with a number of rocks and roots arranged to form hiding-places. A few robust plants would probably not be attacked, although this species is a keen grazer of algae. The water must be medium-hard. Spawning takes place on or near the bottom, where the female collects up the relatively few but rather large eggs and incubates them in her mouth for 22 to 24 days. After hatching, the fry start to feed on small nauplii and other live food of similar size.

A practical reminder
Calculate medication doses accurately. Remove carbon from filters but leave the filters running. Increase aeration to keep the oxygen level high. Change the water gradually to normal following treatments.

Family CICHLIDAE
Pterophyllum scalare
Angelfish
● **Distribution:** South America: Amazon and some tributaries
● **Length:** Up to 6in (15cm)
● **Tank length:** 24in (60cm)
● **Diet:** Worms, crustaceans, insects, plant matter, dried food
● **Water temperature:** 72 to 86°F (22 to 30°C)
● **Community tank**

One of the most popular of all tropical aquarium fishes, the Angelfish was introduced to the aquarium in the early part of the 20th century. It is a laterally compressed, disk-shaped cichlid

Left: **Pterophyllum scalare**
This elegant favorite is now available in many different forms.

with very large fins. Excluding the fins, the body is only one third longer than the height. Including the fins, the total height is about 10in (25cm), although this size cannot be achieved in a home aquarium. The flanks of the common Angelfish are silvery with a brownish tinge and with four prominent black transverse bars. The first bar runs in a curve from the nape across the eye to the insertion of the ventral fins; the second from the front part of the dorsal fin to the anus; the third and broadest from the tip of the dorsal to the tip of the anal fin; and the fourth across the caudal peduncle. The extended rays of the ventral fins are bluish white and the rays of the dorsal fin are yellow-brown to blackish. The sexes are very difficult to distinguish.

This undemanding, peace-loving cichlid should be kept in a shoal in a deep tank with marginal vegetation and plenty of space for swimming. In accordance with its origins in the Amazon region, the water should be soft, but it will tolerate medium-hard water. Spawning takes place on leaves and plant stems that have been previously cleaned. Both parents take part in guarding and fanning fresh water over the eggs, which hatch in 24 to 36 hours. The fry hang from the plants for four or five days and are then taken by the parents to a shallow pit in the substrate. They start to look for food and, at this stage, should be fed on rotifers and small nauplii.

Family CICHLIDAE
Sarotherodon mossambicus
Mozambique Mouth-brooder
● **Distribution:** Eastern Africa
● **Length:** Up to 14in (35cm)
● **Tank length:** 39in (100cm)
● **Diet:** Worms, crustaceans, insects, chopped meat, plant matter, dried food
● **Water temperature:** 70 to 77°F (21 to 25°C)
● **Species tank**

Also known as *Tilapia mossambica,* the Mozambique Mouth-brooder is a particularly hardy cichlid that has been introduced into many parts of the tropics, particularly Southeast Asia, as a food fish. The body is thick-set with some lateral compression, a large head, and thick fleshy lips. In the home aquarium this fish usually attains a total body length of 8in (20cm). Outside the breeding period both sexes are gray or green with a silvery sheen and a dark green marking on the gill cover. At spawning time, the female

Above: **Sarotherodon mossambicus**
This very adaptable freshwater fish has been bred in sea water.

remains the same, but the male becomes an intense blue, the back an even darker blue. The gill cover is iridescent blue-green with a black marking. The ventral fins—and usually also the anal fin—become almost black. The dorsal and caudal fins acquire a bright red border.

This very active cichlid should be kept in a small shoal. It grows very quickly. The tank should have a well-washed gravel substrate, and rocks and roots to provide hiding-places. It should not contain rooted plants, as this is an inveterate digger, particularly at spawning time. A few floating plants, however, would be very suitable. The composition of the water is not important; the species is often found in brackish waters. After spawning, the female takes the eggs up into her mouth for incubation. They hatch in about 10 to 12 days and the fry continue to be protected by the female for a while longer.

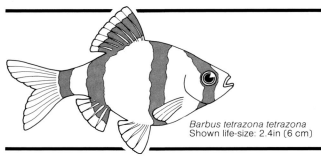

Barbus tetrazona tetrazona
Shown life-size: 2.4in (6 cm)

Family CICHLIDAE

Symphysodon aequifasciata axelrodi
Brown Discus

- **Distribution:** South America: Amazon (near Belém)
- **Length:** Up to 4.7in (12cm)
- **Tank length:** 39in (100cm)
- **Diet:** Worms, crustaceans, insects, plant matter
- **Water temperature:** 77 to 86°F (25 to 30°C)
- **Species tank:** Usually fare better in groups of six or more

The body shape of the Brown Discus is exactly the same as that of the Blue Discus. The general coloration is yellow-brown to chestnut-brown with nine narrow transverse bars. These may be well developed, but are sometimes completely absent except for the bar that runs across the eye. The brown coloration extends onto the basal parts of the dorsal and anal fins. The outer parts of these fins are almost colorless—except for a few rust-red dots—and they are separated from the basal parts by a broad dark brown longitudinal band. The caudal fin is yellowish to greenish. The head has a masklike pattern of iridescent pale spots and lines.

This subspecies of the genus *Symphysodon* requires exactly the same aquarium conditions as the Blue Discus, and its breeding behavior is the same.

The third subspecies, *Symphysodon aequifasciata aequifasciata,* known as the Green Discus, comes from Santarém and Tefé on the Amazon. It is dark brownish green with the same pattern of transverse bars. The caudal fin is translucent with pale dots. The dorsal and anal fins are blackish at the base and olive-green with pale spots towards the edge. There are horizontal dark streaks on the back and the dorsal and anal fins, but these features may be lacking in the middle of the body. The iris is reddish brown in color.

Below:
Symphysodon a. axelrodi
Like other discus fishes this one needs soft, bacteria-free water.

Family CICHLIDAE

Symphysodon aequifasciata haraldi
Blue Discus

- **Distribution:** South America: Amazon (Letitia and Benjamin Constant area)
- **Length:** Up to 4.7in (12cm) often larger
- **Tank length:** 39in (100cm)
- **Diet:** Worms, crustaceans, insects, plant matter
- **Water temperature:** 77 to 86°F (25 to 30°C)
- **Species tank:** Usually fare better in groups of six or more

The Blue Discus is a disk-shaped, almost circular cichlid with strong lateral compression, a small mouth, and a very steep forehead. The dorsal and anal fins have a long insertion. In this form the general coloration is brownish, becoming pale blue with age. The head is somewhat darker with a purple sheen. The flanks are marked with nine dark transverse bars—the first crossing the eye, the last at the root of the tail. The dorsal and anal fins are dark, almost black, with reddish iridescence. The iris is red. This subspecies is characterized by having several horizontal iridescent pale blue lines on the flanks that extend onto parts of the dorsal and anal fins.

This rather delicate cichlid is best left to the advanced aquarium hobbyist. It requires a deep tank with rocks and roots, a dark substrate, some marginal vegetation, and a few isolated plants with large leaves. The composition of the water is extremely important. It must be soft, slightly acid, and filtered through peat (or the substrate can contain peat). Spawning takes place on a previously cleaned leaf or rock, and the eggs hatch in about two days. The fry at first hang from leaves for two or three days and then become free-swimming. At this stage they move to the flanks of the parents where they start to feed on a mucus secretion produced by the parents' skin. The fry soon take small live food as well and gradually become independent of the parent fishes.

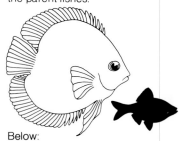

Below:
Symphysodon aequifasciata haraldi
Coloration varies in this species, tending toward pale blue with age.

A practical reminder
Breeding any species requires a true pair of fishes. Learn to sex your fishes accurately. Some species will spawn collectively in a shoal. Condition the sexes separately for two or three weeks before breeding.

Family CICHLIDAE

Symphysodon discus
Discus

- **Distribution:** South America: Amazon at Manaus and Tefé, also in the Rio Negro
- **Length:** Up to 8in (20cm)
- **Tank length:** 39in (100cm)
- **Diet:** Worms, crustaceans, insects, plant matter
- **Water temperature:** 77 to 86°F (25 to 30°C)
- **Species tank**

The shape of the body and fins of *S. discus* is the same as that of the Blue, Brown, and Green Discus. The general coloration is chestnut-brown with pale blue iridescence, which is particularly striking on the flanks. The fifth bar in the middle of the body is broader and darker than the remainder of the bars. The flanks are patterned with wavy iridescent pale blue lines that extend onto parts of the otherwise sky-blue dorsal and anal fins. There is also a pattern of lines on the head.

The aquarium conditions for this species should be the same as those described for the Blue Discus. Spawning and parental care are also similar, although successful rearing may be even more difficult.

The classification of the various members of the genus *Symphysodon* is rather confused. Some authorities maintain that they are all merely color variants of a single species, *Symphysodon discus,* and do not accord them the status of subspecies. It is quite likely that this view will be upheld in the years to come.

Other known forms are the Red Discus, in which the body and the bases of the dorsal and anal fins are deep red, and the so-called Royal Blue Discus, in which the transverse bars are very prominent and the horizontal stripes are brilliant blue.

Above: **Symphysodon discus**
This is the largest and perhaps the most beautiful discus fish, but it is often very difficult to breed.

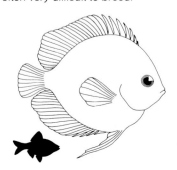

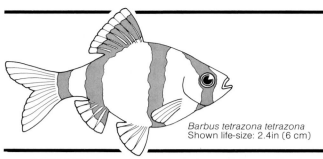

Barbus tetrazona tetrazona
Shown life-size: 2.4in (6 cm)

Family CICHLIDAE

Uaru amphiacanthoides
Waroo

- **Distribution:** South America: Guyana and Amazon.
- **Length:** Up to 10.4in (26cm)
- **Tank length:** 36in (90cm)
- **Diet:** Worms, crustaceans, insects
- **Water temperature:** 81 to 86°F (27 to 30°C)
- **Species tank**

The Waroo is a high-backed, very laterally compressed cichlid with a rather small mouth and, in older specimens, a bulging forehead. The rear parts of the dorsal and anal fins are rounded in the young but pointed in old individuals, and the fins stretch halfway along the caudal fin. In small specimens (about 1.2 to 2in/3 to 5cm long), the body and the pectoral and ventral fins are dark. The other fins are colorless. Half-grown individuals (about 4in/10cm) are yellowish to yellow-brown with some pale or greenish spots. The adults are yellowish to brown with blue-green iridescence. The lower half of the body has a large black, almost triangular marking that is broadest at the front end. There are smaller dark markings just behind the eye and on the upper part of the caudal peduncle. The fins are yellowish or blue-green and the iris is pale red. The sexes cannot be distinguished by color.

This cichlid comes from the same waters as the Discus and Angelfish, and it should be kept in a tank with a few large plants and rocks to provide shelter. The water must be soft, slightly acid, and filtered through peat. Spawning takes place in a dark corner—under a rock or in a broken flowerpot—and both parents guard the eggs, which

Above: **Uaru amphiacanthoides**
This cichlid is usually peaceful but males may fight when spawning.

hatch in 30 to 36 hours. After they have become free-swimming the fry should be given rotifers and small nauplii, but they are not easy fishes to rear successfully.

Family CICHLIDAE

Tropheus moorei
Brbant Cichlid

- **Distribution:** East AFrica, in Lake Tanganyika
- **Length:** Up to 4.7in (12cm)
- **Tank length:** 24in (60cm)
- **Diet:** Worms, crustaceans, insects, plant matter, dried food
- **Water temperature:** 77 to 83°F (25 to 28°C)
- **Species tank**

This relatively high-backed, laterally compressed cichlid has a broad ventral mouth, spatulate teeth, and a steep forehead. The edge of the caudal fin is truncated or slightly concave. The general coloration is dark olive to velvety-black and the middle of the body is marked with a red or yellow band that broadens out on the back and belly. The part of the dorsal fin that lies immediately above the band is an intense red. In general, the females may be more deeply colored than the males.

The Brabant Cichlid is a rather quarrelsome fish in the confines of an aquarium. It is best kept in a shoal in a tank with rocks but no rooted plants; floating plants will help to subdue the light. The water must be hard. Spawning takes place after a courtship that involves vigorous shaking of the fishes' bodies. The female lays only a few eggs (eight to 16), but they are very large—with a diameter of 0.28in (7mm). The female collects the eggs up into her mouth before they have sunk to the bottom and then moves to the genital area of the male. There the sperm are shed and taken into the female's mouth, where they fertilize the eggs. After about four weeks' incubation the eggs hatch, and the fry leave the female's mouth, fully formed and free-swimming. They are then up to 0.6in (15mm) long and ready to feed on a variety of food, such as small crustaceans, chopped white worms, and grindal worms.

Below: **Tropheus moorei**
This hard water cichlid is best kept in a shoal in a species tank.

Left: **Brachygobius xanthozona**
The newly-hatched fry of this fish at first swim in open water and later move down to the bottom.

Family GOBIIDAE
These small fishes come from shallow coastal waters in Europe and particularly in tropical Asia. Some species have the ventral fins fused into a suction organ that allows the fish to adhere to rocks.

Family GOBIIDAE

Brachygobius xanthozona
Bumblebee Fish

- **Distribution:** Borneo, Sumatra, Java
- **Length:** Up to 1.8in (4.5cm)
- **Tank length:** 18in (4.5cm)
- **Diet:** Worms, crustaceans, insects, dried food
- **Water temperature:** 75 to 86°F (24 to 30°C)
- **Species tank**

A very squat, thick-set fish with the body cylindrical in front, laterally compressed at the rear. There are two dorsal fins, clearly separated, the second one lying directly above the anal fin. The caudal fin has a rounded rear edge. As in other members of the family Gobiidae, the ventral fins are fused to form a suction disk.

The sexes can be distinguished at spawning time, the female being stouter than the male. The ground coloration is yellow marked with a very variable pattern of bands and spots. In most individuals there are four blackish bands, the first passing over the head in the region of the eye, the second and third over the body and extending onto the fins, and the fourth across the caudal peduncle. The areas between these bands may have wedge-shaped markings. In general, the dark areas become reduced in size with increasing age.

The tank for this unusual, rather shy fish should have some plants and a few rocks and roots to provide hiding-places; in a community tank this species would remain timid owing to disturbance by the other inmates and would probably die quite soon. The water should contain some added salt (approximately two teaspoonsful to every 2.5 gallons/ 10 liters).

For breeding, the tank can have a few small plants of the genus *Cryptocoryne,* which tolerates the salt, and some rocks. Spawning takes place after a period of courtship, and the 200 to 300 eggs are laid in groups on rocks. The female should then be removed and the eggs will be guarded by the male. They hatch over a period of several days and the fry are free-swimming about 48 hours after hatching. They can be fed at first on very small *Cyclops* nauplii and after five days on brine shrimp nauplii.

THE LABYRINTH FISHES

Above: *Colisa fasciata*, one of the attractive
labyrinth fishes from Southeast Asia.
Right: A quiet, slow-flowing stream in Thailand,
the typical home of labyrinth fishes.

*T*his group of small to medium-sized freshwater fishes is
native to Africa and Southeast Asia, the Philippines, and
Indonesia. Some inhabit estuaries. All members of the suborder
have an accessory respiratory organ, the labyrinth organ, which lies
in the gill cavity and enables the fish to take in atmospheric air
at the surface and extract its contained oxygen. The labyrinth
consists of a number of many-folded lamellae (thin sheets of
tissue) with a rich blood supply. This ability to use atmospheric air
for respiration is highly advantageous in the poorly oxygenated
waters of so many tropical areas. In fact, most anabantoids rely so
heavily on this method of respiration that they will die if denied
access to the air, even if the water is rich in oxygen. In damp,
humid conditions the Climbing Perch of Africa is able to leave
the water and move overland for long distances, thus enabling it to
colonize new waters.

In most of the species the male builds a floating nest at the
surface of the water. This consists of numerous bubbles of air
coated with saliva and it often incorporates a certain amount of
plant matter. Courtship takes place beneath the nest with the male
coiling around the female and turning her upside down. The eggs
are lighter than water and when they are shed they float upwards
and land in the bubble nest. There they are guarded by the male;
even after hatching he still tends the fry, spitting back into the
nest any that stray. In some species the eggs are laid on the
substrate and taken into the mouth (usually of the male) where
they are incubated.

The suborder has four families: the Anabantidae with the
genera Anabas *and* Ctenopoma; *the* Belontiidae *with* Belontia,
Betta, Colisa, Macropodus, Sphaerichthys, *and* Trichogaster;
the Helostomatidae *with* Helostoma; *and the* Osphromenidae *with*
Osphronemus.

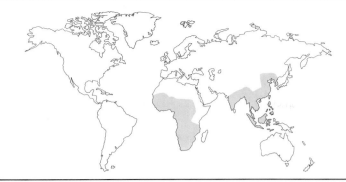

Left: The map shows the distribution of the labyrinth fishes, which are restricted to parts of Africa and southern Asia. They are not as fastidious in their water requirements as the characins. This is due largely to the possession of an accessory respiratory organ that makes them independent of water quality. Only the Gourami of Southeast Asia is economically important as a food fish for human use.

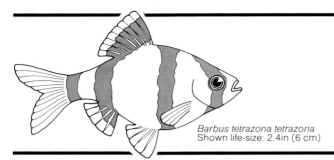

Barbus tetrazona tetrazona
Shown life-size: 2.4in (6 cm)

Family ANABANTIDAE
Anabas testudineus
Climbing Perch

- **Distribution:** India, Sri Lanka, Southeast Asia to southern China
- **Length:** Up to 10in (25cm)
- **Tank length:** 36in (90cm)
- **Diet:** Worms, crustaceans, insects, plant matter, dried food
- **Water temperature:** 75 to 86°F (24 to 30°C)
- **Species tank**

The Climbing Perch is not a true perch and is the only species in its genus. This is an elongated, perchlike fish with large scales and a large mouth with tooth-bearing jaws. The edge of the gill cover is spiny and the pectoral fins are particularly well developed. The general coloration is grayish brown to silvery gray, the edges of the scales being paler. The fins are yellowish or pale brown. The only constant markings are a dark spot on the gill cover and another spot on the root of the tail.

This is a rather shy but quarrelsome fish. During wet weather and usually at night they climb out of the water and move across damp land, propelling themselves with the tail and using the pectoral fins and gill covers primarily as props. In this way they can move from one body of water to another. During such journeys they use the labyrinth organ for respiration. They have also been seen climbing along the trunks of fallen trees. Climbing Perch live mainly in weedy streams, rice fields, muddy ponds, and also brackish water. When the dry season is imminent, they dig down into the mud and remain more or less dormant. They can be kept in a spacious tank with a good lid — to stop them from climbing out — and some dense vegetation. The composition of the water is not critical. Spawning takes place at random among the plants and the eggs hatch in 24 to 36 hours. The fry are neither protected by the parent fishes nor molested by them.

This is an interesting labyrinth fish that is suitable for the home aquarium only when relatively small. It commonly lives for more than five years. It is used as a food fish in some parts of India.

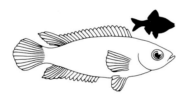

Right: **Anabas testudineus**
This fish needs a secure tank to prevent it crawling or jumping out.

Family BELONTIIDAE
Belontia signata
Combtail

- **Distribution:** Sri Lanka
- **Length:** Up to 5in (13cm)
- **Tank length:** 18in (45cm)
- **Diet:** Worms, crustaceans, insects, dried food
- **Water temperature:** 75 to 83°F (24 to 28°C)
- **Community tank:** Best to keep only young specimens as older fish tend to be quarrelsome

The Combtail is a moderately elongated, laterally compressed fish with an ovate caudal fin. Some of the central rays of the caudal fin extend beyond the edge

Left: **Belontia signata** ♀(t), ♂(b)
Spawnings of this fish may produce about 200 young. The eggs are laid in a bubble-nest or under floating leaves. The male then guards them.

A practical reminder
Cichlid fishes choose their own partners
and should be allowed to do so. Raise a
few of each species from juveniles and
any pairs that 'self-select' are likely to remain
together for life and make good parents.

Family ANABANTIDAE

Ctenopoma nanum
Dwarf Climbing Perch
- **Distribution:** Africa: southern Cameroon, Congo
- **Length:** Up to 3in (7.5cm)
- **Tank length:** 18in (45cm)
- **Diet:** Worms, crustaceans, insects, fish, dried food
- **Water temperature:** 79 to 84°F (26 to 29°C)
- **Species tank**

Dwarf Climbing Perch is another
labyrinth fish. It is elongated and
moderately compressed, and its
dorsal and ventral profiles are
equally convex. The very long
dorsal fin starts just behind the
head and almost reaches the
caudal fin. The anal fin is shorter,
starting at about the middle of the
belly. Both fins are pointed at the
rear in the males and, in general,
are more fully developed than in
the females. The caudal fin is
rounded and the ventral fins are
saberlike, not filamentous as in the
genus *Colisa*. Coloration varies
greatly and may be green, olive-
brown, or red-brown. The head
and flanks are marked with six to
nine dark transverse bars, which
extend onto the bases of the
dorsal and anal fins. The fins are
pale greenish to pale yellowish.
Young individuals have a
conspicuous round spot on the
base of the tail.

This peaceful fish may
sometimes be rather shy, so the
tank should have several areas of
dense vegetation to provide
shelter. It should also have some
roots. The water should be soft,
slightly acid, and filtered through
peat. This species has been bred
on several occasions. The male
builds a bubble-nest at the
surface, but it is not always very
well constructed. The male and
female court beneath the nest.
The female produces several
hundred eggs in batches of about
20. The male guards the eggs
and, subsequently, the fry, which
require very fine live food when
free-swimming. Members of the
related *Ctenopoma oxyrhynchus*
do not build a bubble-nest and
after spawning the eggs merely
float to the surface because of
their high oil content.

Below: **Ctenopoma nanum**
*This warmth-loving labyrinth fish is
highly suitable for an aquarium,
but too shy for a community tank.*

of the fin in older males. The first
rays of the ventral fins are
prolonged to form filaments. The
dorsal and anal fins of the males
are prolonged at the rear and are
pointed. The flanks are gray-green
to olive-green, the back being
somewhat darker. In older
individuals the general coloration
becomes reddish with greenish
and violet shading when seen in
reflected light. The dorsal, caudal,
and anal fins are reddish,
increasing in intensity towards the
edge. There is a distinct dark
marking at the base of the rear
part of the dorsal fin. The other
fins are green. In females the
coloration is duller and the fins are
not so prolonged.

The tank should have patches
of dense vegetation and rocks and
roots arranged to provide hiding-
places. The composition of the
water is not critical. For breeding
the male builds a nest of air
bubbles coated with mucus. The
eggs cling to the nest and are
guarded by the male. They hatch
in about 24 hours and the fry can
be fed at first on small nauplii.
Evidently this species may
occasionally spawn without a
bubble-nest. In this instance, the
eggs are laid under floating leaves
at the surface.

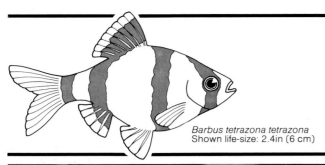

Barbus tetrazona tetrazona
Shown life-size: 2.4in (6 cm)

Family BELONTIIDAE
Betta splendens
Siamese Fighting Fish
- **Distribution:** Southeast Asia
- **Length:** Up to 2in (5cm) in the wild
- **Tank length:** 24in (60cm)
- **Diet:** Worms, crustaceans, insects, dried food
- **Water temperature:** 77 to 83°F (25 to 28°C)
- **Species tank**

The Siamese Fighting Fish is an elongated, laterally compressed fish with a very long anal fin and an almost circular caudal fin. The ventral fins are saber-shaped and the dorsal fin starts behind the middle of the back. By planned breeding and the careful selection of offspring, it has been possible over the course of many years to

Left: **Betta splendens** ♂
Several color forms are available of this highly ornamental fish.

produce forms with enlarged dorsal and anal fins. Such specimens may be up to 2.6in (6.5cm) long. In the wild, the general coloration is red-brown with blue-green iridescence and numerous red, green, or blue dots—usually arranged in rows. The caudal and anal fins have red or brown rays separated by areas of blue-green. The dorsal fin is red-brown, usually with greenish stripes. The female is brownish with faint transverse bars. Males of selected forms bred for aquarium use are available in a wide color range, including green, blue, red or violet.

The males are particularly aggressive and should never be kept together. A single male and one or two females could be kept in a community tank with shallow water and areas of dense vegetation, but the colors show better when a pair is kept in a species tank. The composition of the water is not important. The male builds a bubble-nest near the surface and guards the 400 to 500 eggs laid by the female. The fry can be fed at first on a supply of infusorians and rotifers.

There is a related Fighting Fish, *Betta brederi,* in Java and Sumatra. The male of this species incubates the eggs in his mouth.

Family BELONTIIDAE
Colisa chuna
Honey Gourami
- **Distribution:** Northeastern India, Bangladesh
- **Length:** Up to 2.8in (7cm)
- **Tank length:** 12in (30cm)
- **Diet:** Worms, crustaceans, insects, dried food
- **Water temperature:** 75 to 79°F (24 to 26°C)
- **Species or community tank**

A somewhat stocky, laterally compressed fish, the Honey Gourami has an ovate profile when seen from the side. The dorsal and anal fins have a long insertion, but they are not tall. The rear ends of these fins are not prolonged. The ventral fins are filamentous and considerably longer than the height of the body. The rear end of the caudal fin is slightly concave. The general coloration is pale yellow, with silvery iridescence that becomes more pronounced towards the underparts. The iris is reddish. There is a dark brown longitudinal stripe running from the eye to the root of the caudal fin. The female and the young males are brownish and much duller with a distinct longitudinal stripe. When excited, such as at spawning time, the flanks, caudal fin, and the rear parts of the dorsal and anal fins of

the males become golden-yellow. At the same time, the head, nape, underparts, and the front part of the anal fin become almost black with greenish iridescence. The ventral fins turn orange.

Although this species can be kept in a community tank it is better in a species tank. This gives the males a chance to establish their own territories and to develop their full colors. The composition of the water is not critical. The male builds a small bubble-nest, which is fairly compact. The eggs hatch in about 24 hours and the fry remain in the nest for three to five days, while consuming the contents of the

Above: **Colisa chuna** ♂(l), ♀(r)
This species thrives in a peaceful tank; disturbance causes shyness.

yolk-sac. The male guards the fry until they leave the nest. They should be fed at first on infusorians and rotifers, later on brine shrimp nauplii.

Family BELONTIIDAE
Colisa lalia
Dwarf Gourami
- **Distribution:** Northeastern India, Assam, Bangladesh
- **Length:** Up to 2in (5cm)
- **Tank length:** 12in (30cm)
- **Diet:** Worms, crustaceans, insects, dried food
- **Water temperature:** 68 to 79°F (20 to 26°C)
- **Community tank**

The Dwarf Gourami is stocky and laterally compressed with a longish-ovate profile when seen from the side. The dorsal and anal fins begin in the front part of the body, unlike *Betta,* and are only separated from the fan-shaped caudal fin by a short distance. The ventral fins are filamentous and fairly long—about the same as the body height. The dorsal and anal fins are more fully developed in the male than in the female. The male is scarlet with narrow oblique double rows of blue or green dots that give it a striped appearance. The throat and breast are deep blue-green, and the ventral fins are orange. The female is much duller, usually brownish with oblique gray-blue stripes on the flanks, and even these are visible only in the central part of the body. The front of the underparts is silvery-gray. The

A practical reminder
Egg-scattering fishes are notorious egg-eaters. Use nets, marbles, or thick bunches of plants to trap the eggs. Remove the adults after spawning, and shade the tank, but watch closely for first signs of the young

dorsal and anal fins are rounded at the rear.

This small, peaceful gourami is very suitable for the beginner. It should be kept in a tank with feathery-leaved rooted plants and a few floating plants. Roots and rocks arranged on the bottom will provide shelter, and there must be sufficient open water for swimming. The tank should receive some sunshine. Algal growth on the glass is desirable because these fishes like to graze on it. The composition of the water is not critical. The male builds a relatively deep bubble-nest, often incorporating parts of the neighboring floating plants.

Above: **Colisa lalia** ♂
An extremely popular dwarf species.

After spawning the female should be removed from the tank, and the male then guards the brood. The eggs hatch in about 24 hours, and the fry remain in the nest for three to five days longer. When they leave the nest, they will, at first, require a plentiful supply of infusorians and rotifers.

Colisa fasciata
Banded Gourami
● **Distribution:** India to Malaya
● **Length:** Up to 4.7in (12cm)
● **Tank length:** 24in (60cm)
● **Diet:** Worms, crustaceans, insects, dried food
● **Water temperature:** 72 to 79°F (22 to 26°C)
● **Community tank**

The body of this gourami is longish-ovate with marked lateral compression. The dorsal and anal fins are very long with the rear ends drawn out to a point in the male. Unlike *Colisa chuna,* these fins are rounded posteriorly in the female and young males. The ventral fins are filamentous and, when laid back, reach approximately to the end of the anal fin. Coloration varies. In males the back is brownish and the flanks greenish brown with blue iridescence. A number of oblique, reddish stripes mark the flanks. The gill cover has a bright blue-green pattern. The dorsal fin is bluish; the tips of the spiny rays are white, and the rear part of the fin has red spots and streaks. The ventral fins are mainly orange, the bases whitish. The anal fin is bluish-in front, becoming green to red at the rear. The caudal fin is greenish or reddish yellow with

Above: **Colisa fasciata** ♂
This is a highly prolific fish; broods of 1000 eggs are possible.

red dots. In general, the females are more soberly colored.

This is a hardy gourami with a number of local varieties, which is not surprising in view of its extensive geographical range. It can be kept in a tank with rooted plants and a few floating plants at the surface. Provide roots and rocks for hiding-places. The composition of the water is not critical. The male builds a large bubble-nest, sometimes up to 4in (10cm) across, and guards it assiduously. As soon as spawning has finished and the eggs are in the nest, the female should be removed from the tank. The male adds more air bubbles at the bottom of the nest, so that the eggs are well protected. They hatch in about 24 hours and remain in the nest for four to five days while consuming the yolk-sac contents. The fry then swim free at the surface and require large amounts of infusorians and rotifers; then brine shrimp nauplii.

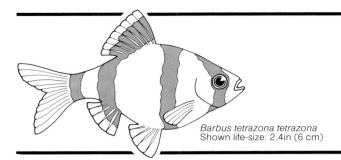

Barbus tetrazona tetrazona
Shown life-size: 2.4in (6 cm)

Family BELONTIIDAE

Macropodus cupanus dayi

Brown Spike-tailed Paradisefish

- **Distribution:** Malabar Coast, Burma, southern Vietnam
- **Length:** Up to 3in (7.5cm)
- **Tank length:** 24in (60cm)
- **Diet:** Worms, crustaceans, insects, dried food
- **Water temperature:** 64 to 79°F (18 to 26°C)
- **Community tank:** Sometimes aggressive; should be watched with smaller species

An elongated, laterally compressed labyrinth fish, the Brown Spike-tailed Paradisefish has a small head and a slightly upturned mouth. The caudal fin is elongated and ends in a spike, hence the popular name. The dorsal and anal fins are also elongated and pointed at the rear. The upperparts are dark brown and the underparts red-brown or red. The flanks are usually chestnut-brown and marked with two dark brown longitudinal bands. One of these bands starts at the upper edge of the gill cover, the other at the mouth. Both extend back to the root of the tail. The caudal fin is reddish at the base and becomes bright red in the center; the elongated rays are bluish. The dorsal fin is marked with small brown dots. The other fins are reddish with green edges. The female is similarly colored,

Above:
Macropodus cupanus dayi ♂
The coloration of both sexes intensifies at spawning time.

but with the dorsal and anal fins more rounded in shape.

This warmth-loving labyrinth fish can be kept in a tank with areas of dense vegetation and a few floating plants, leaving sufficient open water for swimming. The composition of the water is not critical. For breeding the water temperature can be allowed to rise to 86°F (30°C). The male builds a bubble-nest at the surface and guards the eggs while they develop. At this point the female should be removed from the tank. The eggs hatch in about 24 hours and the fry remain in the nest for four to five days longer while they consume the contents of the yolk-sac. They will then feed on infusorians.

The related subspecies *Macropodus cupanus cupanus* comes from India, Sri Lanka, and Malaya. It is usually pale brown with greenish iridescence and dark underparts. The fins are pale gray, although the coloration varies.

Family BELONTIIDAE

Sphaerichthys osphromenoides

Chocolate Gourami

- **Distribution:** Sumatra, Malaysia
- **Length:** Up to 2.4in (6cm)
- **Tank length:** 18in (45cm)
- **Diet:** Crustaceans, insects
- **Water temperature:** 79 to 86°F (26 to 30°C)
- **Species tank**

This is a tall, relatively short labyrinth fish with a laterally compressed body and a ventral profile that is more convex than the dorsal. The head is pointed and the mouth is small. The dorsal and anal fins start in the front half of the body and are slightly pointed at the rear. The ventral fins have well-developed spiny rays and the first soft ray is elongated and filamentous. The sexes are very similar and scarcely distinguishable except that the female is stouter when ready to spawn. Also she usually has a more rounded dorsal fin. The general coloration is chocolate-brown, sometimes red-brown, with dark-edged scales. The flanks have irregularly arranged pale yellow or whitish transverse bars. The first very thin bar extends from iris to iris across the forehead; the second, broader bar usually runs across the gill cover to the insertion of the ventral fins. The other bars are in the rear part of the body. The fins are brown,

Above:
Sphaerichthys osphromenoides
Breeding, which rarely occurs, may produce 20 to 50 young.

except for the rays of the ventral fins, which are yellowish.

This is the most delicate of the labyrinth fishes. It should be kept in a tank with areas of dense vegetation, a dark substrate, and sufficient open water for swimming. The lighting should be subdued, possibly by having some floating plants, and the water must be soft, slightly acid, and filtered through peat. This is a fish for the advanced aquarist only. It was formerly thought to be live-bearing but is now known to be a mouth-brooder. After spawning the eggs are taken up into the male's mouth, where they are incubated for about two weeks. Some say the female also broods eggs. Other reports say that a bubble-nest is built, into which the female spits the eggs that she has held in her mouth. In any case, the fry must be fed at first on infusorians.

A practical reminder
Male bubble-nest-building fishes can be tough on the female if she is not ready for spawning. And after spawning the female should be removed from the tank for her own safety. The male will guard the nest.

Family BELONTIIDAE
Macropodus opercularis
Paradisefish

- **Distribution:** Korea, China, Vietnam, Taiwan
- **Length:** Up to 3.5in (9cm)
- **Tank length:** 24in (60cm)
- **Diet:** Worms, crustaceans, insects, plant matter, dried food
- **Water temperature:** 59 to 75°F (15 to 24°C)
- **Species tank**

This is a moderately elongated labyrinth fish with lateral compression, particularly in the rear half of the body. The caudal fin has upper and lower lobes very elongated. The rear parts of the dorsal and anal fins are also elongated, particularly in the males. The coloration varies greatly. In the males the head and nape are olive with brownish marbling; the flanks are marked with alternate blue-green and red transverse bars. The gill cover has a conspicuous blackish longitudinal marking that shows greenish iridescence and has an orange or red border. The caudal fin is red with dark dots and streaks in the center. The dorsal and anal fins also have dark markings that become increasingly red towards the tips. The ventral fins are red with white tips. In the females the coloration is duller and only the flanks have red transverse bars.

This interesting fish was introduced into the aquarium in Europe in 1869. It can be very aggressive, particularly at spawning time, so it is best kept without other species. The tank should have patches of dense vegetation, including a small number of floating plants, and sufficient open water for swimming. Algal growth on the glass as well as the troublesome planarians which so often infest aquarium tanks will be consumed by the fish. Neither the composition of the water nor the temperature is critical—even 68 to 75°F (20 to 24°C) is sufficient for breeding. The male builds a bubble-nest at the surface and, after spawning, spits the eggs into the nest from below. He then guards them assiduously. They hatch in about 24 hours and after three to five days in the nest the fry become free-swimming and can be fed initially on infusorians.

Left and below:
Macropodus opercularis
Two males of this colorful species.

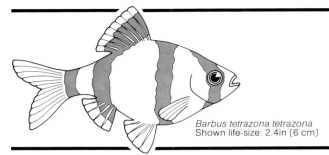

Barbus tetrazona tetrazona
Shown life-size: 2.4in (6 cm)

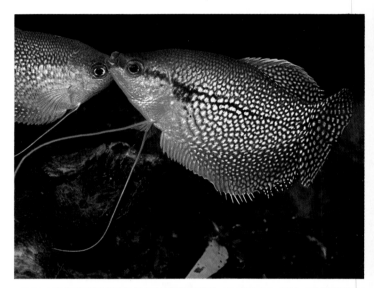

Trichogaster leeri

Pearl Gourami

- **Distribution:** Thailand, Malaysia, Sumatra, Borneo
- **Length:** Up to 4.3in (11cm)
- **Tank length:** 24in (60cm)
- **Diet:** Worms, crustaceans, insects, dried food
- **Water temperature:** 75 to 86°F (24 to 30°C)
- **Community tank**

The Pearl Gourami is a moderately elongated, laterally compressed labyrinth fish. The ventral fins are very long and threadlike. The dorsal fin has a short base and is positioned in the middle of the back, unlike the genus *Colisa*. The anal fin has a very long base and it starts in the front part of the belly. The caudal fin is deeply cleft. The dorsal and anal fins are more fully developed in the male than in the female. The general coloration of the male is reddish brown, but this is overlaid by a pearly, dense pattern of iridescent bluish violet dots. The underparts are orange or red. A somewhat interrupted dark brown longitudinal band extends from the snout across the eye and ends in an enlarged spot on the root of the tail. The pearly pattern extends onto the bases of the dorsal and anal fins. The female is more brownish with silvery-white underparts.

This very attractive labyrinth fish can be kept in a tank with areas of dense vegetation — particularly plants with feathery leaves — and a few floating plants. The composition of the water is not critical. Sexual maturity is reached relatively late. The male builds a large bubble-nest at the water surface. Courtship is particularly stormy and mostly takes place beneath the nest. The female lays a large number of eggs and should then be removed from the tank along with any other fishes — except the male, who will guard the nest. The eggs hatch in about 24 hours. The fry remain in the nest for four or five days and then feed on very small live food.

Below: **Trichogaster leeri**
At spawning time the breast and belly of the male become blood-red in color. This species is also known as the Mosaic Gourami.

Trichogaster trichopterus

Three-spot Gourami

- **Distribution:** Thailand, Malaysia, Java, Sumatra, Borneo
- **Length:** Up to 6in (15cm)
- **Tank length:** 24in (60cm)
- **Diet:** Worms, crustaceans, insects, dried food
- **Water temperature:** 75 to 84°F (24 to 29°C)
- **Community tank:** May harass smaller species

The body of *T. trichopterus* is somewhat stockier than that of the Pearl Gourami, but in other ways is very similar. Both sexes of the Three-spot Gourami have threadlike ventral fins that, when laid back, reach approximately to the middle of the caudal fin. The dorsal fin in the male is taller and more pointed than in the female. The edge of the caudal fin is concave. The general coloration is silvery-olive, becoming darker on the back and paler on the belly. The flanks often have rather indistinct transverse bars. There are two characteristic black spots — one in the middle of the flank, the other on the caudal peduncle. These two spots, together with the eye, account for the popular name. The dorsal, caudal, and anal fins are grayish or green with white or pale orange dots and they show bluish iridescence in reflected light. The subspecies *T. trichopterus sumatranus* (known as the Blue Gourami) is blue with more distinct transverse bars, particularly at spawning time, and iridescent pearly dots on the fins. Another variety, called the Cosby, is blue with dark marbling on the flanks.

This is a peaceful gourami that can be kept in a tank with clumps of rooted plants, a few floating plants, and some roots to provide hiding-places. The composition of the water is not critical, although it has been recommended that the Blue Gourami be kept in soft, slightly acid water. The male builds a bubble-nest at the surface. Spawning takes place below the nest after very vigorous driving by

Above: **Trichogaster trichopterus**
This is a very prolific species. The fry must be sorted into size groups to prevent cannibalism.

the male. The eggs, which have been guarded by the male, hatch in about 24 hours. The fry are free-swimming four or five days later and ready to be fed initially on infusorians.

A practical reminder
Killifish eggs may not hatch the first time they are re-immersed in water. This is nature's way of protecting them against short rain showers. Dry out the eggs again, and re-immersion usually does the trick.

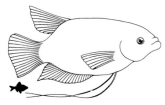

Left: **Osphronemus goramy**
Young specimens of this fish are suitable to mix with larger species.

Family OSPHRONEMIDAE

Osphronemus goramy
Gourami
- **Distribution:** Originally Borneo, Sumatra, Java
- **Length:** Up to 24in (60cm), possibly more
- **Tank length:** 36in (90cm)
- **Diet:** Worms, crustaceans, insects, plant matter, dried food
- **Water temperature:** 66 to 79°F (19 to 26°C)
- **Community tank**

This squat gourami has large scales and a very laterally compressed body. It looks ovate when seen from the side. The head is relatively small, with a distinct projecting chin in old individuals. The ventral fins are elongated and threadlike. Young specimens are not as tall-bodied and they have a more pointed head. The dorsal and anal fins of the males are elongated and pointed posteriorly. The edge of the caudal fin is straight or slightly concave. Adults are brownish or reddish with pale iridescence; the upperparts are a little darker in color and the belly is either pale yellow or silvery. There are several dark spots scattered over the body. Young individuals are reddish brown with a number of dark transverse bars. On the rear part of the anal fin is a more or less circular marking with a yellow or silvery border. The ventral fins are orange; all the other fins are bluish.

Family HELOSTOMATIDAE

Helostoma temmincki
Kissing Gourami
- **Distribution:** Southeast Asia: Thailand, Malaysia, Sumatra, Java, Borneo
- **Length:** Up to 12in (30cm)
- **Tank length:** 36in (90cm)
- **Diet:** Worms, crustaceans, insects, plant matter, dried food
- **Water temperature:** 75 to 83°F (24 to 28°C)
- **Community tank:** Often aggressive, particularly to smaller species.

Well known for its habit of extending its thick fleshy lips and 'kissing,' this gourami is an ovate labyrinth fish. When viewed from the side, it shows strong lateral compression. The flat broad lips are well adapted for browsing on algal mats. These lips also protrude during kissing when the fishes touch lip to lip. This kissing behavior is probably a form of sparring. The forehead is slightly concave particularly in young individuals. The dorsal and anal fins start far forward and extend back to the tail. The caudal fin is slightly concave. The rear parts of the dorsal and anal fins are taller than the front spiny parts. The upperparts are olive-green to gray; the belly is paler. A few, often indistinct, darkish longitudinal stripes appear on the flanks and two short dark transverse bars mark the gill cover. The fins are greenish to grayish yellow. The coloration of old males is somewhat more intense. The sexes are very difficult to

distinguish. There is also a poorly pigmented form of the Kissing Gourami that is uniformly pink and without markings.

This is a largely vegetarian fish, which usually grows to a length of about 4in (10cm) in the home aquarium. It can be kept in a tank with plenty of plants, preferably those with tough leaves. The composition of the water is not important. The fish reaches sexual maturity at three to four years of age. Spawning takes place at dusk or during the night, after a period of stormy courtship. The eggs are lighter than water and they rise towards the surface, many adhering to plants on the way. They hatch in about 50 hours and the fry are free-

Above: **Helostoma temmincki**
The fry of this very prolific fish — up to 1000 eggs per brood — are usually not molested by the parents.

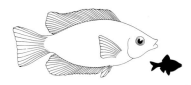

swimming after three to five days. They must then be fed on infusorians and also on pulverized oatmeal scattered at the surface of the water. At first they grow rapidly, but later on more slowly.

This labyrinth fish is, of course, suitable for the home aquarium only when quite small. It has been introduced to many other parts of Southeast Asia and also to Australia as a food fish. When young (about 8in/20cm long) it can be kept in a community tank with floating plants and a large area of open water for swimming. The water composition is not critical. The essential plant part of the diet can include lettuce and soaked oat flakes. The male builds a bubble-nest which often includes pieces of plant. The eggs, which are guarded by the male, hatch in 24 to 36 hours and the fry are free-swimming a few days later. They feed at first on infusorians and rotifers.

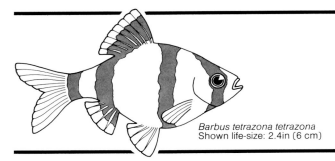

Barbus tetrazona tetrazona
Shown life-size: 2.4in (6 cm)

Suborder ATHERINOIDEI
The suborder Atherinoidei contains a small number of families. Those found in the aquarium are the Atherinidae *Bedotia* and *Telmatherina,* and the Melanotaeniidae with the genus *Melanotaenia.* They live in shallow coastal areas of many parts of the world, including Europe.

Family MELANOTAENIIDAE
Melanotaenia maccullochi
Dwarf Rainbowfish
● **Distribution:** Northern Australia
● **Length:** Up to 2.8in (7cm)
● **Tank length:** 24in (60cm)
● **Diet:** Worms, crustaceans, insects, dried food
● **Water temperature:** 68 to 77°F (20 to 25°F)
● **Community tank**

Also known as *Nematocentris maccullochi,* this is a moderately elongated and laterally compressed fish with almost symmetrical dorsal and ventral profiles. There are two separate dorsal fins. The anal fin starts in the middle of the body and has a relatively long base. The second dorsal fin and the anal fin are separated from the caudal fin by a gap. The first dorsal fin is pointed in the male, more rounded in the female. The small mouth faces slightly upward. The male is silvery-gray with bluish iridescence. The rows of scales on the flanks show pearly iridescence and between them run seven red-brown longitudinal stripes. The gill cover is iridescent blue-green with a bright red spot edged in golden-green. The throat and the edge of the belly are red and the back is brownish. The dorsal and anal fins are red with a greenish base. The female has more subdued coloration.

This is an active, hardy fish that lives mostly in the middle water layers. It can be kept in a shoal in a tank with a sandy substrate and groups of feathery-leaved rooted planted arranged to leave sufficient space for the small shoal to swim about. The water must not be too soft, and should preferably be medium-hard. Add about one teaspoonful of sea salt per gallon (4 liters) of water. Spawning takes place over a period of days, but most of the eggs are laid on the first day, often during the morning. The darkly pigmented eggs are attached by short filaments to feathery leaves. They hatch in seven to 10 days and the fry are free-swimming a few days later. They can be fed initially on *Paramecium,* rotifers and brine shrimp nauplii. At first they grow rather slowly but, after reaching a length of about 0.4in (1cm), the growth rate increases.

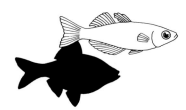

Below: **Melanotaenia maccullochi**
This peaceful fish can be kept as a small shoal in a community tank.

Family MELANOTAENIIDAE
Melanotaenia nigrans
Red-tailed Rainbowfish
● **Distribution:** Eastern Australia, south to Sydney
● **Length:** Up to 4in (10cm)
● **Tank length:** 36in (90cm)
● **Diet:** Worms, crustaceans insects, dried food
● **Water temperature:** 64 to 79°F (18 to 26°C)
● **Community tank**

Also known as *Nematocentris fluviatilis,* this is an elongated torpedo-shaped fish with strong lateral compression. The anal fin, which has a long base, starts approximately below the first dorsal fin, and its pointed tip extends over the base of the caudal fin. The second dorsal fin has the same general shape, but with a shorter base. The caudal fin is forked. In the male the back is yellow to grayish yellow and the belly is whitish. The flanks are iridescent green or blue-green. The relatively large scales have a dark front edge and a red hind edge, forming a netlike pattern. There are several dark longitudinal stripes separated by iridescent zones. The caudal peduncle is green and the gill cover has a triangular blood-red marking with a red, green, and white border. The dorsal and anal fins are yellow with a black edge; the other fins are yellowish. In the female the flanks do not show iridescence on the scales, and the dorsal and anal fins do not have a black border.

This is an active but peaceful fish, which should be kept in a shoal in a tank with a sandy substrate and scattered clumps of feathery-leaved plants. The water must be medium-hard or hard, and neutral in pH, with about five percent added sea water. (This is equivalent to adding 5 teaspoons-ful per 2.5 gallons/10 liters of water). The species is often found in coastal brackish waters. For breeding the temperature should be 73 to 77°F (23 to 25°C). The eggs are attached by short filaments to leaves and they hatch in eight to 10 days. A few days after hatching the fry will be free-swimming and ready to feed on rotifers and brine shrimp nauplii. They are not difficult to rear.

Right: **Melanotaenia nigrans**
In common with M. maccullochi, this species will not molest its brood.

A practical reminder
Keep careful written records of all attempts at breeding new fishes. If you get it right, you may well forget that important factor (such as an increase in temperature) that brought success at last.

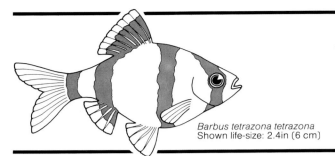

Barbus tetrazona tetrazona
Shown life-size: 2.4in (6 cm)

Family ATHERINIDAE
Bedotia geayi
Madagascar Rainbowfish
- **Distribution:** Madagascar
- **Length:** Up to 6in (15cm)
- **Tank length:** 24in (60cm)
- **Diet:** Worms, crustaceans, insects, plant matter, dried food
- **Water temperature:** 73 to 77°F (23 to 25°C)
- **Community tank**

The Madagascar Rainbowfish is an elongated, laterally compressed fish with symmetrical dorsal and ventral profiles. The head is pointed, the eyes are large, and the mouth faces slightly upward. The very short first dorsal fin is usually folded down. The second dorsal fin and the anal fin are low with long bases. The caudal fin is fan-shaped with a straight or slightly concave rear edge. The coloration of the male varies somewhat, but the back is usually yellowish brown and bordered on each side by a broad dark band. This band is decorated with a number of iridescent golden to grass-green scales and extends back to the root of the tail. There is another less conspicuous dark longitudinal band near the belly. The iris of the eye is golden above and green below. The second dorsal fin and the anal fin have pale yellow bases, but the fins themselves are orange with blackish borders. The main part of the caudal fin is bluish or colorless but the rear border has a semi-circular blue-gray band and a blood-red outer edge. The female is less brightly colored and lacks the dark borders to the fins.

This is an active fish of the upper and middle water layers, which should be kept in a small shoal in a tank with a few feathery-leaved plants and plenty of space for swimming. The water should be medium-hard and quite clear of any cloudiness caused by infusorians, since this species is very sensitive to them. The relatively large, pale yellowish eggs are laid among the plants and hang by short filaments. They are not molested by the parent fishes. The eggs hatch in six to seven days and the fry feed at first on rotifers and a little later on small brine shrimp nauplii.

Right **Bedotia geayi** ♂
This elegant midwater fish takes food from near the water surface.

Family ATHERINIDAE
Telmatherina ladigesi
Celebes Sailfish
- **Distribution:** Southeast Asia, Celebes only
- **Length:** Up to 2.8in (7cm)
- **Tank length:** 24in (60cm)
- **Diet:** Worms, crustaceans, insects, dried food
- **Water temperature:** 68 to 77°F (20 to 25°C)
- **Community tank**

An elongated, laterally compressed fish, the Celebes Sailfish has symmetrical dorsal and ventral profiles. The first dorsal fin is very small and positioned roughly above the ventral fins. The second dorsal fin and the anal fin are much larger. In mature males the first rays of these fins grow filamentous extensions, producing a rather ragged appearance. In females and young males these fins are rounded. The mouth is small and faces slightly upward. In the male the back, the upperpart of the caudal peduncle, and the underparts are yellow. The flanks are yellowish with blue-green iridescence, and marked with a narrow shiny blue-green longitudinal band. The iris of the eye is yellowish green. The first dorsal fin is copper-colored. The second dorsal fin and the anal fins are yellow, becoming more orange-red at the bases; but the first rays of the fins are black. The caudal fin and the ventral fins are yellowish, the former with dark streaks at the upper and lower edge. The pectoral fins are colorless. The female is less brightly colored, and the first rays of the anal fin and the second dorsal fin are not black.

This is a peaceful fish, living mainly in the middle water layers. It can be kept in a shoal in a tank with scattered plants around the edges and a sufficient amount of space for swimming. The water should be medium-hard with about five per cent added sea water. (Equivalent to adding 5 teaspoonsful of sea salt per 2.5 gallons/10 liters of tank water.) Spawning usually takes place in the morning; the eggs are laid in batches over a period of several days. They hatch in 11 or 12 days, and can be fed immediately on very fine live food. They grow slowly and may not reach a length of 0.8in (2cm) until eight weeks.

Above:
Telmatherina ladigesi ♀(t),♂(b)
After a slow start, this fish is sexually mature in seven months.

A practical reminder
There is more to fishkeeping than just fishes. You make lots of friends and develop new skills. The aquarium that was only intended to light up a dark corner will brighten your whole life!

Family TETRAODONTIDAE

The pufferfishes, so called because of their ability to inflate their bodies, occur in tropical seas and brackish waters, with a few species in fresh waters. They have a very powerful beaklike dentition that can crush even the shells of mollusks.

Family TETRAODONTIDAE
Tetraodon fluviatilis
Green Pufferfish
- **Distribution:** Southeast Asia, Philippines, Malay Archipelago
- **Length:** Up to 6.7in (17cm)
- **Tank length:** 24in (60cm)
- **Diet:** Worms, crustaceans, insects, chopped meat, plant matter
- **Water temperature:** 72 to 79°F (22 to 26°C)
- **Species tank**

This is a stocky fish with a very broad forehead and slightly protruding eyes. The dorsal and anal fins are roundish and lie opposite one another. The caudal fin is fan-shaped and there are no ventral fins. The skin is leathery with numerous small spines. The colors vary according to age and locality. In adults the upperparts and head are marked with large brown or blackish blotches on a yellowish green background. The underparts are gray and often spotted, but in young individuals the belly is white. The fins are translucent and yellowish, and the caudal fin may be marked with black spots or have a black border. There are no reliable external sex differences.

In the wild this species lives in fresh and brackish waters. The popular name refers to the ability to inflate the body when disturbed or attacked. It can be kept in a tank with dense vegetation and an arrangement of rocks and roots to provide hiding-places. Young specimens are peaceful, but older ones are usually aggressive towards one another. They appear to do best in brackish water, so the tank water should have one teaspoonful of sea salt added per gallon (4 liters) of water. Spawning takes place after a period of courtship near the bottom. The pale, glassy eggs are laid close to one another on a rock. They are tended by the male and usually hatch in six or seven days. The fry, which resemble tiny tadpoles, are taken by the male to a small pit on the bottom where he continues to guard them. They are not easy to feed but should be offered brine shrimp nauplii and rotifers, or possibly micro-worms.

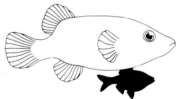

Below: **Tetraodon fluviatilis**
Some invidiuals of this species have lived for nine years.

FURTHER READING

Books

Axelrod, H. et al. *Breeding Aquarium Fishes,* Vols 1-6, T.F.H., 1967, 1971, 1973, 1976, 1978, 1981.

Axelrod, H. et al. *Exotic Tropical Fishes,* T.F.H., 1981.

Dal Vesco, et al. *Life in the Aquarium,* Octopus, 1975.

Duijn, C. van. *Diseases of Fishes,* 3rd edition, Butterworth Group, 1973.

Favre, H. *Dictionary of the Freshwater Aquarium,* Ward Lock, 1977.

Federation of British Aquatic Societies. *National Show Fish Sizes,* F.B.A.S., 1981. *National Show Guide to Cultivated Fishes,* F.B.A.S., 1981. *Dictionary of Common/Scientific Names of Freshwater Fishes,* F.B.A.S., 1982. *Scientific Names of Fishes and Their Meanings,* F.B.A.S., 1980.

Frank, Dr. S. *Illustrated Encyclopedia of Aquarium Fish,* Octopus, 1980.

Gilbert, J. ed. *Complete Aquarists Guide to Freshwater Tropical Fish,* revised edition, Peter Lowe, 1981.

Goldstein, R. *Cichlids of the World,* T.F.H., 1973.

Guery, Dr. *Characoid Fishes,* T.F.H., 1980.

Hervey, and Hems. *A Guide to Freshwater Aquarium Fishes,* Hamlyn, 1973.

Hoedeman, J.J. *Naturalists's Guide to Freshwater Aquarium Fishes,* Sterling Pub. Inc., 1974.

Hunman, Milne, and Stebbing. *The Living Aquarium,* Ward Lock, 1981.

Jacobsen, N. *Aquarium Plants,* Blandford Press, 1979.

Mayland, H.J. *The Complete Home Aquarium,* Ward Lock, 1975.

Mills, D. *Know the Game: Aquaria,* EP Publishing, 1978. *Aquarium Fishes,* Kingfisher Books, 1980. Canada:

John Wiley, 1980. *Illustrated Guide to Aquarium Fishes.* Kingfisher Books/Ward Lock, 1981.

Ramshorst, Dr. J.D. van. *Complete Aquarium Encyclopedia of Tropical Freshwater Fishes,* Elsevier Phaidon, 1978.

Rataj, and Horeman. *Aquarium Plants,* T.F.H., 1977.

Schiotz, and Dahlström. *Collins Guide to Aquarium Fishes & Plants,* Collins, 1972.

Singleton, V. and Mills, D. *How About Keeping Fish,* EP Publishing, 1979.

Spotte, S. *Fish & Invertebrate Culture,* Wiley Interscience, 1970, 1979.

Sterba, G. *Freshwater Fishes of the World,* Studio Vista, 1966. *Aquarium Care,* Studio Vista, 1967. *Dr Sterba's Aquarium Handbook,* Pet Library, 1973.

Thabrew, Dr. V. de. *Popular Tropical Aquarium Plants,* Thornhill Press, 1981.

Vevers, G. *Pocket Guide to Aquarium Fishes,* Mitchell Beazley, 1980.

Whitehead, P. *How Fishes Live,* Elsevier Phaidon, 1975.

Periodicals

The Aquarist and Pondkeeper, Buckley Press, The Butts, Half Acre, Brentford, Middlesex, England.

Practical Fishkeeping, E.M.A.P. National Publications, Bretton Court, Bretton, Peterborough, Cambs., England.

Tropical Fish Hobbyist, T.F.H. Publications Inc., 211 West Sylvania Avenue, P.O. Box 27, Neptune City, New Jersey 07753, U.S.A.

Freshwater and Marine Aquarium, 120 West Sierra Madre Boulevard, Sierra Madre, California 91024, U.S.A.

Roloffia occidentalis ♂

GLOSSARY

Words in *italics* refer to separate entries within the glossary and, in some cases, to scientific names.

Adipose fin Small, non-rayed *fin* carried by some species between the *dorsal fin* and *caudal fin.*

Aeration The introduction of compressed air into the aquarium via an *airstone* to produce water movement and turbulence. This has the effect of allowing carbon dioxide to be released and oxygen to be taken up at the air-water interface.

Aerobic Oxygen-loving, oxygen-dependent. Often applied to bacteria.

Airline Neoprene tubing used to carry compressed air from the air pump to the equipment within the aquarium.

Airstone Block of porous material which, when supplied with air, produces a stream of bubbles.

All-glass Term used to describe tanks made from five panes of bonded glass.

Anabantids Fishes equipped with auxiliary breathing organ in the head. See *Labyrinth fishes.*

Anal fin Single *fin* projecting vertically downward beneath the body.

Annual fishes Fishes with a natural lifespan of one year; those fishes that inhabit waters which completely dry out each summer. See *Killifishes.*

'Apple' snail Species of water snail (*Ampullaria*) often used in *fry*-raising tanks, as it produces quantities of *infusorians* from its droppings.

Artemia salina Brine shrimp.

Barbels Whisker-like growths, often equipped with taste cells, around the mouths of some species, especially catfishes.

Biological filter Method of filtration using bacterial activity instead of a trapping *filter medium.* Usually known as an undergravel filter.

Brine shrimp *Artemia salina.* The eggs can be hatched (in *salt* water) to provide an excellent live food for *fry.*

Cably tidy A junction box for electrical connections to aquarium apparatus (via switches for non-continuously operated equipment).

Caudal fin Single, vertically set *fin* at rear end of fish; the tail.

Caudal peduncle Part of fish's body that connects immediately with the *caudal fin.*

Compost Term often applied to any aquarium base-covering medium.

Conditioning The bringing of fishes into peak physical condition (by isolation and increased feeding of quality foods) for breeding or showing purposes.

Cover glass A sheet of glass placed between the water surface and the tank hood. It reduces evaporation and damage to the lamps from water spray, and prevents dust getting in and fishes jumping out.

Crown The junction between root and stem of aquatic plants; should not be buried in the gravel.

Daphnia *Daphnia pulex,* the water flea; a freshwater crustacean collected and sold commercially as live food for aquarium fishes.

Detritus Layer of material found on the floor of the aquarium, usually dead plant leaves, uneaten food, fish droppings, etc. Also known as mulm.

Dorsal fin Single *fin* projecting vertically from the top of the fish's body; some species may have two dorsal fins.

Driving The pursuit of the female fish by the male, which stimulates the release of eggs when the female eventually succumbs to a spawning embrace, usually in clumps of plants or artificial spawning mops.

Egg-layers Term applied to fishes whose eggs are laid and fertilized outside the female's body. Although the *mouth-brooding* species' fertilized eggs are incubated in the female's mouth, these genera are still classed as egg-layers within the hobby.

Emerse Mode of plant growth in which the roots are anchored in the substrate under water and the leafy shoots and flowers develop above the surface.

Fancy goldfish Any of the cultivated forms of *Carassius auratus,* the Goldfish.

Filter Device for cleaning the aquarium water. Various types are available.

Filter medium Usually a man-made fiber used as a trapping device held within the body of the *filter.*

Fins Propelling and stabilizing external appendage of a fish. Usually seven in number: *dorsal, anal, caudal, pelvic* or *ventral* (2), and *pectoral* (2). An extra fin may be present, either as an additional *dorsal* or as an *adipose fin.*

Fry The young of a fish.

Gallon Measurement of liquid volume.
1 U.S. gallon=3.78 liters.
1 Imperial gallon=4.55 liters.

Gills Fish's organs by means of which dissolved oxygen is extracted from the water during respiration.

Gonopodium The male *live-bearer's anal fin,* modified into a reproductive organ for internal fertilization of the female.

Gravid Pregnant.

Hardness Measurement of the amount of dissolved mineral salts in water.

Heater Heating device, usually a submersible glass- or aluminium-encased electric element controlled by a *thermostat.*

Hood (Reflector) Tank cover housing the aquarium lights, usually with a hinged lid to facilitate feeding.

Infusorians Minute, water-living organisms that include *rotifers* and protozoans. Often used as a first food for young fishes. May be cultured by the aquarist. See *'Apple' snail.*

Killifishes Members of the family Cyprinodontidae. A large number of species of this group are *annual fishes.*

Labyrinth fishes Members of the family Anabantidae (Gouramies, Siamese Fighting Fishes). See *Anabantids.*

Lateral line A vibration-detecting nervous system, whose sensors appear as a row of pierced *scales* along the flanks of the fish.

Length (of fish) Standard length is measured from tip of snout to end of *caudal peduncle; caudal fin* is excluded from this measurement.
Total length is measured from tip of snout to extreme rear end of *caudal fin* (or projections).

Liter Measurement of liquid volume.
1 liter=0.26 U.S. gallon.
1 liter=0.22 Imperial gallon.

Live-bearer Fish whose eggs are fertilized and develop inside the female.

Milt Fertilizing fluid containing spermatozoa released during spawning by the male fish.

Mops Bunches of nylon wool, acting as plant substitutes, in which fishes can deposit fertilized eggs. Mostly used by *Killifish* breeders.

Mouth-brooders (-breeders) Fishes whose females incubate the fertilized eggs in the mouth and buccal cavity.

Mulm See *detritus.*

Nauplii Microscopic, free-swimming larval stages of some crustaceans. Frequently used as first food for very young fishes.

Operculum External bony covering to the *gills.*

Ovipositor Egg-depositing tube extended from the body of some female fishes at breeding time. May also be used to describe milt-depositing tube of the male fish of the same species.

Pectoral fins Paired *fins* immediately behind the *operculum.*

Pelvic fins Paired *fins* on fish's ventral surface ahead of *anal fin.* Often referred to as ventral fins. May be lacking in some marine species.

pH Unit measurement of water's acidity or alkalinity. Neutral is pH7.

Photosynthesis Process by which plants under illumination absorb carbon dioxide and give off oxygen as they build up simple carbohydrates.

Power filter Common name given to any design of *filter* that uses small electrically driven impeller to move water through the filter, as opposed to those operated by compressed air.

Quarantine Period of isolation of new fishes designed to prevent disease introduction into the aquarium.

Rays Spines supporting *fin* tissues.

Rotifers Microscopic, mostly free-swimming animals so called because they have an arrangement of tiny hairs resembling a rotating wheel. Used as live food for *fry.*

Runners Young plants sent out from an established, adult plant.

Salt Sodium chloride (NaC1). Used as a prophylactic bath. Only natural sea salt should be used in aquarium applications.

Scales Thin, overlapping plates covering the fish's body.

Scutes Large, overlapping armored plates replacing scales in some species, particularly catfishes.

Sealant Silicone-rubber adhesive used in bonding glass.

Shoal A large number of one species of fish. Also called a 'school'.

Siphon (tube) Method of transferring water from a higher to a lower level. Can be used to drain tanks or during partial water changes, when it can also be useful in clearing *detritus* from the aquarium floor.

Spawning Act of reproduction in fishes; in aquarium terms may be applied to the whole procedures of courtship, mating, and raising of the young.

Swim-bladder Hydrostatic organ giving neutral density (neither floating up nor sinking down) within the fish's body.

Tail See *caudal fin.*

Thermometer Device for measuring water temperature.

Thermostat Electromechanical device for controlling the supply of electric current to the aquarium heater, thus controlling the water temperature.

Tubifex Small red worms, often found in sewage-infested river mud, used as live food.

Undergravel filter See *biological filter.*

Variety Fishes of same species whose coloration or finnage has been developed into fixed recognizable patterns by selective breeding programs.

Ventral fin See *Pelvic fin.*

Water Flea See *Daphnia.*

Worms Excellent foods for fishes. Sizes may range from cultures of micro-, grindal or white worms up to earthworm proportions.

Aequidens maronii♂

GENERAL INDEX

Page numbers in **bold** type indicate major references; those in *italics* refer to illustrations.

INDEX OF PLANTS

Page numbers in *italics* refer to illustrations.

A beautifully planted freshwater tank

A spawning pair of Poecilia latipinna

INDEX OF FISHES

Page numbers in **bold** type indicate the major references for each fish, including accompanying illustrations. Page numbers in *italics* refer to other illustrations.

CREDITS

Artists
Copyright of the artwork illustrations on the pages following the artists' names is the property of Salamander Books Ltd.

Color artwork
David Nockels: 34, 35, 36, 37, 42-3(B), 44, 45

Colin Newman (Linden Artists): 16-7(B), 18-9, 20-1, 23, 29, 42(T)

Tony Payne (Tudor Art Studios Ltd.): 46, 47, 49

Brian Watson (Linden Artists): 10, 11, 12-3, 14-5, 24, 40-1

Line artwork
Alan Hollingbery: 17(TR), Maps: 55, 93, 121, 133, 145, 161, 185

Sarah-Gay Wolfendale: 52-197

Photographs
The Publishers wish to thank the following photographers and agencies who have supplied photographs for this book. The photographs have been credited by page number and position on the page: (B) Bottom, (T) Top, (C) Center, (BL) Bottom left etc.

Heather Angel/Biofotos: 21, 22, 25 (T, Murray Watson), 34, 98(B) 101(T), 124, 125(B), 152, 174(T), 195

Bruce Coleman Ltd: 50 (Jane Burton), 55

(Luiz Claudio Marigo), 65 (Hans Reinhard), 78-9 (T, Burton), 80-1 (T, Hans Reinhard), 90-1 (T, Hans Reinhard), 92 (Hans Reinhard), 100 (Jane Burton), 108-9 (T, Hans Reinhard), 113 (T, Hans Reinhard), 121 (Sandro Prato), 133 (Fritz Vollmar), 145 (M. S. L. Fogden), 147 (T, Hans Reinhard), 154 (T, Jane Burton), 155 (T, Hans Reinhard), 161 (Peter Davey), 185 (Fritz Vollmar), 193 (T, Hans Reinhard)

Eric Crichton © Salamander Books Ltd.): 8, 12, 22, 23, 26, 27, 28, 29, 30, 31, 32, 33, 38, 39

Interpet Ltd: 38(TL)

Jan-Eric Larsson: 25(B), 47(R), 56, 58(BL), 60(BL), 62, 68, 69(T), 86(BL), 98(T), 107, 117(T), 120, 160, 172-3(B), 174(BL), 174-5(B), 175(CR), 180(R), 183(T), 189(B), 197(B)

Arend van den Nieuwenhuizen: Half-title page, title page, copyright page, contents page, 16, 19, 24(TL), 35, 37, 44, 45, 46, 47(L), 52, 53, 54, 57, 58-9(T), 59, 60-1(T), 61(BR), 63, 64, 66, 67, 69(B), 70, 71, 72, 73, 74-5(B), 75, 76(BL), 77(BR), 78(BL), 79(B), 80(BL), 81(BR), 82, 83, 84, 85, 87(BR), 88(B), 89(B), 90(B), 91(BR), 94, 95, 96, 97, 98(B), 101(B), 102, 103, 104(T), 105(T), 106(B), 109(BR), 110, 111, 112, 113(B), 114, 115, 116, 117(B), 118, 119, 122, 123, 125(T), 126, 127, 128, 129, 132, 134, 135, 136, 137, 138, 139, 140, 141, 142, 143, 144, 146, 146-7(B), 148, 149, 150, 151, 153(TL, BL), 154(B), 155(B),

156-7(T), 157, 158, 159, 162, 163(T), 166(T), 167, 168(T), 169(T), 170, 171, 172(T), 173(T), 175(T), 176(C, B), 177, 178, 179, 181, 182, 183(B), 184, 186(B), 187(B), 188, 189(T), 190, 191(B), 192, 193(B), 196(B), 198, 200, 203, 204

Barry Pengilley: 43, 76-7(T), 86-7(T), 88-9(T), 99, 104-5(B), 130(T), 131(T), 156(BL), 163(B), 165, 166(B), 180(L), 186-7(T), 194, 196-7(T), endpapers

Seaphot: 108(L)

Ian Sellick: 176(T)

W. A. Tomey: 10, 11, 17, 24(C), 36, 40, 48, 74(T), 93, 106(T), 130(B), 153(TR), 164, 168-9(B), 191(T)

Acknolwedgments
The Publishers would like to thank the following individuals and organizations for their help in the preparation of this book: J. Reddick, Aquatic and Pet Supplies Ltd; J.N. Carrington, Interpet Ltd; Dr. C. Andrews. Tetra Information Center; John Allan Aquariums Ltd; Mr. Dutta, Fish Tanks Ltd; Freshwater and Marine Aquarium magazine, Practical Fishkeeping magazine; Ian Sellick, British Cichlid Association; Federation of British Aquatic Societies (F.B.A.S.); Roger Paine, F.B.A.S. judge; South-East London Aquarist Society; East Dulwich Aquarist Society; Janet Parr (for typing the manuscript of part one); Carol Warren (for design assistance); Maureen Cartwright (for copy-editing); Stuart Craik (for preparing the index).

PRINTED IN BELGIUM BY

INTERNATIONAL BOOK PRODUCTION